Unlivable Lives

Unlivable Lives

Violence and Identity in Transgender Activism

LAUREL WESTBROOK

University of California Press

University of California Press
Oakland, California

Library of Congress Cataloging-in-Publication Data

Names: Westbrook, Laurel, 1980– author.
Title: Unlivable lives : violence and identity in transgender activism /
    Laurel Westbrook.
Description: Oakland, California : University of California Press, [2021]
    | Includes bibliographical references and index.
Identifiers: LCCN 2020017642 (print) | LCCN 2020017643 (ebook) |
    ISBN 9780520316584 (cloth) | ISBN 9780520316591 (paperback) |
    ISBN 9780520974159 (epub)
Subjects: LCSH: Transgender people—Violence against—United States.
    | Transgender people—Social aspects—United States. | Identity
    politics—United States. | Gender identity—Political aspects—United
    States. | Gender identity—Social aspects—United States. | Sexual
    minorities—United States.
Classification: LCC HQ77.965.U6 W47 2021 (print) | LCC HQ77.965.U6
    (ebook) | DDC 305.3—dc23
LC record available at https://lccn.loc.gov/2020017642
LC ebook record available at https://lccn.loc.gov/2020017643

Manufactured in the United States of America

30 29 28 27 26 25 24 23 22 21
10 9 8 7 6 5 4 3 2 1

This book is for every woman who is terrified to be alone in public, every person of color whose heart skips a beat at the sight of a white person, every LGBQ person who worries about being outed to the wrong person, and every trans person who expresses their identity only in private, fearing the consequences of being visibly trans. May your lives become more livable.

Contents

Illustrations

Preface

When I started gathering data for this project, I used computers in libraries on my university's campus. That lasted no more than two days because, reading these accounts of violence, I cried. Sometimes it was wracking sobs (muffled as best I could), and sometimes I managed to collect the press releases, flyers, reports on violence, and online memorials in silence, as tears streaked down my cheeks. I felt wrong disturbing other patrons with my grief, my sense of social propriety kicking in as they regularly stared at me (although, oddly, none ever asked me what was wrong). Part of me wanted to cause a disruption, though, yearning to shout to all of them about the horrors I was reading about and beg them to help me prevent future violence. But my sense of appropriateness and fear of being kicked out of the library quelled such desires. More important than my discomfort over being disconcerting, though, was my conviction that I owed it to the murder victims to properly mourn their deaths, and I could not do that in the stifling atmosphere of the library. I knew that I would sob uncontrollably if I thought too long about how terrified they must have been; how much dying in the ways they did must have hurt; how much their friends and family must miss them; and how incredibly horrible it would be to have the last person you see, the last person who touches you, be a person who despises you (or what you represent) enough to kill you. I felt that they deserved that sobbing, so I moved my data collection to the more private setting of my home office.

I tell this story because I want to make it clear that I care about these victims and that I care about everyone who lives in fear that they will be next. I started this project with a practical application of my research in mind; I hope that my work can be used to improve anti-violence activism in order to reduce violence and make lives more livable and full of joy. Some readers may not believe that about me once they are partway through this book, so I want to try to make it clear here. We are used to stories about social movements being a "good versus evil" narrative in which activists valiantly fight against oppression. We are not used to the critical lens being turned on those activists, particularly not trans activists. As transgender studies is a relatively new field in the social sciences and humanities, we have not gotten to the point where we often see academic critiques of trans activists' tactics. Such appraisals are relatively more common for longer running movements and more established fields of study, such as feminism.[1] Moreover, because trans people are seen as one of the most oppressed groups in US society, assessing trans activism is interpreted by some as misguided; when there are so many people working against transgender rights, why am I critiquing those who are fighting for them? Although challenging, I think this work is necessary because if we really want to make the world a better place, we also have to assess the work done by "the good guys" (and gals and all other genders), including activists fighting to decrease inequality. Many of the tactics used by activists that I highlight are very effective in terms of bringing attention to the issue of violence experienced by trans people. And the awareness that has been brought to this horrible problem is commendable. However, the tactics have also had unintended, potentially destructive consequences. It is vital that we attend to these as well. It is necessary to note when social movements are possibly damaging the very groups they are working to protect. Activism in some form is needed to end violence experienced by transgender people, but it does not necessarily have to be identity-based and does not have to utilize the tactics I detail in this book. In order to properly honor murdered transgender people and to work to prevent future violence, we must turn a critical lens on the causes and consequences of identity-based anti-violence activism.

Acknowledgments

I am deeply indebted to the many wonderful people in my life who generously offered their support and feedback on this project. I began the journey that became this book as an undergraduate at the University of California, Berkeley. In my senior year, about to complete a double major in sociology and mass communications with a minor in LGBT studies, I was steeped in knowledge about social inequalities but unsure what to do with my love of learning. I was fortunate enough to take the senior honors thesis courses in sociology with Mary Kelsey and in mass communications with Allison McCracken. Together, they taught me the joys of research and of sharing one's findings with others. Bolstered by their mentorship, I applied to graduate school. I was overjoyed when I was accepted to my top choice, my intellectual home: the Sociology Department at University of California, Berkeley. At the time, Berkeley was a perfect fit for the work I wanted to do. It housed what was seen as the best sociology program in the country for studying gender and was also one of the few high-ranking departments that had a faculty member studying sexuality using a post-structuralist lens. Moreover, my scholarship has always been inter-disciplinary, and Berkeley's Department of Gender and Women's Studies and the Designated Emphasis in Women, Gender, and Sexuality program allowed me space to expand my intellectual horizons.

So many people at Berkeley helped me grow intellectually that it is impossible to thank them all. Special thanks, however, go to Dawne Moon, Barrie Thorne, Wendy Brown, Raka Ray, Michael Burawoy, Charis Thompson, Leslie Salizinger, Susan Stryker, Claude Fischer, Minoo Moallem, Mel Chen, Evelyn Nakano Glenn, Michael Lucey, Karl Britto, Percy Hintzen, Mel Stanfill, C.J. Pascoe, Aliya Saperstein, Damon Mayrl, Rachel Sullivan, Shannon Gleeson, Benjamin Moodie, Christine Quinan, Robin

Mitchell, Ariane Cruz, Sonal Khullar, Lowry Martin, Gita Pai, Kelly Rafferty, Huma Dar, Monica Stufft, Nicholas Wilson, Ryan Centner, Phillip Fucella, Sarah Staveteig, Patricia Munro, Brian Folk, Seio Nakajima, Sarah Ovink, Dori Aspuru-Takata, Rebecca Bodenheimer, Rebekah Edwards, Kristin Fujie, Gladys Nubla, Sarah Townsend, Yen-Ling Tsai, Suowei Xiao, Mona Bower, Allegra McLeod, Sara Kendall, Jack Jackson, Asaf Kedar, Diana Anders, Carla Yumatle, Geo Ciccariello Maher, Yves Winter, Matt Baxter, Zhivka Valiavicharska, Yasmeen Daifallah, Tim Fisken, Jason Koenig, Jennifer Denbow, and Maia Sieverding, Ryan Calder, and the rest of the 2007–2008 Berkeley Journal of Sociology Editorial Collective.

I would also like to thank the faculty in the Feminist Studies Department at the University of California, Santa Barbara, who through their pre-doc fellowship program provided an intellectual home away from home for me during my last year in graduate school; Isaac Reed, Erika Summers-Effler, and the rest of the organizers of the 2008 Junior Theorists Symposium, who afforded a space for the kernels that became chapter 2 to grow; and Sarah Fenstermaker and CL Cole.

In terms of gathering materials for this book, I am indebted to the excellent research assistance of Christine Noack, Katie Winchel, Kaylin Haff, and Jamie Munson. I am also beholden to the people who run the Internet Archive (aka the Wayback Machine). Without them, many vital pieces of transgender history would be lost. A special thank you also goes to Aaron Devor for sharing his personal copies of the *FTMi* newsletter from 2006 to 2008.

I am exceptionally grateful to Jennifer Randles, who has been a dear friend since we shared a graduate student office at Berkeley. Jennifer believed in this project from the beginning and was my rock and my flashlight throughout writing this manuscript. Thank you, Jennifer, for reading my messy first drafts and for cheering me on throughout this process! Huge thanks also go to Amy Stone, Miriam Abelson, Kristen Schilt, and stef shuster for reading drafts of chapters of this book and providing excellent insights and feedback.

Thank you to my family, particularly my mom and brother, for their love and support. Finally, thank you to Soren, my amazing nesting partner and one of the great loves of my life. Your infinite kindness, care, affection, and compassion are treasures for which I will forever be grateful. I am thankful for everything You have taught me about living.

Abbreviations

FTMI	FTM International
GEA	Gender Education and Advocacy
GenderPAC	Gender Public Advocacy Coalition
GLAAD	Gay and Lesbian Alliance Against Defamation
GSA	Gay Straight Alliance
HRC	Human Rights Campaign
IFGE	International Foundation for Gender Education
NCAVP	National Coalition of Anti-Violence Programs
NCTE	National Center for Transgender Equality
NTAC	National Transgender Advocacy Coalition
ROD	Remembering Our Dead
SPLC	Southern Poverty Law Center
TDoR	Transgender Day of Remembrance

1. Unlivable Lives

The Origins and Outcomes of Identity-Based Anti-Violence Activism

On October 28, 2009, President Barack Obama signed the Matthew Shepard and James Byrd, Jr. Hate Crimes Prevention Act into law. At the signing, he stated:

> We must stand against crimes that are meant not only to break bones, but to break spirits—not only to inflict harm, but to instill fear. . . . And that's why, through this law, we will strengthen the protections against crimes based on the color of your skin, the faith in your heart, or the place of your birth. We will finally add federal protections against crimes based on gender, disability, gender identity, or sexual orientation. Because no one in America should ever be afraid to walk down the street holding the hands of the person they love. No one in America should be forced to look over their shoulder because of who they are or because they live with a disability.[1]

On March 7, 2013, he again signed into law a piece of legislation intended to reduce violence experienced by specific Americans, this time through a reauthorization of the Violence Against Women Act. At the signing, Vice President Joe Biden, who had participated in drafting the original bill in 1994, argued: "With all the law's success, there are still too many women in this country who live in fear of violence, who are still prisoners in their own home; too many victims that we have to mourn. . . . So when Congress passed this law that the President will sign today, they just didn't renew what I consider a sacred commitment to protect our mothers, our daughters, our sisters. They strengthened that commitment."[2]

Leading up to the passage of both of these laws were extensive efforts by anti-violence activists, including families of victims, survivors of violence, and organizations focused on the rights of women, people of color, religious groups, people with disabilities, gay men and lesbians, and transgender people.[3] This activism included numerous vigils and protests, often incorporating pictures of victims of violence, attendees holding candles in honor of victims, and speakers beseeching the crowd (and the attending journalists) to never forget these acts of violence. Activists argued that the violence against members of their identity group was caused by hatred and that, since society is plagued with a disdain for difference, all group members were potentially at risk. They actively sought news coverage of acts of violence in hopes of educating the public about their cause. Finally, to try to reduce the violence, activists lobbied members of Congress, victims and their families testified before Congress, and organizations gathered and distributed statistics about crimes—all with the aim of writing into law protections for certain groups of people.

These movements to stop violence against women and to add race, religion, ability, sexual orientation, and gender identity to hate crime legislation are all forms of what I term *identity-based anti-violence activism*: activism done to reduce violence against a particular identity group. Identity-based attempts to reduce violence have become so commonplace as to seem a natural way to combat it. Indeed, the vast majority of anti-violence activism in the United States occurs within the framework of identity politics. However, this form of activism can have a number of unintended consequences. In this book I turn a critical lens on these actions, asking: What happens when identity politics and anti-violence activism are combined?

I answer this question through analysis of an original data set of more than one thousand documents produced by thirteen national organizations working between 1990 and 2009 to reduce violence experienced by transgender people in the United States. I define *trans activists* as those people who advocate for the rights of those who fall under the umbrella category *transgender*. For the purposes of this book, I refer to the group of people advocated for by trans activists as transgender and trans. Although these terms may not always have been claimed by the people on whose behalf trans activists have advocated, they are the categories used by the activists themselves. Throughout the book I use quotes from activists that contain language now considered offensive (e.g., "transgendered"). I include it without marking it with "[sic]" both to be respectful to the speakers and to highlight how language about identity groups changes over time. When relevant, I bring in illustrative examples from other identity-based anti-violence movements, such as the civil rights movement, the women's rights movement, and the gay rights movement.[4]

In my focus on all of these movements, I take up two central questions about the unique consequences of combining identity politics with anti-violence activism: (1) How might anti-violence activism shape beliefs about the identity group and experiences of being a member of that group? and (2) How do ideas about the identity group, as well as the particular logics of identity politics, influence the tactics of fighting violence, including ways of getting attention for the cause and proposed methods of reducing violence? In other words, what are the effects of President Obama's and Vice President Biden's depicting certain groups (and not others) as living in fear? How is the experience of being a person with a disability, a woman, gay or lesbian, transgender, and/or of color influenced by the message that you are always at risk for violence and that many people hate you for your social category? What beliefs about the groups and the dangers they face made protection by the government the logical remedy?

Although violence is usually only studied in terms of what philosopher Michel Foucault called *repressive power,* the stories we tell about violence are highly productive of ideas and practices. Narratives about violence can have far-reaching consequences, shaping beliefs about victims, perpetrators, and potential solutions.[5] For example, in my analysis of identity-based anti-violence activism, I find that social movement actors use frames and narratives to try to produce an idea of the identity group as valuable humans with a right to live a fulfilling life free of fear.

Faced with what philosopher Judith Butler termed *unlivable lives,* activists attempt to make those lives more livable through identity-based anti-violence activism.[6] For less well-known categories, such as transgender, they do so first by educating the public about the existence of this identity, increasing the group's visibility. For all marginalized identities, activists work to reduce the stigma against them. Historically, many oppressed groups have been seen socially as villains. American culture has portrayed transgender people as monstrous "evil deceivers," both trans and gay people as dangerous to children, and black people as criminals.[7] In response, identity-based activists have worked to construct these groups as socially valuable rather than as villains. Part of the activism of these groups has been to say "we aren't dangerous, you are," flipping the script in terms of who is the villain and who is the victim.[8]

By increasing visibility and highlighting vulnerability, these groups hope to garner rights and decrease violence against them.[9] However, in their fight to mark violence against their group as morally wrong, identity-based anti-violence activists utilize a number of techniques that, though highly effective in getting attention for the cause, can also have significant unintended consequences. These run counter to the goals of reducing violence and making the lives of group members more livable. Social movement actors both intentionally and unintentionally engage in *emotion work*, shaping the feelings held by, and about, the group they are advocating for.[10] Rather than decreasing fear, the tactics used in identity-based anti-violence activism can actually increase it, leaving members of the identity group convinced that a violent fate is inevitable. This is not a *livable life.* As Butler argued: "In the same way that a life for which no categories of recognition exist is not a livable life, so a life for which those categories constitute unlivable constraint is not an acceptable option. . . . The task . . . seems to me to be about distinguishing among the norms and conventions that permit people to breathe, to desire, to love, and to live, and those norms and conventions that restrict or eviscerate the conditions of life itself."[11]

In addition to utilizing tactics that exacerbate fear, identity-based anti-violence activists often focus on only one identity category and usually on only a few famous victims. In doing so, they unintentionally misrepresent patterns of violence that, if attended to, could aid reduction efforts. Furthermore, in their attempts to value the victims of violence, activists often focus their efforts on mourning the dead through holding vigils and demanding that the government recognize the violence against their group. Thus, the tactics utilized by those merging identity politics with anti-violence work have encouraged a suppression of alternative techniques that may be more effective in reducing or, preferably, eliminating the violence. Moreover, as I argue throughout this book, these efforts do not achieve their main goal of increasing livability. In the conclusion, I take up the question of how to successfully reduce violence without unintentionally making an *unlivable life* for those we seek to protect. Key to a livable life is what Butler termed *possibility*, or "the ability to live and breathe and move," which she argues is central to "freedom."[12] As Butler stated: "Possibility is not a luxury; it is as crucial as bread. I think we should not underestimate what the thought of the possible does for those for whom the very issue of survival is most urgent."[13] My suggestions include attending to intersectionality in analyzing patterns of violence, highlighting moments in which violence was reduced or deterred, encouraging positive representations of the identity group, and forming coalitions around reducing violence outside of an identity politics model.

IDENTITY-BASED ANTI-VIOLENCE ACTIVISM

The vast majority of anti-violence activism in the United States occurs within the framework of identity politics. Although there is extensive research on specific identity-based anti-violence organizations, particularly those working on behalf of women, gay men and lesbians, and people of color, no one has yet examined how the combination of identity politics and anti-violence work may shape understandings of the group and practices of activism. In this book I build a theory of the practices and consequences of identity-based anti-violence activism by combining three sources of knowledge: (1) my insights from analyzing the transgender rights movement; (2) scholarship on social movements more broadly; and (3) existing research on activism seeking to reduce violence against people of color, women, and gay men and lesbians.

Within what sociologist Joel Best has termed the *social problems marketplace*, countless organizations and individual activists compete for attention for their causes.[14] This struggle encourages the use of tactics designed to mark their issues as highly important and deserving of public notice, media coverage, and government resources. These include certain ways of protesting, types of narratives to tell about the importance of their causes, methods of raising money, decisions about whom to try to reach with their messages, and ways of framing their issues, all of which coalesce into *tactical repertoires*.[15] Which tactics are effective is shaped by historical context, the culture in which they are taking place, and the *political field* in which they operate. Sociologist Raka Ray defined a political field as an environment comprised of "the state, political parties, and social movement organizations" and populated by actors with differing levels of access to power.[16] In the twentieth and twenty-first centuries, identity politics has deeply influenced the political field of the United States, and anti-violence activists have adapted their tactical repertoires to match.

Engaging in identity-based activism has become a seemingly obvious way to try to enact social change within the current political field. Factors like race, gender, and sexual orientation stratify US society, and resources are more readily allocated to those at the top of the hierarchy within each of those social systems than to those lower down. Thus, for most Americans groups fighting for women's rights; other groups fighting for the rights of people of color; and still other groups fighting for the rights of gay men, lesbians, bisexuals, and transgender people seems like a logical way for non-dominant groups in society to gain access to resources and reduce discrimination. Within academia, however, identity politics is more contentious. Those in favor of maintaining identity groups argue that identity politics is a necessary tactic for empowerment because it helps maintain community, creating a base from which to gain strength to fight oppression.[17] In addition, identity-based tactics can be quite successful in the political field.[18]

Although this form of activism can be highly effective in garnering support for struggles against oppression, it can also negatively affect activists' responses to that oppression. In particular, identity politics can discourage an awareness of *intersectionality*.[19] The dominant model of identity politics encourages a focus on discrimination against only one identity category. In highlighting a single identity category, activists ignore the role that multiple socially constructed systems of stratification, such as race, gender, sexuality, age, ability, and class, play in maintaining inequalities faced by their group members. This failure to attend to multiple systems of stratification makes it challenging to implement effective solutions. For example, activists working to reduce domestic violence experienced by women have tended to focus only on gender, not on how citizenship status, race, and class may also play a role.[20] Moreover, by only attending to one system of oppression, activists often unintentionally perpetuate others, such as lesbians and gay men working to expand a police state that disproportionately punishes people of color.[21]

An additional academic dispute over identity politics centers around whether it is desirable to maintain a group (and group identity) originally created through domination. Historically oppressed identity groups came into being through being marked as "other" by those in power. Can activism change the meaning of those identity categories enough to free them from that coercive birth? In this debate, scholars have argued that identity politics is disempowering and unintentionally reproduces the very sources of oppression it is trying to end. They see attempting to create social change by organizing around identity as reifying categories of oppression, treating them as essential characteristics of people.[22] By essentializing these categories, activists engaged in identity politics are unable to undo the categories on which their oppression is based.[23] Moreover, scholars argue that identity groups often become invested in their own domination through struggles to be recognized within the social problems marketplace, as it is through claims of woundedness that they are able to be recognized and heard in the political field and the larger culture.[24] For example, education scholar Valerie Harwood detailed how those struggling for the rights of queer youth tell narratives of violence, parental abuse, and risk for suicide in their activism, rather than stories about the joy of being queer.[25] In the current cultural and political moment, what she termed *wounded truths* are particularly resonant when struggling for rights. Thus, activists tell narratives of pain instead of pleasure, which can seriously impact group members' sense of self.

Identity groups have commonly taken up the issue of violence experienced by members of their group. Civil rights organizations such as the National Association for the Advancement of Colored People (NAACP) engaged in extensive campaigns against lynching and police brutality, causes most recently addressed by the Black Lives Matter movement.[26] Women's rights organizations have focused on making others aware of, and opposed to, sexual assault and domestic violence, issues that have garnered widespread attention recently through the #MeToo movement.[27] Gay and lesbian organizations have demanded the right to move safely in public spaces as well as the termination of police harassment, both factors in the push for the inclusion of sexual orientation in the 2009 hate crime law.[28] And as I detail in this book, trans activists have worked to end violence against transgender people, particularly murder. By highlighting violence that has been either ignored or seen as socially acceptable, these movements work to shift cultural norms such that it is understood to be immoral to assault a member of their group.

In doing so, they face the pressures of the social problems marketplace and have utilized specific tactical repertoires in their struggle to get attention for their cause. Social movement actors often borrow tactics from previously successful movements, particularly those with similar goals. In their struggle against violence, women's rights activists adopted framings and tactics used in the civil rights movement; similarly, gay and lesbian anti-violence activists borrowed from both the civil rights movement and the women's rights movement.[29] By using historically effective tactics, social movements on behalf of marginalized people increase their ability to be heard within the political field. However, as I demonstrate in this book, although effective, these tactics often have negative unintended consequences which, if not addressed, impact members of each successive movement.

TRANS ACTIVISM AGAINST VIOLENCE

In the United States, the first organization-based trans activism began in the 1960s in the form of self-identified transsexuals fighting for access to hormones, surgery, and the ability to change the sex listed on their identification documents, as well as working to educate doctors and the general public.[30] In the 1970s more radical activist groups were formed that engaged in public protests and demonstrations.[31] After a period of relative silence throughout the 1980s, trans activism emerged once again in the early 1990s, this time under the umbrella term *transgender*.[32] Although access to medical care was still a goal of the latest incarnation of this movement, as was fighting employment discrimination, by far the most common issue taken on by trans activists was physical violence against transgender people.

The murder of Brandon Teena in the early hours of December 31, 1993, pulled together the trans activist community and solidified a focus on violence.[33] Trans activists labeled Brandon Teena, a man who was assigned female at birth, as transgender and drew on networks and organizations established during the early 1990s to mobilize around the murder, coordinating vigils, demonstrations, press releases, and letters to the editors of mainstream news publications.[34] From 1994 on, violence against transgender people became a central issue in trans activism. Most of this anti-violence activism has centered around murder rather than more common incidents of nonfatal violence; in fact, almost all anti-violence documents produced by trans activists included mention of fatal violence.

This shift toward focusing on violence can be seen in transgender community publications, such as *FTMi* and *TV-TS Tapestry*. From 1990 to 1993, *FTMi*, a popular newsletter for trans men, covered no incidents of violence, but after the murder of Brandon Teena it began to regularly feature stories about violence, particularly homicide. Similarly, in the four issues published in 1991, *TV-TS Tapestry*, a long-running magazine for members of the trans community, ran a total of two stories about violence; one described three homicides and the other mentioned the possibility of someone being killed if discovered to be trans. For the next three years, stories about violence were rare. Issues in 1992, 1993, and 1994 included one, two, and three such stories, respectively, and only one murder victim was mentioned by name in any of those three years (Brandon Teena in 1994). By contrast, the winter 1995 issue alone contained details on five separate murders. Moreover, that issue featured an explanation for renaming the magazine *Transgender Tapestry*, which included a list of notable events from the year. At the top of the list was the murder of Brandon Teena.[35]

The sudden shift in news coverage by the trans community press was not because there was an increase in fatal violence after 1994. There were nineteen murders in 1990, including four in the San Diego area alone; fourteen in 1991; fifteen in 1992; and twenty in 1993, whereas there were seven in 1994, fourteen in 1995, and eight in 1996.[36] Instead, the new focus on violence in these publications was the result of trans activists' attention to violence and the resulting belief that the risk of experiencing violence was central to what it is to be transgender.

As I demonstrate in this book, when trans organizations shifted in the 1990s to working to end violence, trans activists adopted a framing that began in the 1980s and was circulated by other identity-based social movements: the claim that violence against minority groups is motivated by hate and that hatred of difference is a society-wide problem.[37] Trans activists argued that it is category membership—the essence of the person—rather than individual interactions between the victim and perpetrator that sparked the violence. Sociologist Kathleen Blee demonstrated that the "racial fungibility of victims" is a defining characteristic of current understandings of "racial violence."[38] Similarly, trans activists produced an idea that trans people are hated for their group membership, so any transgender person could be interchangeable with any other trans victim of violence being described.

In addition to adopting the rhetoric of other identity-based anti-violence activists, trans activists also implemented their tactics, including focusing media and activist attention on "ideal victims" rather than representative cases; ignoring or denying other possible causes for violence besides membership in a single identity category; highlighting victims rather than perpetrators in a way that elided patterns of perpetration; portraying violence as being at "epidemic" levels; and actively participating in what scholar-activists Angela Davis and Elizabeth Martinez dubbed the *oppression Olympics*.[39]

With the adoption of other activists' tactics came the adoption of their proposed solutions. Trans activists organized vigils, worked to educate the public about levels of violence experienced by transgender people, and lobbied for the addition of "actual or perceived gender" and "actual or perceived gender identity" to hate crime legislation. As a result of their activism, actual or perceived gender and gender identity were added to hate crime legislation in thirteen states between 1990 and 2009: Minnesota (1993), California (1998), Missouri (1999), Vermont (1999), Pennsylvania (2002; although it was ruled unconstitutional in 2008), Hawaii (2003), New Mexico (2003), Connecticut (2004), Colorado (2005), Maryland (2005), New Jersey (2008), Oregon (2008), and Washington (2009), as well as the District of Columbia (1990) and Puerto Rico (2002). Moreover, after more than fifteen years of activism, actual or perceived gender and gender identity were added to US federal hate crimes laws in 2009 in the form of the Matthew Shepard and James Byrd, Jr. Hate Crimes Prevention Act.

STUDYING TRANSGENDER IDENTITY-BASED
ANTI-VIOLENCE ACTIVISM

In this book I detail and analyze this history through a systematic collection of documents produced by national social movement organizations engaged in anti-violence activism on behalf of transgender people in the United States between 1990 and 2009. These documents include web pages, press releases, flyers, transcripts of speeches, blogs, e-mails to group members, magazine articles, newsletters, reports on violence, and instructions on how to run vigils and protests. Analyzing publicly available documents produced by trans activists allows me to investigate what messages about the relationship between trans identity and violence were circulated among both transgender and cisgender people.[40] Although this analysis cannot speak to motivations for actions, documents are not subject to revisionist recollections and so are ideal for examining the messages about violence experienced by trans people that were circulated during this period.

My selection of social movement organizations covers the majority of activism being done on the national level around violence against transgender people during the twenty-year period from 1990 to 2009. I include organizations that engaged in this sort of advocacy whether or not it was their sole focus and whether or not they self-identified as a trans group. These organizations include FTM International (FTMI), publisher of the newsletter *FTMi*; Gay and Lesbian Alliance Against Defamation (GLAAD); Gay Straight Alliance (GSA); Gender Education and Advocacy (GEA); Gender Public Advocacy Coalition (GenderPAC); Human Rights Campaign (HRC); National Coalition of Anti-Violence Programs (NCAVP); National Center for Transgender Equality (NCTE); National Transgender Advocacy Coalition (NTAC); Remembering Our Dead (ROD); Southern Poverty Law Center (SPLC); Transgender Day of Remembrance (TDoR); and *Transgender Tapestry*. For details about each organization, see appendix A. I focus on national, rather than local, organizations, as national organizations are more likely to influence mainstream media coverage, federal and state policies, and the style of activism utilized by local groups.[41] By examining this diverse group of organizations, I am able to explore the variety of narratives about violence experienced by trans people as well as the range of tactics utilized to attempt to reduce that violence on a national level.

Trans activists' fight against violence is an ideal site for exploring identity-based anti-violence activism, as trans activists engaged in a very public campaign, producing a large number of advocacy documents aimed at both trans communities and the general public. Most of the documents from this activism are available for analysis because the movement began in the recent past. Importantly, trans activists borrowed and built on the rhetoric of other groups engaged in identity-based anti-violence activism, such as those working to end violence against women, people of color, and gay men and lesbians. Thus, an analysis of trans activist documents is also, by extension, an investigation of some of the language and techniques used by other identity-based anti-violence groups.

My examination of the twenty-year period from 1990 and 2009 traces this activism from the beginning of the transgender anti-violence movement through its crowning achievement: transgender-inclusive federal hate crime legislation. The early 1990s witnessed a burst of transgender rights organizing, including extensive anti-violence activism. By collecting data starting in 1990, I have been able to analyze the lead-up to, and the very beginning of, this identity-based anti-violence movement. My dataset also captures the progression of the movement as well as the relative lull in anti-violence activism that began in the mid-2000s. Several organizations either disbanded or began to falter around 2004, a trend that continued to 2009. GEA disbanded in 2004, and the ROD website stopped adding new victims in 2005. *FTMi* published its final issue in 2008; *Transgender Tapestry* did the same in 2009. Finally, NTAC issued its last press release in 2004 but engaged in lobbying through 2009, and after several years of relative quiet in terms of anti-violence organizing, GenderPAC officially disbanded in 2009. The push for transgender-inclusive hate crime legislation in the years leading up to 2009 included a flurry of activity from the remaining organizations. After that success, however, some activist groups turned their attention to other causes, while others, negatively impacted by the economic crisis that began in 2007, reduced their anti-violence efforts.[42]

I gathered all the available materials that these thirteen organizations produced between 1990 and 2009 related to violence experienced by trans people from both digital and physical archives. *Violence* for these purposes was defined as physical force used against another person. Although there are many types of violence, including *symbolic violence*, activists focused on physical violence, particularly fatal physical violence, and so my analysis reflects that.[43] The digital sources for data included versions of these organizations' websites archived on the extensive internet archive the Wayback Machine, as well as Alternative Press Index, AltPress Watch, GenderWatch, GLBT Life, and the Queer Resources Directory.[44] The physical archives were located at the San Francisco Gay, Lesbian, Bisexual, Transgender Historical Society, the Bancroft Library at the University of California, Berkeley, and the San Francisco Public Library. Most of the issues of *FTMi* and *Transgender Tapestry* were accessed at the Bancroft Library and the San Francisco Public Library, respectively.

Though this collection strategy limits my analysis to what was available on websites and in digital and physical archives, almost all trans activism during this period had an online component.[45] Moreover, because of the value placed on archiving activist materials in the later part of the twentieth century, documents from these organizations have been carefully preserved. Thus, although it is unlikely that I collected every single document about violence produced by these organizations, I was able to gather the vast majority that were made available to the public. Because publicly available documents have the most potential to shape dominant understandings of the identity group and of violence, findings based on these documents best reflect the influence of transgender anti-violence activism.

In total, I collected and analyzed more than one thousand individual documents that mentioned violence against trans people from the thirteen activist organizations. The length of these ranged from less than a page to almost one hundred pages. I organized and analyzed the documents with the assistance of the qualitative software program Atlas.ti, which is especially helpful for managing and coding a large number of texts. I took a grounded theory approach to my analysis of the documents produced by transgender anti-violence activists, focusing on what beliefs both about violence and about what it means to be transgender were reflected and produced in these texts.[46] I carefully coded both for aspects of documents that were extremely common, such as descriptions of vulnerability, as well as those that were exceedingly rare, such as discussions of "pride" and attention to intersectionality. I analyzed the texts with particular attention to two types of rhetorical techniques commonly attended to by social movements scholars as well as those engaged in textual analysis: *frames* (how people answer the question "What is going on here?") and *narratives* (templates for storytelling that follow set arcs). I describe both of these concepts in detail in chapter 2.

In their book *Shaping Abortion Discourse*, sociologists Myra Marx Ferree, William Gamson, Jurgen Gerhards, and Dieter Rucht traced the production of discourse around abortion in six forums (media, social movements, religious groups, political parties, scientists, and the legal realm). They defined a *forum* in the following way: "A forum includes an *arena* in which individual or collective actors engage in public speech acts; an active audience or *gallery* observing what is going on in the arena; and a *backstage*, where the would-be players in the arena work out their ideas and strategize over how they are to be presented, make alliances, and do the everyday work of cultural production."[47] Although Ferree and colleagues did not cite sociologist Pierre Bourdieu, their concept of the forum is similar to his concept of the *field* in that both a forum and a field are socially constructed designations of realms in which unequal actors struggle for access to power.[48] I focus my analysis of activist organizations on the arena of the social movements forum, examining how it is shaped by the larger political field and cultural factors such as beliefs about the identity group. I also explore the potential effects that pubic speech acts made in the arena may have on beliefs about the identity group and ideas about the best ways to work to prevent violence. Finally, I detail the ways in which identity groups' actions in the arena are attempts to influence other forums, mainly the mainstream media and politicians, as they work toward the goal of marking transgender people as socially valuable and deserving of protection from harm.

In addition to my analysis of the documents produced by trans activists engaged in anti-violence work, I have supplemented my findings with an original dataset of all the known murders of people who would be seen by the activists I studied as falling under the transgender umbrella. I gathered information about these homicides from activist documents, the mainstream media, and police records. My methods for collecting and analyzing these homicide data are detailed in appendix B.

In this book I use my extensive collection of documents from trans activists engaged in anti-violence work to expand understandings of anti-violence activism done by and for transgender people. In doing so, I merge my analysis of documents produced by trans activists with existing research on anti-violence activism done by other identity groups in order to explore what happens when activists combine identity politics with a struggle to end violence, asking: What are the unique consequences of fighting violence with a focus on a single identity? What beliefs about both the identity group and violence are produced in the intersection of identity politics and anti-violence activism? How might the use of identity politics to struggle against violence shape practices, including those of being a member of that group and violence-prevention efforts?

ORGANIZATION OF THE BOOK

The narratives activists tell about violence *matter*, in all meanings of the word. They mark certain acts of violence as worthy of attention and mark certain physical features as socially relevant.[49] Chapter 2 takes up this argument, exploring how, although we traditionally see violence as a tool to repress people, the narratives we tell about violence also have the potential to produce beliefs and behaviors, extending the effect of violence beyond the initial act. By studying the narratives told about a violent event, which could be conceived of as the ripples in a pond after a rock is thrown in, researchers can explore the far-reaching consequences of a single act of violence. Narratives about different types of bodies, such as racialized or gendered bodies, engaging in and being victim to violence shape understandings of who does violence and who is vulnerable to violence. Consequently, they also influence proposed solutions to violence as well as practices of being a member of a social category. Chapter 2 details how narratives about violence have influenced understandings and practices of gender, race, and sexuality; how violence can produce not only feelings of victimization but also empowerment and resistance; and the particularly powerful effects of narratives about homicide.

Despite arguments made by activists that all trans people are at equal risk of violence at all times, trans activists did not give all victims the same level of attention. Social movements often focus on *ideal victims* (those seen as especially sympathetic) and tell *landmark narratives* (those thought of as exceptionally compelling) in order to gain the most attention for their cause.[50] These tactics have unique consequences when utilized within identity-based anti-violence activism, as they influence understandings of what it means to be a member of the identity group and impact proposed solutions to the problem. In chapter 3 I examine which cases trans activists highlighted in their work to reduce violence. I find that two murder victims, Brandon Teena and Gwen Araujo, are mentioned in activist narratives significantly more frequently than other victims. Their stories become a lens by which activists view violence, such that they discuss subsequent murders as "another Brandon Teena" or "just like Gwen Araujo." This phenomenon is notable because these two murders are quite exceptional and not reflective of the patterns of fatal violence experienced by trans people. The uniqueness of their stories may be what caused them to become more famous, but it has serious consequences as activists develop solutions based on these two cases and trans people shape their lives so that they do not become "another Brandon Teena."

In chapters 4 and 5 I explore the understandings of what it means to be transgender that were produced in identity-based anti-violence documents. Due to the logics of identity politics, whereby only one identity is highlighted at a time, activists engaged in identity-based anti-violence activism tend to focus on a single identity as the root of violence experienced by their group. As I demonstrate in chapter 4, activists depicted "transgender" as an internally homogenous category by portraying all trans people as at equal risk of violence at all times. Despite evidence that economically disadvantaged transgender women of color are the most at risk for violence of any group of transgender people and the knowledge that transgender people may be attacked because they are perceived as "gay" rather than as "transgender," I found that anti-violence activists argued that transgender people who experience violence do so because of their transgender status alone. Activists did this using several techniques, including labeling victims as transgender, dismissing causes besides anti-transgender hatred, and grouping diverse victims together. These tactics helped draw attention to the issue of anti-transgender violence by downplaying the role of perceived sexuality, race, and class. Moreover, they encouraged all trans people to be concerned about violence due to the implication that every trans person is at equal risk. Overlooking certain patterns of violence has serious consequences, however, including constructing transgender as what I term a *homogenous subjecthood* and deflecting attention from possible solutions that knowledge of the patterns would suggest. The narrative that all trans people are at equal risk of violence at all times has been widely adopted by the mainstream media as well as academics. Circulation of these beliefs about risk escalates levels of fear and reduces the chances of successfully decreasing violence by deterring attendance to multiple causes. Moreover, identity-based anti-violence activism encourages narratives in which *identity*, rather than other possibilities, is the motivation for violence. This discourages non-identity-based explanations and solutions and, by focusing on the role of *difference* in motivating violence, hinders an exploration of violence within groups.

In addition to constructing transgender as a homogenous category, activists also depicted its members as intrinsically vulnerable to violence. Activists worked to portray transgender people as socially valuable and to mark violence against them as morally wrong, constructing what I term a *valuable subjecthood*. However, as I detail in chapter 5, the unique combination of identity politics and anti-violence activism also had the unintended consequence of portraying vulnerability to violence as central to membership in the category transgender, facilitating the construction of what I term a *vulnerable subjecthood*. Though all people in society may suffer violence at any time, we only think of certain groups as inherently vulnerable to violence. Members of those social categories experience higher levels of fear than those not marked with vulnerable subjecthood and develop elaborate strategies for avoiding violence. The practices of anti-violence activists are likely to solidify these feelings of vulnerability. Due to competition in the social problems marketplace, trans activists utilized a number of techniques that, although effective in gaining attention for their cause, also produced an idea that transgender people are at constant risk of being killed. Epitomized by the annual Transgender Day of Remembrance, in which activists mourn murdered trans people and encourage participants to *identify with the dead*, the labor done by social movement actors to mark transgender as a valuable subject category unintentionally also produced it as a potentially unlivable category defined by fear. This is particularly notable considering that data indicate transgender people do not experience more fatal violence than cisgender people, possibly due to the extremely high homicide rate for cisgender people in the United States.[51]

Descriptions of violence imply a cause, and causal narratives suggest solutions. As such, the practices of identity-based anti-violence activism shape understandings of how to respond to violence. In chapter 6 I examine what solutions activists regularly advocated for and which did not receive much attention. I find that between 1990 and 2009 trans activists focused mainly on adding gender identity as a protected category to hate crime legislation. This turn to the government for protection has notable ramifications as these solutions literally write the group's vulnerability and status as hated into law and expand the power of the criminal justice system, an institution known to disproportionately criminalize transgender people.[52] Moreover, in their argument that violence experienced by trans people is motivated by hatred of the category, activists assumed that perpetrators knew what transgender is, a dubious assumption in the early years of activism. Other common responses to violence suggested by activists focused on marking transgender as a valuable subjecthood through mourning the dead and making victims count through enumeration of those crimes and educating others about levels of violence. In doing so, they followed in the footsteps of other identity-based anti-violence movements.[53] They differ, however, from those movements in that they did not regularly advocate "pride" or "coming out" as a solution, nor were their organizations focused on "fighting back."

In the conclusion I highlight some trends in trans activism since 2009, showing how the movement has and has not altered. I do so through an analysis of all the trans anti-violence documents produced in 2018 by the organizations I studied for this book. Due to pressures to acknowledge intersectionality, trans activists have begun to highlight aspects of race, class, and gender that were not focused on by most organizations between 1990 and 2009. However, for the most part, proposed solutions have stayed the same, as has the narrative of vulnerability and the tendency to focus on extreme cases. As such, much of chapter 7 is focused on detailing alternative approaches to anti-violence activism. The main purpose of this book is to help reduce violence experienced by trans people, with the idea that improving anti-violence activism is one path toward making trans lives more livable. I draw on all of the findings from the previous chapters to offer alternative approaches. Some of these come from "outliers" in the textual data—trans activists engaging in unusual, but potentially better, tactics—whereas others come from insights from other social movements, including more contemporary trans activism, and from my own critiques of the unintended consequences of identity-based anti-violence activism. These suggestions include redoing identity-based anti-violence activism to construct what I term a *multifaceted subjecthood*. This can be accomplished by acknowledging the diversity within the category transgender and reducing the negative impacts of narratives about vulnerability by highlighting successful resistance to violence and telling narratives of transgender joy. In addition, I propose unlinking identity politics from anti-violence activism. My hope is that these suggestions for alternative practices will be useful for rethinking how we work to reduce violence and make more lives livable.

2. Violence Matters

Producing Identity through Accounts of Murder

Imagine that as you scroll through your feed on a popular social media site, you see a headline for a news article that reads "Community Mourns Homicide." As those in your social network have deemed this story important, you click on it and begin to read. The story contains details about both the victim and the perpetrator, including their gender, race, and sexuality. How does this information shape your understanding of the violence that occurred? Suppose you share identity categories with the victim. How does that make you feel? Do you fear that something similar might occur to you? How does the fact that the violence was fatal influence your emotions? What about your behavior toward people who share identity categories with the perpetrator; might you interact with them differently in the future? Now suppose that you have heard similar stories your whole life, and people have told you that individuals with your identities are highly vulnerable to violence. How does the repetition of narratives about acts of fatal violence against people like you influence your beliefs and behaviors?

In this chapter I explore why and how these questions *matter*, in all meanings of the word. Most people who consume popular media are exposed to narratives about violence every day. These stories may constrain our actions, stopping us from behaving in certain ways. However, they are also productive, encouraging certain behaviors as well as constructing ideas about what it means to be part of a particular identity category. It is this consequence of violence that is missing from most scholarship on the topic. Violence, contrary to common understandings, is a form of *productive power*, meaning it influences thoughts and actions. Traditionally, academics have seen violence as a tool used to oppress people and stop them from doing what they want to do. Although violence does have that effect, it also has the ability to encourage beliefs and behaviors. Nowhere is this more evident than in the stories we tell about violence. Though the initial act of violence may only affect those directly involved, retellings of that violence by activists and in the media have further-ranging social effects. This occurs because the way we talk about violence teaches people about who is likely to be a perpetrator and who is likely to be a victim.[1] It also teaches us how to interpret violence, often through the lenses of social categories such as gender, race, and sexuality. For example, the violence experienced by a straight, white man during a war is seen as proof that he is "strong" and a "hero," whereas violence experienced by a gay, white man at the hands of a homophobic bigot is seen as evidence of his being "weak" and a "victim." Moreover, not only do beliefs about gender, race, and sexuality shape understandings of violence; the stories we tell about acts of violence also affect our beliefs about various groups of people in our society, including what it means to be a person of color, a woman, gay, and transgender. These beliefs then influence behavior, such as discouraging women, but not men, from walking alone at night.[2]

REPRESSIVE VERSUS PRODUCTIVE POWER

Violence is typically studied with a focus on *repressive power*, paying little attention to *productive power*. Repressive power, in philosopher Michel Foucault's work, limits ways of acting; focuses on controlling the body; and says "no," stopping us from acting on our desires.[3] In contrast, productive power produces ways of thinking and acting; focuses on affecting the mind; and says "yes," encouraging certain desires. Through shaping the mind, productive power controls the body and constructs subjects.[4] Foucault argued that although power that prohibits action is much more visible and is what people usually think of when talking about "power," it is the weaker of the two forms.[5] He argued that to fully understand the role of power, we must look at what it produces, including our ideas about the world as well as our actions in it.

If we were to place acts into the supposed mutually exclusive categories of repressive power and productive power, nothing, it seems, would more clearly belong in the repressive grouping than physical violence, especially fatal physical violence. Violence, both actual and threatened, is often a means of stopping actions. This can range from spanking children in an attempt to end certain behaviors to violent suppression of entire groups of people through dictatorship or war. However, even Foucault's clearest example of repressive power—the public execution—is also a moment of productive power.[6] Publicly killing someone convicted of crime can induce terror, stopping potential future criminal actions. However, it can also prompt rebellion, particularly if the punishment is viewed as unwarranted. Moreover, the narratives told about the execution likely shape beliefs about the government that authorized the killing, solidifying its claim to power or calling its morality into question.

To make sense of the concept of productive power, it is helpful to first understand Foucault's conception of power itself. Foucault argued that power, contrary to dominant understandings of it, is exercised, not held. He detailed how power is enacted through all actions and "comes from everywhere."[7] Although not all actors have the same access to all forms of power, and different forms of power are more or less easy to exert from particular social positions, power is exercised not only top-down, but also laterally and bottom-up. Foucault took special care to contest the belief that "resistance" is against or outside of "power," contending instead that resistance itself is an act of power.[8]

Much of the productive aspect of power occurs through *discourses*, which are "practices that systematically form the objects of which they speak."[9] Discourses are sets of knowledge that have an internal logic and structure that produce particular social realities, including identities, desires, practices, and the materiality of bodies, while also limiting or erasing others.[10] Post-structuralist scholars argue that discourses, through their repetition and their tie to biological phenomena such as bodies, come to seem natural and thus often remain unquestioned, taking on the label of truth. In this way, "truth . . . is something which societies have to work to produce."[11] But discourses are not static; they are processes and sites of struggle between subjects. Although those subjects themselves are shaped through discourses, they are not determined by them and so can create social change through the processes of language.

A discourse can be identified both through the orderedness of its knowledge and through the orderedness of the practices it produces. As linguist Sara Mills explained, "A discursive structure can be detected because of the systematicity of the ideas, opinions, concepts, ways of thinking and behaving which are formed within a particular context, and because of the effects of those ways of thinking and behaving."[12] Mills argued that discourses should be studied because of what they reveal about the society that constructs them: "The main reason for conducting an analysis of the structures of discourse is not to uncover the truth or the origin of a statement but rather to discover the support mechanisms which allow it to be said and keep it in place. These support mechanisms are both intrinsic to discourse itself and also extra-discursive, in the sense that they are socio-cultural."[13] Beyond better comprehending the culture that produces these discourses, it is also vital to study discourses due to their profound consequences in terms of shaping people's lives. This book applies both this method of identifying discourses and this justification for the importance of a study of discourses to understanding violence, identity, and the relationship between the two. Utilizing this approach, I examine how identity-based anti-violence activism constructs beliefs about what it is to be a member of the identity group the activists are working to protect. I explore how those beliefs produce particular emotions, including fear, and behaviors, such as violence-prevention practices.

REPRESSIVE POWER IN STUDIES OF VIOLENCE

Most scholarship on violence only explores its repressive aspects. As such, there is a focus on how violence constrains rather than produces subjects and, relatedly, on how violence is the effect, rather than the cause, of ideologies, norms, beliefs about groups, and categories of people. Many scholars of violence against members of historically marginalized groups argue that violence is caused by hatred, "phobias," or "isms," and that it oppresses group members.[14] The vast majority of academic work on violence experienced by trans people focuses on the repressive aspects of violence, including arguing that it works to "erase" or "make invisible" transgender lives and possibilities.[15] By contrast, the existing literature tends not to attend to how ideas about, and practices of, "transgender" may be produced in moments of, and narratives about, violence.[16] Based on this extensive literature, it is clear that violence does constrain and oppress subjects. However, we should also explore how these acts of violence produce social categories, subjects, norms, and behaviors, including violent actions themselves.

There is a startling silence within post-structuralist scholarship about the productive aspects of violence. For example, philosopher Judith Butler's work on the production of gender included discussions of violence.[17] But Butler focused only on how ideas about gender can cause violence, to the detriment of an investigation of how practices of violence can produce and reproduce gender. Foucault himself, despite arguing that all acts are acts of power and that productive power is the more pervasive form, was largely mum on the question of violence. When he did discuss whether violence is a form of productive power, he was inconsistent. In "The Subject and Power," he both argued that violence is not productive and then conceded that productive power may include acts of violence. Regarding the repressive vein, he stated that "a relationship of violence acts upon a body or upon things; it forces, it bends, it breaks on the wheel, it destroys, or it closes the door on all possibilities."[18] On the same page, though, he argued that "obviously the bringing into play of [productive] power relations does not exclude the use of violence."[19] This ambivalence is also present in *Discipline and Punish*. In his discussion of how punishment has changed, Foucault worked hard to detail how acts of violence are part of sovereign/repressive power but not disciplinary/productive power. At the same time, though, he described productive effects of acts of violence, such as witnessing violent public executions teaching the public that the way to achieve their goals is through violence.[20] Moreover, he mentioned that *subjection* (i.e., the making of the subject) can be achieved through "violence or ideology."[21] It may be that the ambivalence in Foucault's own work is one factor that has discouraged scholars from examining the productive aspects of violence.

VIOLENCE AS A FORM OF PRODUCTIVE POWER

In this book I challenge this silence regarding the productive aspects of acts of violence within empirical studies as well as post-structuralist theory. The suggestion that physical force should be studied as productive power is, of course, not entirely new; however, it remains undertheorized. A small number of academics have argued that we must examine the role of power in producing ideas about—and practices of—violence.[22] These scholars have found that violence, through our interpretations of it and the stories we tell about it, produces beliefs about the use of force, including what counts as violence and conceptions about who are "victims" and "perpetrators." Further, they have revealed that these ideas shape practices, including doing violence, victimhood, and attempted violence prevention. Of course, the repressive/productive divide in scholarship is not absolute; there are often of hints of productive power in scholarship that otherwise focuses on repressive power.[23]

One exception to the silence on violence as a form or productive power is criminologist Gail Mason's *The Spectacle of Violence: Homophobia, Gender and Knowledge*, which examined "the constitutive capacity of physical violence" in lesbians' accounts of being attacked by others.[24] Mason argued that "violence is both a corporeal injury which inflicts direct harm upon individual bodies, and a discursive statement that infiltrates the processes of subjectification through which these bodies are constituted."[25] As such, violence produces subject positions and constructs identity categories, such as sexual identities. Moreover, violence shapes ideas about some identities being especially vulnerable to, as well as appropriate targets for, violence and other identities as being likely, and proper, perpetrators of violence.

In her analysis, Mason explicitly excluded fatal violence, arguing that "the violent extinction of life demands an analysis of its own."[26] This book picks up where Mason left off, building on and extending past conceptions by exploring questions of how violence, particularly murder, "matters."

In *Bodies That Matter: On the Discursive Limits of "Sex"*, Butler offered two meanings of the discursive process of mattering.[27] The first is that certain parts of bodies become culturally important, marking people as members of specific categories. Although all bodies are different in many ways, current social structures only highlight certain differences as socially meaningful and place people in categories based on those differences. For instance, by defining genitals and skin color as meaningful, discourses produce subjectivities and create the matter of bodies. By this Butler did not mean that words make flesh, but that categories, by making certain parts of flesh meaningful, make those parts of flesh exist socially. Discourses also make certain bodies *matter* in the sense that they produce ideas of social worth and value. By either supporting or condemning violence, narratives create an idea of who is socially worthy of protection from violence and who is an appropriate target. Extending Butler's arguments, we can thus ask: How does violence, including fatal violence, make the matter of bodies and make certain bodies matter? How do acts of violence produce subjectivities, including beliefs about, and experiences of, being a member of an identity group? How do narratives of violence shape the practices of violence, victimhood, and violence prevention? My analysis reveals that identity-based anti-violence activists tell narratives about violence that emphasize the role of identity, including gender, race, and sexuality, in the violence. These identities are often indicated by bodily aspects, such as genitals and skin color, and activists point to those factors as provoking the violence, making them matter. Like other identity-based anti-violence activists, trans activists often tell narratives about murders when attempting to gain attention for their cause. This focus on fatal violence and the emphasis on a single identity category shapes beliefs about what it means to be transgender, portraying trans lives as constrained and unlivable.

FRAMES AND NARRATIVES

Frames and narratives are two ways that violence constructs the matter of bodies and marks certain bodies as mattering. Framing an act of violence provides a particular interpretation. That interpretation is often circulated socially through narratives, which extend the consequences of a single violent act. Like the ripples in a pond after a rock is thrown in, narratives about violence spread beliefs about what sorts of violence occur, to whom, and why.

Frames

Sociologist Erving Goffman used the notion of *frames* to refer to the ways in which people understand or explain a situation or action. Frames answer the question: "What is it that's going on here?"[28] In doing so, frames provide an interpretation that highlights certain aspects while ignoring others. A useful way to conceptualize this is the trimming of a photograph to fit it into a picture frame that is too small or zooming in on a digital photograph so that only part of the picture is in the frame. By narrowing our focus to particular aspects of a complex situation, frames emphasize some facets. However, in not presenting the whole picture, frames elide other features of a situation. For instance, in attempting to explain school shootings, people tend to utilize one of a few frames, including attributing the violence to mental health issues or guns. These frames both help people interpret the violence and cause people to ignore other possible causes.

Social movement activists regularly utilize frames to promote particular understandings of the issues for which they advocate.[29] In identity-based anti-violence activism, one of those frames, not surprisingly, is *identity*. In these moments, activists stress how being a member of a certain social category influenced the violence, while downplaying the role that other factors may have played. Transgender anti-violence activists engaged in this practice regularly, labeling murder victims as "transgender" even if they did not identify as such and attributing the violence to "hatred" of transgender people, omitting information that might point to other causes.

Frames have far-reaching consequences. Social movement framings greatly influence understandings of violence held by individuals not in the social movement.[30] Moreover, frames influence proposed solutions to violence.[31] For instance, identity-based framings of causes for violence often encourage proposals for identity-based solutions such as hate crime legislation aimed at "protecting" particular groups of people. Although some scholars treat the use of frames as conscious and deliberate, it is important to note that this is often not the case.[32] In addition, even when frames are intentional, one cannot control their outcomes. Thus, frames can have significant unintended consequences.[33]

Narratives

Attention to narratives is another way to examine the productive role of acts of violence. *Narratives* tell a story about events, are constructed for a particular audience, and are recounted by a narrator.[34] They are told about something seen as significant enough to describe, and in the retelling the events become even more important because narratives focus the audience's attention on them.[35] Narratives are comprised of a number of frames and thus highlight certain parts of the situation while ignoring others. When people talk or write about violence, they often create a narrative to explain it—a coherent storyline that usually has a high level of cultural resonance and does not include all possible "facts" but instead is a selection of information about events, presented together in a way that makes sense at a particular historical moment.[36] These narratives then circulate culturally, shaping beliefs and practices, including practices of violence, victimhood, and violence prevention.[37]

An examination of narratives is imperative to the study of the productive aspects of violence because telling a story of how the violence happened shapes beliefs about why people are violent and which types of violence are or are not socially acceptable.[38] These narratives can take many forms, including stories told about one's own experiences of violence, everyday conversations about violent acts experienced by others, news coverage of violence, and activist narratives.[39] As they characterize the victims and the perpetrators, narratives about violence shape ideas about the people involved in particular acts of violence and in this way can influence the practices of both doing violence and being a victim of violence.[40]

Narratives about violence, to the extent that audience members share identities with either the perpetrators or victims of violence, can produce feelings of powerfulness or vulnerability in those who have never personally experienced physical violence.[41] In this way, the effects of violence, including fatal violence, stretch far beyond the harm to, or death of, one or more people. For example, cultural narratives about famous school shootings such as Columbine, Sandy Hook, and Parkland have deeply influenced the experience of being a student or a parent of a student in the United States. Schools that have never had even a threat of a shooting regularly engage in active shooter drills, and parents live in fear that their children will not survive school that day.

Telling narratives is common within social movements. In the social problems marketplace there are acceptable plots, and those working to end violence against their identity group tend to reproduce those plots in their struggle to be heard.[42] The most successful narratives are those that are the most culturally resonant.[43] Illustrating this, there are a number of different versions of the murder of Mathew Sheppard, but one has become dominant. Journalist Stephen Jimenez argued in *The Book of Matt* that Sheppard was a regular user and possible dealer of methamphetamine and knew the men who killed him (doing drugs with them and possibly having a sexual relationship with one of them).[44] However, the story of a gay rights martyr makes more cultural sense and better serves anti-violence activists' cause. Thus, the dominant narrative of "strangers meeting a defenseless gay man, being panicked by his homosexuality, and executing him in a fit of hatred" is the one circulated by the mainstream media, activists, and politicians.[45]

In US culture, the standard plot of a violence narrative includes at least one victim and one perpetrator. We tend to see violence as binary; one is either a doer of violence or the one to whom violence is done, not both.[46] Once codified as legitimate victims, individuals or groups are seen as innocent and worthy of protection.[47] An identity group being repeatedly characterized as victims or perpetrators in narratives of violence shapes perceptions of future violent acts such that members of that group are assumed to be either innocent or guilty. These repeated characterizations can make all members of a group be perceived as "always already" victims or perpetrators. For instance, despite the fact that women successfully resist the vast majority of rape attempts, newspaper articles about sexual assault are almost always about completed rapes and rarely mention resistance.[48] As sociologists Jocelyn Hollander and Katie Rodgers argued, in their narratives about violence "newspapers 'victimize' the targets of sexual assault even when they fight back, constructing them as victims (and particular kinds of *feminized* victims) rather than resisters."[49] These narratives have serious consequences, teaching that women are victims, men are perpetrators, and women are unable to resist rape; these lessons then affect men's and women's behavior.[50]

By highlighting a cause, narratives about violence imply a solution. If one tells a story in which violence was caused by hate, one implies that a solution would be to reduce hate. In this way, narratives about violence shape the practices of violence prevention. Sociologists Joel Best and Valerie Jenness and Ryken Grattet demonstrated that through their framings and narratives, activists were central actors in the construction of the idea of "hate crimes," including defining the types of acts that would be considered hate crimes, attributing causes to those crimes, and getting attempted solutions institutionalized.[51] Anti–hate crime activists constructed a new type of crime and a new type of victim and proposed crime prevention policies. Moreover, activists' framing of the problem shaped those proposed solutions.

In addition to official policies, narratives about violence also influence individual prevention practices. For example, due to the prevalence of "stranger danger" stories of men raping women, women restrict their behaviors in an attempt to protect themselves from sexual assault.[52] These strategies, which I term *rape avoidance labor* and others have termed a "rape schedule," range from avoiding being alone in public at night to checking the back seat of the car before getting in.[53] Often these strategies are at odds with actual data on sexual assault, which demonstrate that most rapes are perpetrated by someone known to the victim.[54] Moreover, these strategies rarely include learning to fight back, since despite evidence that resistance is highly effective in stopping a rape attempt, most narratives about sexual assault do not include successful resistance.[55]

In this book I demonstrate that it is vital to attend to narratives in activists' statements about violence experienced by transgender people. Doing so reveals how these narratives both reflect and produce ideas about gender and violence. Moreover, they shape practices of gender and violence, including practices of being transgender and attempts at violence prevention. Importantly, the profusion of narratives about violence experienced by transgender people has not been offset by narratives of transgender joy. This imbalance produces an unlivable life filled with fear.

VIOLENCE SHAPES SUBJECTHOODS

Violence, as a form of productive power, *matters* in the sense that it both highlights certain parts of bodies and ascribes social meaning to them. As such, violence plays a role in constructing systems of stratification, including gender, sexuality, and race, as well as in constructing the subjects within those systems.[56] These systems are bound together through *intersectionality*.[57] As sociologist Patricia Hill Collins argued: "While violence certainly seems central to maintaining *separate* oppressions—those of race, gender, social class, nationality/citizenship status, sexual orientation and age—violence may be equally important in structuring *intersections* among these social hierarchies. Rather than viewing violence primarily as part of distinct social hierarchies of race and gender, violence may serve as conceptual glue that binds them together."[58] Each body is *comaterialized* through the multiple social labels it carries; race, class, gender, sexuality, age, and so forth together make the matter of bodies. Every unique comaterialization has a different relationship to violence. Through this, perceptions of people shaped by their particular location in systems of power affect the types of violence they are at risk for as well as what sorts of violence they might enact.

Violence, both threatened and actual, is an important part of current systems of stratification. It functions as a means of enforcement of gender norms, is used to control sexual practices and maintain sexual hierarchies, and is used to regulate racialized subjects.[59] But gendered violence and violence related to sexuality and race tend to be conceptualized only as repressive, not productive.[60] These forms of violence are thus seen as simply reflecting, rather than producing, these systems of inequality. For example, scholars have argued that gendered beliefs cause rape, including the ideas that men need sex and are strong enough to force sex on women. However, rapists are not acting on an innate vulnerability of their victims; instead, the act of violence itself produces that vulnerability.[61] The focus solely on how beliefs about gender, sexuality, and race cause particular forms of violence impairs our ability to reduce violence. In our search for effective violence-reduction strategies, we must also attend to how violence itself produces and perpetuates gender, sexuality, and race as social systems.

By examining it as a form of productive power, we can see that violence constructs ideas about, and practices of, gender, sexuality, and race. Both actual acts of violence and the stories we tell about them create the materiality of subjects. Violence genders, sexualizes, and racializes by highlighting parts of the body, such as skin color or genitals, and aspects of identities, such as sexuality, as both socially meaningful and indicative of vulnerability or dangerousness. For example, sociologist Jocelyn Hollander argued that in mainstream US society, everyday conversations about violence construct a perception that women are inherently vulnerable to violence and men are inherently dangerous, despite the fact that men experience more violence than women.[62] Women are discussed as vulnerable in three key ways. First, they are portrayed as defenseless through descriptions of them as "naturally" smaller and weaker than men. Second, more stories are told about women, rather than men, experiencing violence. Finally, men are more often described as dangerous, implicitly constructing women as vulnerable due to the belief that men and women are "opposite." This perception of vulnerability affects how women go about their daily lives; in response to this perception, women adopt a number of risk-mitigating behaviors, including limiting their use of public spaces and internalizing an awareness of the constant potential for violence against them. As sociologist Alex Campbell argued, these "multiple 'safe-keeping' acts . . . have come to be a performative condition of normative femininity."[63] Just as rape avoidance labor constitutes femininity, the doing of violence constructs masculinity. Through interviews with heterosexual men who had engaged in domestic violence, sociologists Kristin Anderson and Debra Umberson found that these "batterers attempt to construct masculine identities through the practice of violence and the discourse about violence that they provide."[64] Thus far, the limited literature on how violence produces gender has focused on "women" and "men." In this book I extend these examinations by attending to another gendered construction resulting from violence: beliefs about, and practices of, being "transgender" versus "cisgender." I argue that the category transgender and its counterpart cisgender are produced in identity-based anti-violence activists' narratives about violence. Like men, cisgender people are portrayed as perpetrators and unlikely to experience violence. By contrast, like conventional depictions of women, transgender people are described as victims and highly vulnerable to violence.[65]

In addition to constructing gender, violence also produces sexuality and race. Everyday conversations about violence portray gay men and lesbians as vulnerable to violence, and "homophobia-related violence" marks gay men and lesbians as "appropriate" targets for violence.[66] In a similar vein, philosopher Frantz Fanon argued that through the violent act of colonization, colonizers create the colonized.[67] This practice dehumanizes the colonized and also marks them as racially "other" to the colonizers. Likewise, sociologist Kathleen Blee stressed that "violence can be about *establishing* race rather than being an *effect* of preformed racial categories."[68]

PRODUCING FEAR THROUGH IDENTIFYING WITH THE VICTIM

Violence is particularly productive of subjectivities and the practices of subjecthood when members of a social category *identify with the victim*. This often occurs through hearing narratives about violence against members of your identity group. Because of the logics of identity politics, people hearing about such violence are likely to believe that they are also vulnerable to violence and, as a consequence, feel fear. Scholars have termed this process *vicarious victimization*.[69] For example, when women hear about violence against other women, they may experience fear and therefore alter their actions to reduce the risk of violence.[70] This is largely because dominant understandings of violence include the belief that being a member of the category "woman" makes one more susceptible to violence and because women hearing about an act of violence against another woman are encouraged to see themselves as at similar risk for experiencing violence. By contrast, hearing about an act of violence against a man may not make a woman fear violence more than she already does, unless, of course, she shares another pertinent identity category with him.

Narratives about violence against members of an identity group produce fear in those who share that identity. Through stories about violence, those who have been vested with *vulnerable subjecthoods* are taught to be afraid.[71] Illustrating this, sociologists Nicole Rader and Stacy Haynes demonstrated that "both gender and fear of crime are learned" and "fear of crime socialization occurs each time an individual hears a story about victimization."[72] The dominant cultural narratives about gender and violence are that women are weak and vulnerable to violence, and men are strong and dangerous.[73] These narratives produce high levels of fear among women and low levels of fear among men, despite the fact that men are more likely to experience violence.[74] Moreover, when narratives of violence in the mainstream media disproportionately focus on "stranger danger," white victims, and perpetrators of color, white women have higher levels of fear, and all women are more likely to be afraid of men who are black, Latinx, and/or not known to them.[75] Notably, these patterns of fear do not align with actual patterns of victimization. Terror then shapes behaviors, constructing a *geography of fear* in which women avoid places and people they have been taught are dangerous.[76] These constrained actions constitute femininity and construct women as *"subjects of fear."*[77]

Social movements working to reduce violence often encourage members of identity groups, such as women, gay men and lesbians, people of color, and transgender people, to identify with victims of violence by arguing that it is category membership that motivates violence. They do this by arguing that the violence was caused by homophobia, racism, or transphobia or that all women are vulnerable to violence. As a result, such anti-violence activism has the unintended consequence of constructing vulnerable subjecthoods for the very populations it is attempting to protect, making their lives less, rather than more, livable. This feeling of vulnerability means that members of these identity groups do not feel safe around other identity groups portrayed as dangerous to them, because the risk for violence is attributed to *who* someone is (which is often outside of their control), rather than *what* they have done (which feels controllable). In some instances, this may cause people to refuse to adopt a particular identity in hopes that such a refusal will protect them from violence. Sociologists Lory Britt and David Heise argued that identity-based activists hoping to mobilize people to action intentionally provoke fear, and narratives about violence are especially effective in producing fear. However, they warned that "the trouble is that fear leaves people feeling vulnerable, so they may prefer flight over fight."[78]

We can illustrate the process of producing fear by identifying with the victim by comparing two types of narratives and frames, (1) those about violence against a group thought to be hated by others and (2) those about violence experienced by a group for which a relationship between their identity and risk for violence has not been articulated. Take, for instance, the very different narratives told about two of the most deadly mass shootings in the United States: the shooting at Pulse, a gay nightclub, on Latin Night in 2016, and the shooting at an outdoor country music festival in Las Vegas in 2017. Victims of both mass shootings shared a particular identity (respectively, gay and country music fan), as opposed to those killed in shootings that could be interpreted as more "random," such as a shooting of pedestrians in a large city.[79] However, only one shooting was framed as motivated by the shooter's hatred of an identity group. Because there is not a widespread belief that country music fans are hated enough to provoke fatal violence, people did not assume that the Las Vegas shooting was motivated by hatred of an identity group. By contrast, because of existing understandings of homophobia, people did assume that the Pulse shooting was motivated by hatred of gay people. Although there is substantial evidence that the shooter picked the club randomly and that the shooting was motivated by anti-American, not homophobic, beliefs, many people still attribute the shooting to homophobia.[80] This interpretation has had substantial consequences for people who share identities with the Pulse victims. Not only did those who experienced the Pulse shooting see this as a confirmation of their vulnerability due to being part of marginalized communities, so too did many LGBT people who were not at the club, especially LGBT people of color. By contrast, there has not been a similar feeling of vulnerability among country music fans. This is particularly notable considering the subsequent shooting in 2018 at a country western bar in Thousand Oaks, California. Despite the facts that the 2018 shooter also targeted a location patronized by country music fans and that the victims of the Thousand Oaks shooting included some who had survived the Las Vegas shooting, neither shooting fostered a sense of identity-based vulnerability.

THE PARTICULAR POWER OF HOMICIDE

Fatal violence is often seen as the most repressive form of violence. Indeed, Foucault argued that "it is over life, throughout its unfolding, that power establishes its domination; death is power's limit, the moment that escapes it."[81] In death, power can no longer shape the subject. However, individuals who experience violence are not the only subjects influenced by that violent act. Violence, including fatal violence, has wide-ranging consequences through its incorporation into discourse, and narratives about murder are an exceptionally rich, although underexplored, site for the examination of the productive aspects of violence.

Far from being the least productive form of power through violence, murder has the potential to be its most. Compared to nonfatal violence, the taking of life is more likely to be covered by mainstream media, talked about by activists, and discussed in everyday conversation. Thus, it is not true that "dead men tell no tales." In fact, dead men (and those of all other genders) generate an enormous number of tales, particularly if their deaths are especially culturally resonant and/or unusual. Thus, although homicide is the end of an individual, that ending becomes a potent site for meaning making.[82]

The practice of identifying with the victim is one way fatal violence can be productive. Although death ends power's control over the victim of violence, when other subjects *identify with the dead*, adopting the idea "that could be me," fatal violence shapes subjectivities. Murders, because of their fatal nature, evoke more terror in those who hear about them and identify with the dead. Those who identify with the dead may potentially become fearful, cautious subjects, perceiving themselves as "always already" victims.

In identity-based anti-violence activism, narratives about homicide are extremely common due to their capacity to evoke interest and compassion. However, they also have substantial unintended consequences. Unlike stories of violence in which the victim successfully resisted, narratives about fatal violence are lacking a message of hope and what Butler argued is vital for a livable life: "possibility."[83] Moreover, they do not point toward tools for violence prevention. Narratives about nonfatal violence have the potential to portray the victim as a hero; by contrast, the main character in stories of murders is, at best, a martyr. Those different characterizations evoke distinct emotions for those who identify with the victim. To illustrate this, think back to how you felt at the beginning of this chapter when reading about the hypothetical homicide of someone who shared your identity categories. Furthermore, unlike stories of resistance, narratives about murder do not include a message about how to stop violence. Stories of homicide may include lessons about what increases risk, including behaviors and identities, but they do not tell listeners what they can do to protect themselves. As such, they can be highly disempowering.

UNEXPECTED OUTCOMES OF VIOLENCE

Examining violence as a form of productive power can challenge the dominant assumption held by many scholars that experiencing violence marks one as vulnerable or weak.[84] In addition to eliciting fear, violence has some less intuitive effects, including fostering resistance and feelings of strength. Because of the multiple meanings of violence and the variety of ways people interpret it, experiencing an act of violence does not always mark one as vulnerable. Although acts of violence, either directly experienced or heard about, often result in fear, they also may produce resistance. For instance, as a consequence of violence within their neighborhoods gay men and lesbians banded together in the 1970s to fight against it.[85] In this way, violence helps produce collectivities and feelings of togetherness. Thus, rather than causing people to cower and conform, as is often assumed, acts of violence may incite people to organize and resist as a group. This can then produce identity categories united in their resistance, rather than in their vulnerability.

In addition, many people who experience and survive violence interpret that as a sign of their strength rather than their vulnerability. This is especially true for members of identity categories that have not been vested with a vulnerable subjecthood and are therefore not perceived as weak. For example, if a man who is a soldier is taken hostage by an enemy force and tortured but survives and returns to his country, he is usually celebrated for his strength. Moreover, others also interpret his endurance as symbolic of the country's might, and this understanding is shared in the narratives they tell about the violence. Similarly, many men who have been in fistfights with other men use stories about these fights to demonstrate their masculinity and strength, even if they "lost" the altercation, and heroes in action films who experience extraordinary levels of violence are seen as strong because of those encounters.[86] Thus, being a victim of violence does not always produce feelings of weakness. Whether experiences of violence produce a sense of vulnerability or invincibility depends on a variety of other factors, including the circumstances of the violence and dominant discourses about the people involved.

Violence may also be less likely to produce feelings of weakness when it occurs between members of the same social category or when, despite meeting the definition of "violence," it is not interpreted as violent. Because we homogenize subject categories, we see members of the same category as equally able to enact violence and equally vulnerable to violence. As such, physical force by one member of a social category against another of the same social category is often not seen as resulting in actual harm. In fact, because dominant understandings of violence are so tied to that which occurs across categories, people may not even interpret some same-category violence as violence at all. For instance, men hitting each other is often understood as "just play," whereas the same set of actions involving a man and a woman may be seen as violence. Thus, just as violence produces beliefs about social categories, our beliefs about social categories also shape what we see as "violence." When acts of physical force are not interpreted as violent, they are much less likely to mark the victim as weak or vulnerable.

VIOLENCE MATTERS

Violence *matters*, meaning that violence, through its incorporation into discourse via frames and narratives, materializes bodies and shapes subjectivities. Violence produces, and constructs beliefs about, social categories and identities. It influences senses of weakness and strength, levels of fear, behaviors, and the likelihood, and forms, of resistance.

A common form of resistance in the current political field is identity-based anti-violence activism. In the following chapters I detail how this form of activism, in its attempts to reduce harm, often reproduces the very messages that violence against an identity group is thought to send, including beliefs about vulnerability of members and homogeneity of the identity group. In my analysis of documents produced by identity-based anti-violence activists about transgender people, I find that transgender became visible as a category of personhood through narratives of violence against transgender people. These narratives constructed transgender as a vulnerable subjecthood and defined trans subjects exclusively by their gender.

Activists worked to make transgender people legible as people (i.e., as valuable members of society), in hopes that such recognition would reduce violence. They did this through telling many stories about violence against transgender people, focusing on fatal violence. The narratives they told in this attempt to construct a *valuable subjecthood* also produced particular ideas about what it means to be transgender, linking transness with vulnerability and reducing the livability of that life. These narratives function as *scenes of subjection* in which a vulnerable subjecthood is produced through tellings and retellings of experiences of violence.[87] These scenes both produce transgender people *as subjects* and define them as *subject to* violence. Activists promoted the idea that violence experienced by transgender people is caused solely by perpetrators' hatred of transgender people, ignoring other possible causes, including race and sexuality. Indeed, in activist narratives, identifying the victim as transgender was practically equivalent to identifying the cause of the violence. This framing then shaped proposed solutions to violence. As activists identified hatred as the main cause of the violence, they focused on getting gender identity added to hate crime legislation. Thus, identity-based anti-violence activists' narratives about violence are moments of productive power, shaping beliefs about the identity group and influencing anti-violence strategies. In the next chapter I examine a particular form these narratives took: the focus on a few famous victims of violence.

3. Atypical Archetypes

The Causes and Consequences
of Famous Victims of Violence

In 1995 trans activists organized a number of vigils during the trials of the men who murdered Brandon Teena. These demonstrations and related press releases garnered widespread media attention. Among the demonstrators was Kimberly Peirce, who went on to direct an award-winning feature film about the murder.[1] *Boys Don't Cry*, considered by many to be one of the best films of 1999, brought violence against transgender people into the national spotlight and was many viewers' first encounter with a media representation of a sympathetic trans character. The attention paid to the murder of Brandon Teena advanced the cause of anti-violence activism on behalf of transgender people and shaped understandings of this form of violence. However, it is important to ask why this particular case of violence against a trans person became so famous. Of all the transgender people who experienced violence in the early 1990s, why did Brandon Teena become so well-known, whereas others did not? Moreover, what are the consequences of some victims becoming much more famous than others?

In this chapter I explore these questions by comparing the victims of violence regularly mentioned by trans activists to those who received little or no attention. I find that of all the transgender people who experienced violence between 1990 and 2009, murder victims were mentioned regularly whereas survivors of violence rarely appeared in activist documents. Moreover, due to forces within the political field and the mainstream media, of the 289 murders of transgender people that occurred during this period just 2—those of Brandon Teena and Gwen Araujo—received high levels of attention from activists, journalists, policy makers, and academics. To explore how similar or different famous victims are from those rarely mentioned by activists, I utilize my original dataset of all the murders of transgender people during that period.[2] Notably, although the murders of Brandon Teena and Gwen Araujo are often treated as archetypal, they are actually highly atypical. Focusing on victims of violence who are not representative of the larger problem they come to signify has substantial consequences in terms of the construction of ideas of what it means to be transgender, beliefs about the causes of this form of violence, and proposed solutions to violence. The narratives about famous victims share three major outcomes with tactics I detail in the next three chapters: they homogenize what it means to be transgender, they produce beliefs about vulnerability, and they shape solutions. I explore the specific ways narratives about famous victims do these things in this chapter, before exploring in depth the other ways activists constructed a homogeneous subjecthood (chapter 4) and a vulnerable subjecthood (chapter 5), and the ways these framings influenced proposed violence-prevention tactics (chapter 6).

THE INFLUENCE OF "IDEAL" VICTIMS AND LANDMARK NARRATIVES

Criminologist Nils Christie coined the concept of the *ideal victim* to describe those who are more likely to receive social recognition and be seen as legitimate victims in need of protection.[3] Christie noted that the attributes associated with the "ideal" victim are culturally specific, but that they often include vulnerability and innocence (the example he gave was "a little old lady"). In addition, Christie identified common factors of offenders in crimes for which the victim comes to be seen as the "ideal" victim, namely that the perpetrator is a stranger and has the opposite traits of the victim (i.e., is strong and immoral—the quintessential big, bad wolf). In the United States, those cast as "ideal" victims are disproportionately white, young, and female, whereas "ideal" perpetrators are poor men of color.[4] Criminologists have embraced this concept, highlighting how it results in a *hierarchy of victimization*.[5] Those seen as more "ideal" victims receive disproportionate attention and care from the media, the general population, and the criminal justice system.[6]

Victims who experience particularly horrifying forms of violence are also likely to receive high levels of attention. A few of these cases become what sociologist Lawrence Nichols termed *landmark narratives*.[7] A landmark narrative is a case that comes to be seen as representative of an entire social problem, such as 9/11 for terrorism in the United States or Columbine for school shootings. Although atypical, these cases become shorthand for the issue, often becoming synonymous with the social problem. In terms of identity-based anti-violence activism, each movement tends to have an individual victim or group of victims that function as landmark narratives.[8] For example, the murders of Matthew Shepard and James Byrd Jr. have become the landmark narratives for violence against gay men and lesbians and against people of color, respectively. Because these cases are well known, they deeply influence how people understand these particular forms of violence and thus influence their proposed solutions. The murders of Shepard and Byrd came to be seen as motivated by hatred, and this understanding helped shape proposed violence-prevention policies, eventually resulting in the hate crime legislation that is named after them: The Matthew Shepard and James Byrd, Jr. Hate Crimes Prevention Act of 2009.

FAMOUS VICTIMS

Reading through the materials produced by trans activists between 1990 and 2009, one cannot help but notice that certain victims are mentioned much more frequently than others. Of the more than 1,000 anti-violence documents I examined, 729 include references to a specific victim. Almost all of those were homicides. Moreover, two victims, Brandon Teena and Gwen Araujo, are mentioned in a full 35 percent of the documents that mention victims. This far exceeds mentions of other victims; Brandon Teena is mentioned 2.4 times more often than the next most commonly mentioned victim, F.C. Martinez.

Brandon Teena was labeled female at birth and as a teenager began wearing his hair short, dressing in men's clothing, and going by men's names (including Charles, Billy, Tenor, and Brandon).[9] In 1993 he traveled to Falls City, Nebraska, where he met and began dating Lana Tisdale. After a short time in Falls City, Brandon was arrested for check forgery and booked as a woman.[10] After his arrest, rumors spread around town that he was female. At a Christmas Eve party, two friends of Lana's, Marvin "Tom" Nissen and John Lotter, confronted Brandon and ordered Lana to go into a bathroom and "check" whether Brandon was "really" male. Lana reported back that Brandon was male. Tom did not believe her and grabbed Brandon while John pulled down Brandon's pants, exposing Brandon's genitals. The men would not release Brandon until Lana looked and said that Brandon was female. Tom and John then took Brandon into the woods and raped and beat him. Brandon reported the assault to the sheriff, but no arrests were made. Brandon then fled to Humboldt, Nebraska, to stay with his friend, Lisa Lambert, her friend, Philip DeVine, and Lisa's nine-month-old baby. On New Year's Eve, Tom and John went to Lisa's house and shot Lisa, Philip, and Brandon. Tom repeatedly stabbed Brandon's body after they shot him. When they were arrested, Tom entered into a plea bargain, admitted to the murders and the plot to kill Brandon, and testified against John. Both men are currently in prison. John was sentenced to death, and Tom was given life in prison without parole.

Gwen Araujo came out to her family as transgender at age fourteen. At seventeen, Gwen met and started partying with Jaron Nabors, Michael Magidson, José Merél, and Jason Cazares in Newark, California, thirty-five miles southeast of San Francisco. After having oral sex and anal sex with her, these men began wondering whether Gwen was "really" male. On October 3, 2002, they confronted her, refusing to let her leave their house until she showed them her genitals. Gwen would not, and so they sent one of their girlfriends into a bathroom with Gwen to ascertain her sex. The girlfriend reported back that she felt testicles and so stated that Gwen was male. The four men then attacked Gwen, beating her in the head with a can of food, a frying pan, their fists, and their knees. They then bound her, strangled her to death, and drove to the woods to bury her body. Rumors of the killing quickly spread around the local high school, but no one went to the police. Finally, a member of Gwen's family heard the rumors and reported the killing. The four men were arrested. Jaron Nabors pled guilty to manslaughter and testified against his friends in exchange for a reduced sentence of eleven years in prison. The first trial against the other three accused perpetrators resulted in a mistrial. In the second trial, Michael Magidson and José Merél both were found guilty of second-degree murder without a hate crime enhancement. They were sentenced to life in prison. Jason Cazares's trial resulted in another mistrial. To avoid another trial, Jason then pled no contest to manslaughter and was sentenced to six years in prison.

ATYPICAL ARCHETYPES

These two cases are what many people think of when they think of violence against transgender people. However, how representative are they? Although accurate information about trans people's experiences of violence is challenging to acquire, the best data currently indicate that about 13 percent of transgender survey respondents have experienced some form of physical assault in the previous year.[11] As these are survey responses, none of those assaults were fatal. Current estimates state that about 1.4 million people in the United States are transgender; using survey results, we can estimate that about 182,000 of them have been victims of violence in the last year.[12] Given an average of about fifteen murders a year between 1990 and 2009, it is clear that most violence against transgender people is not fatal. As I discuss later, treating homicide as representative of all violence experienced by trans people can have severe consequences, including inadequate anti-violence policies and high levels of fear among transgender people, their family, and their friends.

Though clearly unrepresentative of overall trends of violence, how similar are these famous cases to other trans homicides in the United States? To answer that question, I turn to my original dataset of transgender homicides. Comparing the murders of Brandon Teena and Gwen Araujo to these other homicides, there are some key similarities, particularly in terms of body modification, the gender of the offender(s), and the relationship between the perpetrator(s) and the victim. However, there are also substantial ways in which they are not representative, including victims' gender, race, and age as well as the number of perpetrators, level of *overkill*—cases in which the perpetrator killed the victim and then continued violent acts against them—and whether the culprits were convicted.

Both Brandon and Gwen had not had genital surgery and, based on most accounts, had not had other gender confirmation surgeries or taken hormones. This pattern is echoed across the other homicides during this period. Of the 289 transgender people killed between 1990 and 2009, just 4 of them are known to have had genital surgeries. Moreover, just 35 of the victims are known to have done other body modifications (including taking hormones and/or having chest surgeries). The remaining 87 percent of victims are not known to have engaged in any of these body modification practices. Thus, in this way both Brandon and Gwen are representative of the group of trans people who appear to be most at risk of experiencing fatal violence.[13]

These two famous murders are also similar to the other homicides in terms of the gender of the perpetrator(s). Of the 176 homicides for which the genders of the perpetrator(s) are known, cisgender men comprise 95 percent of perpetrators.[14] The murders of Brandon and Gwen echo this stark gendered pattern, as both Brandon and Gwen were killed by cis men. This alignment between famous cases and more general patterns is likely both due to the large gender gap in perpetration and because cisgender men best fit the criteria of the "ideal" perpetrator, in that they are seen as strong and dangerous.[15]

Finally, one of the cases (Gwen Araujo) is similar to most of the other murders in terms of the relationship between the perpetrator(s) and the victim. Of the 136 homicides in which the relationship between the victim and the perpetrator(s) is known, in the vast majority of cases (71%) the victim and perpetrator(s) had a sexual relationship of some kind prior to the homicide. Like in most trans homicides between 1990 and 2009 in the United States, Gwen had sexual interactions with some of her killers. Thus, those who see her murder as representative of murders of trans people are correct in identifying that most murdered trans people are killed by someone with whom they have had a sexual interaction.

It is here that the similarities end. Overall, although iconic, these two famous cases are highly atypical. Though the murder of Gwen Araujo is representative of the general pattern in terms of the relationship between victim and perpetrator(s), the murder of Brandon Teena could not be more unique. Though the sexual relationship between Brandon and Lana was a factor, unlike most murders of trans people, Brandon did not have a consensual sexual relationship with his killers. This case is highly unusual in that in no other murders of trans people in the United States between 1990 and 2009 did the perpetrators first rape the victim and then murder the victim in an attempt to cover up the rape.[16] Moreover, in no other case did friends of someone who had a sexual relationship with the victim act alone in killing the victim in response to a perceived gender deception.

In almost every other way these homicides can be compared, the famous murders, particularly the most famous of them all (Brandon Teena), are very different from most murders of transgender people in the United States. One stark difference is in terms of the gender of the victim. Using the cases of Brandon and Gwen as models, one might assume that trans men and trans women are equally at risk for fatal violence. This assumption would be mistaken. Of the 289 transgender people who were killed in the United States between 1990 and 2009, 285 (98.6%) were transfeminine and 4 (1.4%) were transmasculine.[17]

Another crucial way in which the famous cases are not representative of the larger social problem is the race of the victim. Of the 277 victims whose race is known, 58 percent were black. By contrast, 18 percent were, like Gwen Araujo, Latinx, and 17 percent shared Brandon Teena's racial category of white.[18] Thus, using Brandon and Gwen as models for these types of murders portrays victims as decidedly lighter skinned than is actually the case. Despite the fact that the majority of the victims were black, no black victim came even close to the level of recognition given Brandon and Gwen.[19]

Not only are the famous victims lighter skinned than most victims, they are also younger. Of the 284 victims whose ages were known, ages ranged from twelve to sixty-five, with an average age of thirty-one. Brandon Teena was twenty-one when he was killed, and Gwen Araujo was just seventeen.

Thus, the most famous victims are a full ten to fourteen years younger than the average victim. As I discuss later, this discrepancy between typical victims and famous victims occurs because those who are particularly young or old better match the notion of the "ideal" victim.

Finally, the famous cases are also atypical in terms of the number of perpetrators and the level of violence used in the homicide. If one used these cases as models for murders of this kind, one would make the inaccurate assumption that most murders of trans people are committed by pairs or groups and include extreme levels of violence. However, of cases with a known number of perpetrators, the vast majority (81%) have only one perpetrator. There are just two cases with four known perpetrators, one of which is the murder of Gwen Araujo. Less atypical but still unusual is the murder of Brandon Teena, which in terms of number of perpetrators, looks like just 13 percent of known murders of trans people between 1990 and 2009 in the United States. Moreover, despite activists' assertions that murders of transgender people almost always included overkill, it was relatively rare. Most transgender homicide victims were not subjected to violence well beyond what is necessary to kill a person, such as being stabbed after being shot to death, as Brandon was, or being assaulted with multiple weapons and strangled, as Gwen was.

The attention paid to these two cases resulted in another feature in which they are atypical: convictions for these crimes. Although all six perpetrators in the famous cases were convicted of their crimes, just 42 percent of murders of trans people between 1990 and 2009 resulted in a conviction.[20] Similarly atypical, particularly in the case of Brandon Teena's murder, are the sentences. Of all the murders, just four resulted in the death penalty for at least one perpetrator. John Lotter, who killed Brandon Teena, is one of those four. High levels of activist and news media attention on a case increase the chances of a perpetrator being arrested, charged, and convicted.[21] Thus, it is likely that the relative fame of Brandon Teena and Gwen Araujo resulted in the further atypicalness of their cases.

SOCIAL FORCES THAT PRODUCE THESE PATTERNS:
THE SOCIAL PROBLEMS MARKETPLACE, IDENTITY
POLITICS, AND THE MAINSTREAM MEDIA

Competition within the Social Problems Marketplace

Social movements must compete for attention within the social problems marketplace. As a result, they tend to highlight the most horrifying cases of the problem their movement is focused on, as more shocking examples garner more notice. For anti-violence activists, that means the cases of violence they highlight are often murders. Thus, although usually the least common form of violence experienced by members of an identity group, homicides attract the most attention. Moreover, particularly horrifying homicides that include multiple acts of violence and/or overkill, such as the murders of Brandon Teena and Gwen Araujo, come to represent all violence experienced by the group. Unlike what happens in most murders of trans people, Brandon's killers sexually assaulted him first and stabbed him after they shot him. Similarly, Gwen's killers severely beat her before strangling her. Because these landmark narratives become well known, people may assume, erroneously, that most violence against trans people is fatal and includes multiple acts of violence.

In addition to the forces of the social problems marketplace encouraging a focus on particularly horrifying violence, the competition within it also encourages a focus on "ideal" victims, as they are perceived to elicit the most sympathy and therefore will make the most gains for the social movement.[22] Those subjected to fatal violence are more likely to be seen as "ideal" victims. Unlike those who fought back and survived, it is easier to portray murder victims as weak and innocent and the perpetrators as strong and evil. This increases the likelihood that activists will focus on homicides. However, only certain homicide victims are seen as "ideal." Indeed, some activists commented that the pressure to only draw attention to the most "ideal" victims influenced which victims they highlighted and how they did so. In 2000, Joy Vannelia Hughes wrote an essay for the Remembering Our Dead (ROD) website about the murder of Alina Marie Barragan, who was killed by a cis man she met at a bar. The piece, titled "The Whole World Wasn't Watching," questions why the murder had not attracted much attention. One reason she highlighted is resistance within the trans community to drawing notice to non-"ideal" victims: "It has been suggested to me that because Alina acted in such a risky way by leaving with this man, that we shouldn't 'make a lot of noise' about this murder."[23]

Between 1990 and 2009, the pressure from both activists and the larger social problems marketplace to focus only on "ideal" victims resulted in the two most famous victims, compared to all of the victims during this period, being relatively lighter skinned, younger, labeled female at birth, and dead. In the United States, darker skin has long been associated with criminality, whereas lighter skin (particularly that of white people, as well as that of lighter skinned people of color) is often perceived as reflecting inherent innocence.[24] Characterizations used to justify slavery—including portrayals of black people as sexually deviant, gender nonconforming criminals and white people as normatively gendered, properly sexual, and law abiding—still circulate today, shaping perceptions.[25] This likely influenced the fact that the most famous victim, the one who has come to be seen as representative of all violence against transgender people, was white. We can see the importance that race plays in relative famousness by looking at the murder of Nireah Johnson. This case shares a number of attributes with the murder of Gwen Araujo, yet it garnered very little activist attention (just seven documents mention Nireah, compared to ninety-eight that mention Gwen). Johnson was the same age as Gwen (seventeen), was killed just nine months after Gwen, and was killed in a particularly brutal way by multiple perpetrators.[26] Like Gwen, Johnson had been sexual with one of the perpetrators and then was "discovered" to be transgender.[27] One of the main differences between the two cases, however, is that Nireah, unlike Gwen, was black.

Like race, age is also treated as a proxy for innocence in US culture, with the relatively young and relatively old being perceived as the most innocent. Relative youth or age is also associated with weakness, as the very young and very old are seen as frailer than those in the middle of the spectrum. As a result, it is these victims who garner the most attention. The transgender rights movement was no different in this regard, as evidenced by the fact that Brandon and Gwen were a full decade younger than the average victim. Activists regularly highlighted the youth of particular victims during this period. In the "notes" section of the entries on the ROD website, ages of victims were occasionally included. Tellingly, though victims of all ages were included, no victim over the age of twenty-four had their age listed in the notes section. This portrayal of age is highly unrepresentative of most victims of this type of crime, whose average age was thirty-one. Echoing this trend, Riki Wilchins, the executive director of GenderPAC, went so far as to say, "The murder of any human being because of their race, class, orientation, or gender is terrible, but especially when the victim is so young."[28] Statements like these reinforce the belief that people should be more concerned about violence against members of particular age categories.

Like the very young and very old, those labeled female at birth are also seen in US culture as weaker and are often perceived to be more innocent than those labeled male at birth (who are associated with criminality). This common feature of the "ideal" victim plays out in revealing ways in the case of transgender anti-violence activism. Although one might think that trans women, due to their femininity, would be seen as more "ideal" victims, that is not the case. Many Americans associate trans people with the sex they were labeled at birth, particularly in sexual interactions.[29] The fact that Brandon Teena's case is so famous, despite its exceptional uniqueness, is likely related to this belief. Much of the general public, when hearing about the murder, likely thought of Brandon as female, despite his identity as a man. As such, he is a more sympathetic victim than a trans woman.

Brandon Teena and Gwen Araujo share another common characteristic with other "ideal" victims—they are normatively attractive. In US culture, good looks are associated with good character; thus beautiful people are seen as more "ideal" victims.[30] Although there is no way to rate the average "attractiveness" of the victims during this time period, it is undeniable that, within US culture, Brandon and Gwen would both be considered very good-looking. This was even noted by activists. Though trans anti-violence activists did not regularly comment on the beauty of victims, when they did, the two victims they most often called good-looking were Brandon and Gwen. The executive director of GenderPAC regularly referred to Brandon as a "beautiful young man."[31] Even more common was highlighting Gwen's attractiveness. Gwen was repeatedly called beautiful. Interestingly, these statements, like those about Brandon, were often coupled with a statement highlighting her youth. A National Transgender Advocacy Coalition (NTAC) press release called her "an attractive girl," and activist Monica Helms described her as "beautiful and young."[32] Some activists even noted that her youth and appearance may have influenced her famousness. Activist David Steinberg questioned why Gwen's murder garnered more attention than other violence experienced by transgender people and suggested, "maybe it's because Gwen was attractive, relatively well-adjusted, and just 17 years old."[33]

Finally, the most compelling narratives about victimization are those in which the victim(s) are seen as good and the perpetrator(s) are seen as evil. One way of demonstrating that is cases in which the perpetrators were significantly stronger than the victims. This helps explain one of the other ways in which the most famous victims are not representative of the larger social problem. Unlike what occurred in most of these crimes, Brandon and Gwen were attacked by multiple perpetrators. The narrative of four against one lends to a heightened sense of injustice, thus making cases with multiple perpetrators more effective in the social problems marketplace.

Established Activist Networks

Of course, whether or not a victim fits the criteria for an "ideal" victim is not the only factor that determines whether that victim becomes iconic. As sociologists Elizabeth Armstrong and Suzanna Crage argued, for a particular event to become central to an identity group's *collective memory*, not only must the group consider the event to be worth remembering; to achieve iconic status, the group that values the event must also have the capability to organize around it at the moment it occurs.[34] Armstrong and Crage illustrated this argument by highlighting that before the Stonewall riots in 1969, there were a number of similar moments in which members of the gay community (broadly defined) fought back against police oppression. However, Stonewall is the incident that is remembered because when it occurred activists were able to create an event that ultimately memorialized it: a march through the streets of New York that eventually became the modern Gay Pride Parade. One can apply Armstrong and Crage's argument to other social movements. For example, although Rosa Parks's protest on a bus in Montgomery, Alabama, in 1955 was not the first protest of its kind, it is the one that is remembered because it occurred at a time when the members of the civil rights movement were able to rally around it. Activists quickly organized the Montgomery Bus Boycott, a protest that brought national attention to the cause. Thus, though these events are often told as what I term *flashpoint stories*—narratives about the event that is said to have "sparked" the movement—they are not what started the movements. Instead, the movements needed to be well established before the iconic event so that activists were able to mobilize around it.

Like the gay and civil rights movements, the modern transgender rights movement also has a moment that is often pointed to as the beginning: the murder of Brandon Teena. Trans people faced cultural backlash through what historian Susan Stryker called "the difficult decades" of the 1970s and 1980s.[35] However, activists in the early 1990s started uniting under the banner of the recently coined term *transgender* and began to increasingly focus on violence as one of the main issues facing transgender people.[36] During this time, Brandon Teena was murdered and activists quickly informed the trans community through publications such as *FTMi* and *Tapestry*, circulated mainstream press releases, and organized demonstrations at the trials of both perpetrators.[37] These demonstrations helped bring national attention to the issue of violence against transgender people and further solidified the young transgender rights movement. As activist Nancy Nangeroni described this time in the newly named *Transgender Tapestry*: "When forty transgender folk gathered in Falls City to show their solidarity and commitment to standing up for 'genderqueers,' it kicked off the most exciting year ever for activism by the TG [transgender] community. The last few months have seen unprecedented breakthroughs for people not just identifying as crossdressers or transsexuals but for a rapidly expanding circle of folks who now for the first time think of themselves as 'trans-gendered' (i.e. transgressing gender norms)."[38] It is likely that if Brandon had been killed before 1993, he would not have become as famous as he did. However, by the early 1990s trans activists had begun to see murders as what Armstrong and Crage call *commemorable events,* and those activists were organized enough to be able to mobilize demonstrations, including those at the Nebraska trials.[39]

One might think that the reason trans activists began to focus heavily on violence right after the murder of Brandon Teena was that fatal violence against transgender people was increasing during this time. However, that is not the case. There were on average 17 murders of trans people a year between 1990 and 1993. By contrast, the average was 9.67 a year between 1994 and 1996—the years in which the transgender rights movement shifted its focus to violence and began to regularly organize vigils and demonstrations. Thus, the attention focused on violence was not a result of these years being particularly violent but rather because the transgender anti-violence movement was at that point organized enough to effectively draw attention to the cause.

Although much of their focus was on the murder of Brandon Teena, that homicide was not the only one transgender anti-violence activists drew attention to during that time. The murders of Deborah Forte and Chanel Pickett both received high levels of activist attention, including vigils and rallies numbering up to 250 people.[40] However, victims seen as less "ideal" tend not to garner sustained attention over time. Though Deborah Forte and Chanel Picket received lots of attention initially, between 1990 and 2009 they garnered only a fraction of the mentions of Brandon Teena (about one-fifth). Although white, Deborah did not align as closely with the idea of the "ideal" victim, as she was fifty-six years old, labeled male at birth, and killed by a single perpetrator. Though Chanel was young (twenty-three years old), her case was likely not focused on because, again, there was a single perpetrator and, probably more important, she was black. Thus, over time Brandon Teena's murder was considered more commemorable than the others because he better fit the criteria for an "ideal" victim. The convergence of activists being sufficiently organized and Brandon's correspondence with the criteria for "ideal" victims resulted in Brandon's murder becoming the landmark narrative for the social problem.

Identity Politics

Although the constraints of the social problems marketplace influence all anti-violence activism, that which is done under the mantle of identity politics is also shaped by factors unique to identity-based anti-violence activism. For those engaged in such activism, "ideal" victims need to be clear members of the identity category and be harmed because of their identity category membership. Identity politics has particular require-ments, and those cause certain individuals within the identity group to become more visible than others. At the time of writing this, the two most famous living trans people are Laverne Cox and Caitlyn Jenner. Their rela-tive fame is not an accident. Instead, it is a product of a number of forces, including closely adhering to particular understandings of what it means to be transgender. Both identify as transgender, have had genital surgery, and are highly gender conforming (e.g., outside of her acting jobs, one almost never sees Cox in pants; instead she almost always wears dresses or skirts and blouses).

Like Laverne and Caitlyn, the two most famous victims of violence were both seen as having a clear transgender identity and followed the norms of their gender identity. Though Brandon Teena never identified as "trans-gender" (the term was not well known at the time), he did live full time as a man. After his death, activists claimed that he identified as transsexual. Similarly, Gwen Araujo lived full time as a girl and came out to her family as transgender at fourteen. Brandon and Gwen were also highly gender conforming. In the parlance of the time period, both of the famous vic-tims "passed" well. They were not genderqueer in their presentation of self and instead conformed to the expectations of their gender category. On the night she was killed, Gwen wore makeup and a skirt paired with other feminine items of clothing. She wore her hair long and plucked her eyebrows. Similarly, Brandon wore masculine clothing (there are multiple photos of him wearing ties) and was usually read by others as a boy/man. In addition, the logics of identity politics encourage anti-violence activists to focus on cases that were clearly motivated by bias against members of the identity group. Brandon was raped by the two perpetrators right after they "discovered" that he was trans; they later killed him in an attempt to cover up the rape. Similarly, Gwen was killed the same night that her perpetrators "discovered" that she was trans.

The role of identity, both in terms of clearly holding it and being attacked because of it, can be seen by contrasting the two most famous cases to the next most famous, that of F.C. Martinez. In many ways, one would expect F.C. to be at least as famous as Brandon and Gwen, as F.C. was even younger (sixteen), was normatively attractive (the GSA web-site described F.C. as "a very striking Navajo teen"), was relatively light skinned, and was killed in a particularly horrifying way (their head was beaten in with a rock and they were left to die in a canyon).[41] However, F.C. did not hold a clear trans identity and was not gender conforming, and the motivation for the murder was not clearly anti-trans. Unlike Brandon and Gwen, F.C.'s gender presentation tended to be more of a blending of masculine and feminine elements. Though feminine, F.C. was thought of by most as male-bodied and, unlike Brandon and Gwen, F.C. did not choose a highly gendered name (instead, they used their initials). Moreover, F.C. alternately identified as gay, nádleeh, and two-spirit. Although nádleeh and two-spirit were claimed by activists under the transgender umbrella, F.C.'s additional identity as gay and the fact that they did not clearly claim an identity as a girl made it less likely that F.C.'s murder would garner the same level of focus. Thus, due to the forces of identity politics, those who most conform to dominant ideas of what it means to be a member of the identity group are those who are most likely to garner activist attention.[42] As activist Jamison Green stated in 2007: "Why has the trans community taken Brandon Teena as an icon? Because Brandon claimed himself as one of us."[43] As I detail later, this has the effect of reifying beliefs about what it means to be transgender as well as beliefs about what "anti-trans" violence looks like.

The pressures of identity-based anti-violence activism also made it less likely that F.C. would become as famous as Brandon or Gwen because the murder was not clearly motivated by anti-transgender hatred. After the murder, the perpetrator bragged to others that he had "bug-smashed a joto" (meaning that he had beaten a "fag" with a rock)—pointing to homophobia, rather than transphobia, as the stimulus for the crime. The investigation into the murder never revealed how or why the perpetrator and F.C. ended up in a canyon in Cortez, Colorado, or why Shaun Murphy attacked F.C. There were many theories about the motivation, including racism (F.C. was Native American and Shaun was Latinx, although often labeled white by activists), homophobia (because Shaun referred to F.C. as a joto/fag), and transphobia (because trans activists labeled F.C. as trans). Due to the lack of clear anti-trans bias, F.C.'s murder is not as well-known within the trans community or by the general public as those of Brandon Teena and Gwen Araujo. As identity-based anti-violence activist groups focus on only one identity, "ideal" victims must be targeted solely for their membership in a single identity category. This makes it less likely that cases with multiple possible causes will become famous. Notably, this may further increase the focus on white victims in anti-violence activism done on behalf of women, gay men and lesbians, and transgender people, as people are unlikely to question whether the crime was racially motivated.

The Mainstream Media

The mainstream media also shape which victims become iconic. Thousands of news articles have been written about the lives and deaths of Brandon Teena and Gwen Araujo.[44] That level of coverage, above and beyond that received by other trans victims of violence, likely contributed to Brandon and Gwen's relative fame both within the trans community and with the general public. As a 2007 GLAAD press release stated: "Brandon Teena, a transgender man, has become one of the most visible victims of anti-transgender violence due to the media response to his death and the subsequent success of a documentary and Oscar®-winning film (*Boys Don't Cry*) about his life and death."[45] There is a circular aspect to this; murders that receive a lot of attention from activists are more likely to get news coverage, and in turn, cases that receive a lot of news coverage are also likely to get activist attention, as those cases are seen as resonating with the general public. Thus, in the interaction between the activist and journalist spheres, famousness begets famousness.

In addition, scholars have demonstrated that there is a close alignment between the criteria for "ideal" victims and the factors that make it likely a victim will be covered in the news.[46] Thus, the factors previously discussed contributed to the level of news coverage garnered by the famous cases. In addition, the mainstream news often covers atypical cases. One of the central criteria used by journalists to determine whether to cover something is whether it is "new."[47] Typical, everyday occurrences are not deemed newsworthy because they are not new. Consequently, the two cases that received the most news coverage were also highly atypical (e.g., in terms of gender, age, and number of perpetrators).

Part of this atypicality is a factor shared by both Brandon Teena and Gwen Araujo that does not appear in any of the other murder cases between 1990 and 2009: what news stories called an "ongoing deception." Many of the perpetrators during the period studied knew that their victims were trans before the murder occurred. For those who "discovered" their victim's trans status shortly before killing them, most had not known their victim for very long. By contrast, both Brandon and Gwen were read by their killers as cisgender for a period of time before they were outed as transgender. This perceived "deception" and the length of it were particularly fascinating to the mainstream press. In the 1990s and 2000s the mainstream media in the United States often framed murders of trans people as motivated by "deception," claiming that trans people "lied" about their sex.[48] However, almost all of the cases described in the mainstream media as involving "deception" were sexual relationships of short duration, such as the victim and perpetrator engaging in a physical sexual encounter for the first time or the perpetrator or victim propositioning the other for a sexual relationship (either with or without the exchange of money).

Although cases framed by journalists as involving "deception" often received a moderate amount of news coverage, it seems that the ways in which Brandon and Gwen were "ideal" victims, combined with the ongoing nature of their perceived "deception," resulted in particularly high levels of news coverage of these two cases. Though there is no way to know for sure why having an ongoing relationship before being "discovered" to be transgender garners more news coverage, it is likely that for straight, cisgender journalists, these cases represent a sort of gender horror. Ongoing "deceptions" challenge people's certainty that they can use gender presentation as a proxy for sex assigned at birth. By contrast, cases in which the victim and perpetrator have just met and then the perpetrator quickly "discovers" the "deception" reinforce people's faith that they can determine someone's sex based on looking at them. Short-term "deception" narratives indicate that it does not take much interaction to "discover" someone's "true" sex. By contrast, journalists highlighted how Brandon and Gwen had everyone "fooled" for a period of time. This ability of bodies to "fool" is particularly horrifying in sexual encounters. Some perpetrators who "discovered" that the person they were being sexual with had different genitals than they were expecting reacted with violence because they feared that such a sexual encounter would mark them with the stigma of homosexuality, and they engaged in violence to ward off or erase that stigma.[49]

To further examine the role that ongoing "deceptions" plays in the famousness of these cases, let's return for a moment to the question posed by Joy Vannelia Hughes: Why didn't the murder of Alina Marie Barragan become a well-known case? The murder occurred in a similar time period as that of Gwen Araujo (2000), and like Gwen, Alina was young (nineteen) and Latinx. In addition, the two murders occurred in the same geographical area (about thirty minutes apart in the San Francisco Bay area), and like Gwen's, Alina's mother was very outspoken about the case. Moreover, this case was framed as "deception" in the media; Alina met Kozi Santino Scott in a bar, went home with him, had sex, and was killed when Kozi "discovered" that Alina was transgender. However, this case garnered significantly less coverage. According to an Access World News search, whereas Gwen's case was described in almost three thousand stories between 1990 and 2009, Alina's was mentioned in just fifteen. Although the different number of perpetrators (one vs. four) may play a role in this discrepancy, as might the original mistrial in Gwen's case, it seems that one of the key factors is the length of time the perpetrator(s) knew the victim.[50] Thus, in addition to fitting the criteria for an "ideal" victim, those who experience violence are more likely to become famous in the mainstream media if their story includes especially sensational aspects, further distorting understandings of violence against a particular group.

OTHER IDENTITY-BASED ANTI-VIOLENCE ACTIVISM

The patterns that I have described are not unique to trans anti-violence activism. Indeed, they occur in much identity-based anti-violence activism. A notable example is the murder of Matthew Shepard in 1998. Like Brandon Teena and Gwen Araujo, Matthew Shepard had many characteristics of the "ideal" victim. Matthew was young (twenty-one), white, and normatively attractive. He also had additional aspects of presumed innocence; he was a college student and middle class. Moreover, there was a clear discrepancy between his strength and that of his two killers; Matthew was relatively small (five feet two), and the attack was two against one. Finally, Matthew's death was particularly gruesome, Matthew held a clear identity as gay, and activists were sufficiently organized at the time of his death to publicize and protest it. As a consequence of all these factors, Matthew Shepard's murder is exceptionally famous in the United States. From 1998 through 2009, more than twenty thousand articles were published about his life and death, and a Google search in 2019 for "Matthew Shepard" produced 897,000 results (by contrast, a search for "Gwen Araujo" and "Brandon Teena" garnered 61,000 and 160,000 results, respectively). However, also like Brandon and Gwen, Matthew's murder is atypical in terms of violence against gay men and lesbians. Most violence against gay men and lesbians is not fatal, and of the murders that occur, most victims are not young, white college students beaten, tied to a fence, and left to die.

UNINTENDED CONSEQUENCES

The fact that the most famous cases of violence tend to be unrepresentative of violence against the identity group has a number of unintended consequences. It produces inaccurate understandings that detrimentally (1) influence ideas about what it means to be a member of the identity group, (2) affect academic understandings of violence, (3) shape proposed solutions, (4) guide what comes to count as a "bias" crime, and (5) further reinforce the narrow criteria for who is an "ideal" victim.

Shaping Subjecthood

Because of their fame, iconic victims influence understandings of what it means to be a member of the identity group. Compared to most victims, the narratives about the lives and deaths of famous victims often have relatively high levels of detail. As I describe in chapter 4, most trans victims were portrayed by activists as holding no identities other than transgender. However, Brandon Teena and Gwen Araujo were given ages, races, and so forth. As such, they potentially influence understandings of what it means to be transgender in a different way than the general discourse of anti-violence activists.

As detailed previously, one of the factors that increases the chances of a victim becoming famous is if they are a clear member of the identity group. In the case of trans anti-violence activism, famous trans victims are portrayed as intrinsically trans, as opposed to being fluid in their identities or embracing numerous identities (e.g., F.C. Martinez). In this vein, philosopher C. Jacob Hale critiqued activists' treatments of the Brandon Teena case, arguing that although Brandon spent the last years of his life in "a butch/ftm border zone" and did not clearly identify as either butch or transgender, he was claimed by both identity groups.[51] Hale maintained that this politically motivated rhetorical move denied Brandon's subjectivity by posthumously forcing him into an identity he did not claim while alive. Moreover, Hale demonstrated that narratives about Brandon as clearly a butch lesbian or a female-to-male transsexual work to harden the borders between these two identity categories and erase both the overlap that exists between them and the ambiguity in Brandon's own life. Hale reasoned that this restricts the possibility of living in the butch/ftm border zone and, in so doing, discourages the embracing of diversity and social change because strict labeling encourages normalization. Thus, the fact that only victims who are clear members of the identity group, or who can be portrayed as such, become famous has deep implications for the construction of the identity group itself. Rather than being seen as including genderqueer, gender diverse, nonbinary, and agender people, "transgender," as represented by the portrayal of iconic victims, came to mean only transgender people who identify as men or women. This both reflected and likely shaped larger cultural trends. Despite early definitions of transgender including a wide range of people who identified as something other than what they were labeled at birth, a binary gender identity (i.e., as a man or a woman) has become central to dominant conceptions of what it means to be "transgender."[52]

In addition to obscuring the diversity of gendered expressions under the transgender umbrella, the focus on "ideal" victims also obscures the diversity within the category in terms of age, race, and norms around gender conformity and attractiveness. The most famous victims are disproportionately young, light skinned, normatively attractive, and gender conforming. As they are often the most well-known trans people at a particular historical moment, this may influence who feels comfortable claiming the identity of transgender. Although murder victims are rarely seen as models to aspire to, when they become the face of an identity category they may shape who feels like they belong in that category.

Even more significant in terms of shaping subjecthood is the fact that the most famous transgender victims of violence were murdered as opposed to having fought off their attackers and survived. During much of the period studied, the most famous trans people in the United States (not just the most famous victims of violence, but the most famous trans people, period) were homicide victims and, importantly, victims who had been killed in especially brutal ways. As I discuss in detail in chapter 5, for members of the identity category this likely produced high levels of terror and constructed transgender as a vulnerable subjecthood. This is a very different outcome from identity-based activism that is not focused on violence, in which the people they make famous can be living heroes rather than martyrs. Thus, the merging of identity politics with anti-violence activism, along with the forces within the social problems marketplace that encourage activists to highlight murder victims, has dire consequences for the very people those activists are working to protect. Rather than celebrating the living or accurately representing patterns of violence, they associate their identity category with vulnerability and cause violence to seem disproportionately fatal. In response, people considering adopting the label transgender may choose not to for fear of being killed. In addition, those who do embrace the identity may exist in constant dread of being murdered, which is not a livable life. Indeed, sociologists interviewing transgender people about their experiences have found that although most of their respondents had not experienced violence, many had a high level of fear of violence. When asked why, transgender men regularly referenced the murder of Brandon Teena and transgender women talked about the killing of Gwen Araujo.[53] Similarly, transgender activist and actress Laverne Cox has stated that after watching *Boys Don't Cry*, she thought, "Oh, my God, I'm going to die."[54]

The Stories Spread

Narratives about famous victims do not just shape the beliefs held by members of the identity group; they also spread to outsiders. Thus, narratives about famous victims influence non-identity-group understandings of the identity group and the violence they experience. The most famous victims are often the only ones those outside the identity group hear about, and depending on the level of fame, they often hear a lot about those few victims. Due to high levels of news coverage as well an Oscar-winning film, many in the United States have heard of Brandon Teena. There was also extensive news coverage of the murder of Gwen Araujo. Similarly, during the 2000s there were likely very few people in the United States who had not heard of Matthew Shepard. However, most probably did not know many details of his death, just that he was killed for being gay.

As landmark narratives, these famous victims come to serve as shorthand for the larger social problem of violence experienced by members of the identity group. When activists speak to outsiders about these crimes, they often invoke famous cases to help their audience understand what they are talking about. In 2003, GLAAD added a page on its website aimed at the mainstream media detailing how to cover hate crimes. The introduction to the page read: "As we approach the observance of several historic markers in high profile hate crimes against our community—five years since the murder of Matthew Shepard, nearly ten years since the death of Brandon Teena and close to one year since the tragic murder of Gwen Araujo—GLAAD has prepared this media reference guide to address the myriad complex issues relating to incidents motivated by anti-LGBT bias."[55] Although the shorthand of landmark narratives is helpful in orienting audiences to the topic at hand, the fact that these cases are unrepresentative of the larger problem of violence experienced by the identity group has numerous important consequences. They are likely to make both members of the identity group and nonmembers believe that these sorts of horrific crimes occur more often than they do.

In the case of violence against trans people, an inaccurate statistic has circulated both within and outside of trans communities. In 2003 HRC published "Transgender Basics," which was intended to educate cisgender people about discrimination against transgender people. The section on hate violence informed readers that "transgender individuals living in America today have a one in 12 chance of being murdered. In contrast, the average person has about a one in 18,000 chance of being murdered."[56] Although woefully inaccurate (as I detail in chapter 5), this statistic resonated with trans and cis people alike. The false statistic seemed true in part because the famous victims of anti-trans violence were murder victims, suggesting that most violence against trans people is fatal. Moreover, for many cis Americans, the trans people they had heard of were victims of fatal violence. This is likely to cause cis people to treat trans people with some level of pity and may have a particularly detrimental effect on parents of trans children. The atypical youth of famous victims, combined with inaccurate statistics such as "one in twelve," may terrify parents and make them want to discourage their child's trans behavior/identity for fear that their child will be killed "just like Brandon Teena and Gwen Araujo." As sociologist Ann Travers argued: "One of the main reasons otherwise-LGBT-positive parents sometimes resist their children's trans identities is because they are afraid of what lies in store for them. . . . In spite of shifting social contexts that provide some measure of recognition and tolerance, parents fear that their children will be subject to discrimination, hatred, and violence—in short, that their life chances will be profoundly compromised."[57] Notably, activist narratives about violence leave these parents ill equipped to help their children protect themselves, as the message has been that all trans people are at risk of violence at all times. Without knowledge of patterns of violence, family and friends of trans people struggle to help safeguard their loved ones.

Shaping Scholarship

Landmark narratives about violence also influence academic understandings of the problem. This is particularly true for forms of violence that are not systematically tracked. As national victim surveys rarely ask about certain identities such as transgender, lesbian, gay, and/or bisexual, representative data on experiences of this violence are scarce. Similarly, although some hate crime legislation requires collection of data on these crimes, most violence experienced by marginalized groups is not considered a hate crime from a legal standpoint and so is not recorded as such. Thus, academics interested in studying violence against LGB or T people are faced with either trying to collect national data themselves (a highly laborious task) or using case studies as their points of analysis. Historically, most have chosen the latter route, and due to their fame, most of the case studies selected are landmark narrative cases. A Google Scholar search shows more than fifteen hundred articles and books that mention Brandon Teena, including numerous ones that analyze his murder as a way to understand violence against transgender people. Authors who have used Brandon's story in this way include Judith Butler, Jack Halberstam, and James Sloop. A representative example of how academics use famous victims as case studies is a 2014 article by criminologists Carrie Buist and Codie Stone. In it, the authors examined "the cases of three transgender victims of violence—Brandon Teena, Gwen Araujo, and Cece McDonald."[58] From these three cases, the authors drew conclusions about "the experiences of transgender people within the criminal justice system as both victims and offenders" in general. If these were typical cases, such an approach might lead to valuable gains in knowledge. However, as I have demonstrated, iconic cases are usually highly peculiar in a number of ways. As such, using them in research to understand violence against an entire group can lead to erroneous conclusions.

The impact of inaccurate academic understandings of violence that can come from only examining iconic cases is not limited to scholarly circles. Academics share their knowledge with others, including through giving interviews for news stories, testifying in court trials as expert witnesses, and advising policy makers. Academic understandings also influence activism both in terms of activists reading academic publications and academics producing materials for activist publications, such as Jody Norton's article in *Transgender Tapestry* in 1999 that compared the murders of Brandon Teena and Matthew Shepard. In it, she highlighted how both were killed "by a pair of under educated young white men with prior criminal involvement" and argued that it is this pairing, in which the men play off each other's need to prove masculinity and heterosexuality within a same-sex friendship, that is at the heart of the violence.[59] These conclusions are concerning because, at least in the case of murders of trans people, most perpetrators act alone, and thus there must be other factors causing this violence.

Structuring Solutions

By shaping understandings of this violence, the focus on only a few victims may also influence proposed solutions to the problem. We can see the influence that famous victims likely have over policy construction by noting the titles of legislation aimed at reducing this violence—from the Matthew Shepard and James Byrd, Jr. Hate Crimes Prevention Act to the Gwen Araujo Justice for Victims Act. Indeed, a 2007 GLAAD press release argued that "the case of Gwen Araujo, a transgender woman, has become a rallying cry for the importance of including transgender protections into hate crime legislation."[60]

Narratives about violence include implied causes and thus make certain solutions seem more logical. If the famous victims were representative in terms of the larger patterns of violence, such a consequence would be unconcerning. However, the forces shaping which victims become famous tend to encourage particularly nonrepresentative victims becoming iconic. As such, those who use famous victims as models for understanding the larger social problem are likely to incorrectly identify patterns of violence and thus suggest solutions that are less effective than those that would come from focusing on all victims.

Those treating iconic victims as representative of violence experienced by trans people may correctly concentrate their efforts on those factors in the murders of Brandon Teena and Gwen Araujo that are typical. Focusing on only these two cases, they could generate solutions: (1) addressing the patterns of trans people who engage in little or no body modification involved in casual sexual encounters being at higher risk for fatal violence; (2) focusing educational efforts on cisgender men, as they are often perpetrators; and (3) identifying (correctly) that some of this violence is caused by straight cisgender men feeling "deceived" by transgender women. As I discuss in chapter 7, although abhorrent, this feeling of "deception" must be addressed if we are to reduce violence against trans people.

However, there are many more ways in which the most famous cases are atypical. Cultural studies scholar Jack Halberstam critiqued one aspect of this: the geography of famous victims. Halberstam analyzed texts about Brandon Teena's life and death and concluded that they constructed "an urban fantasy of homophobic violence as essentially Midwestern."[61] By portraying rural spaces as dangerous for people like Brandon, these narratives suggested that urban spaces are safe. A similar argument can be made about narratives around the murder of Matthew Shepard. If one were to treat these constructions of transphobic and homophobic violence as truth, one might focus violence-prevention efforts on rural areas and/or encourage LGBT people to avoid the Midwest. These steps would be unlikely to prevent violence, however, as most of the murders of trans people during the period studied occurred in relatively urban spaces and on the coasts of the United States. Indeed, between 1990 and 2009 there was only one murder of a trans person in Nebraska (Brandon) and none in Wyoming. Moreover, of the four major regions of the continental United States, the Midwest was actually the least deadly (with thirty-nine trans homicide victims).[62]

In addition to geography, there are a number of additional ways in which iconic victims are atypical. Primarily, most violence experienced by trans people is not fatal. Activists focus on fatal violence because it garners the most attention within the social problems marketplace. However, the vast majority of violent incidences are not homicides. This focus on fatal violence may result in proposed solutions that aim mainly at reducing fatalities rather than much more common forms of violence. Although homicides should be eliminated, so should other forms of violence. It is likely that different forms of violence experienced by an identity group have (slightly) different causes and thus must be addressed in different ways.

The fact that the "ideal" victim is one who is attacked by a number of perpetrators may also influence prevention efforts, particularly at the personal level. Individual trans people who want to avoid the fate of Brandon Teena and Gwen Araujo may avoid groups of cisgender men. However, most murders of trans people involve a single perpetrator. Thus, one's risk of violence is unlikely to be decreased by avoiding groups.

The ways in which the most famous cases have influenced solutions can be seen in other identity-based anti-violence activism as well. For example, women raped by strangers, as opposed to someone they know, are seen as more "ideal" victims and so historically have been the focus of activists and the media.[63] As such, violence-prevention actions concentrated on such crimes. Police were deployed to make the "streets safer," and women were encouraged to not walk alone at night. However, most perpetrators of sexual assault are actually known to the victim.[64] Thus, although the efforts born out of iconic understandings may have prevented some crimes, they were not able to address the majority of sexual assaults.

Similarly, there are substantial consequences to the fact that in order to become an iconic victim made famous by identity-based anti-violence activists, one must clearly experience violence motivated by bias or hatred against their identity group. Due to the focus on hate-based homicides, hate crime legislation is the commonsense solution to violence experienced by people of color, gay men and lesbians, and transgender people. However, as I detail in chapter 6, this violence-prevention strategy is ineffective and has concerning unintended consequences. Moreover, the near-exclusive focus on hate crime legislation caused activists to overlook potentially more effective approaches.

Reifying the Archetype

The detrimental effects of focusing on a few cases that fit the criteria of the "ideal" hate crime extend beyond the current moment. The success of certain narratives within the social problems marketplace is likely to cause them to be reproduced over time. When only certain kinds of victims receive cultural attention, it becomes likely that the victims focused on in the future will look similar. By the very virtue of their fame, iconic victims influence the "ideal" victim archetype. When this is merged with the practices of landmark narratives and the logics of identity politics, the combination is likely to influence which crimes in the future are seen as "actual" hate crimes and which are not. It is possible that violence that does not fit the narrative will not get reported to police, investigated, or described in the media. Thus, violence against those members of an identity group that is not unusually horrific or is done against someone who does not fit the idea of what a "true" member of that identity is may have a harder time getting attention. The practices utilized in order to succeed within the social problems marketplace are self-perpetuating. When activists only highlight violence against victims of particular genders, races, and/or ages, the cultural tendency to disproportionately value those bodies is reinforced. Similarly, by attending only to the most horrifying forms of violence, the tendency to only care about more ghastly crimes is reproduced (rather than seeing all violence as bad and worth working to stop). Finally, the victims who are most highlighted by those engaged in identity-based anti-violence activism are those who were attacked for reasons that are indisputably related to bias against the identity group. However, violence is complicated and often has many causes. Although transphobia is a factor in much of the violence experienced by transgender people, it is often only one of many other factors. In order to attend to these factors, we must focus on more than just the most famous victims. Moreover, as I discuss in the following chapter, when doing so we must also attend to diversity within identity categories.

4. Homogeneous Subjecthood

How Activists' Focus on Identity
Obscures Patterns of Violence

> The problem with identity politics is not that it fails to transcend
> difference, as some critics charge, but rather the opposite—that it
> frequently conflates or ignores intragroup differences.
>
> —KIMBERLÉ CRENSHAW (1991, 1242)

In 1998, Gwendolyn Smith established the Remembering Our Dead (ROD)
web page to draw attention to murders of transgender people. The page was
visually arresting. Viewers first saw a dark grey, almost black, screen on
which a small, gray transgender symbol inside a triangle was overlaid with
the statement: "Those who cannot remember the past are doomed to repeat
it.—*George Santayana.*" A click on the triangle opened another dark grey
page filled with hundreds of names in small, white type. Behind the names
were ghostly black-and-white photographs of transgender murder victims.
Smith designed the page to look like the Vietnam Veterans Memorial, and
scrolling through hundreds of tiny names gave one the same overwhelming sense of sorrow brought on by standing in front of the thousands listed
on the wall in Washington, DC.[1] Clicking on a name opened a new page
that listed the location of the murder, cause of death, date of death, and
source of the information. Many entries are fewer than twenty words long,
highlighting that the victim was transgender but giving little other information about them.

From its inception through the mid-2000s, ROD was the most well-
known and frequently visited website for information about violence against
trans people. The site sent a clear messages to visitors about the causes of
such violence as well as what it means to be transgender. The "about" page
stated: "There is no 'safe way' to be transgendered: as you look at the many
names collected here, note that some of these people may have identified as
drag queens, some as heterosexual crossdressers, and some as transsexuals.
Some were living very out lives, and some were living fully 'stealth' lives.
Some were identifying as male, and some, as female. Some lived in small
towns, and some in major metropolitan areas. . . . Over the last decade,
one person per month has died due to transgender-based hate or prejudice,

regardless of any other factors in their lives."[2] In this chapter I explore how activists' focus on *identity* in their anti-violence activism, such as the ROD website's exclusive focus on transgender category membership as the motivation for violence, shaped beliefs about what it is to be a member of the identity group as well as influenced beliefs about violence.

Identity-based anti-violence activism encourages framings in which identity, rather than other possibilities, is the cause of violence, thus discouraging non-identity-based explanations and solutions. Moreover, due to the logic of identity politics and the constraints and expectations of the political field, activists engaged in identity-based anti-violence activism tend to claim that bias against one, and only one, identity group is the cause of an act of violence. Since all members of the group are in the same identity category, they are all portrayed as equally at risk for violence motivated by bias against that category. Historically, women's rights organizations have promoted an idea that "*all* women are potential rape victims" and that "any woman or child can be the victim of gender violence."[3] The gay rights movement borrowed this framing, arguing that "*all* gays and lesbians—as well as anyone presumed to be gay or lesbian—are at risk at *all* times."[4] The claim that all group members are at equal risk for violence discourages an awareness of intersectionality.[5] Gay and lesbian anti-violence activism focused solely on homophobia as a cause for violence, ignoring the roles played by race and gender in violence experienced by gay men and lesbians.[6] Similarly, activists working to stop domestic and sexual violence against women elided the ways in which factors such as race and class influence these forms of violence.[7] Like the focus on famous victims described in the previous chapter, attention to a single identity shapes beliefs about who comprises the identity group as well as solutions to violence. As sociologist Beth Richie demonstrated, activist claims that every woman is at risk for sexual and domestic violence "led to the erasure of low-income women and women of color from the dominant view."[8] Moreover, when only focusing on one system of oppression, activists often unintentionally perpetuate others. As a consequence, the proposed solutions to these forms of violence have tended to be those that would best serve the least oppressed within the identity category.[9]

Between 1990 and 2009, transgender anti-violence activists argued that acts of violence against transgender people were caused solely by hatred of transgender people. Activists promoted this message through several techniques, including labeling victims as transgender, dismissing causes besides anti-transgender hatred, and grouping diverse victims together. This is an effective message for getting members of the identity group to care about the problem of violence, since it states that all transgender people are at equal risk at all times and so all should be equally concerned. However, the homicide data I compiled reveal that transgender women of color were the most at risk for violence of any group of transgender people and that transgender people were often attacked in sexual encounters, including when sex was being exchanged for money. Overlooking these patterns of race, gender, sexuality, and class had serious consequences. It constructed transgender as a *homogenous subjecthood* whereby all transgender people are seen as the same and any individual member is seen as interchangeable with another member of the identity group. Due to the focus on violence, this homogeneous subjecthood was portrayed as highly vulnerable, further shaping beliefs about what it means to be transgender. In addition, the focus on a single identity facilitated an "us versus them" mentality that when coupled with anti-violence activism can produce high levels of fear and conflict between groups. Moreover, it obscured potentially effective solutions, encouraging activists to advocate for hate crime legislation rather than for policies that would address the intertwined roles played by race, gender, class, and sexuality in this violence. Despite these negative consequences, activists who attempted to abandon the identity politics approach faced fierce opposition. In one case, this conflict resulted in the downfall of one of the most influential groups in the struggle to reduce violence experienced by transgender people: GenderPAC.

EXPLAINING VIOLENCE WITH IDENTITY

Asking why activists highlight the role of identity in violence may seem pedantic, as identity-based anti-violence activism has become so ubiquitous as to seem natural. However, it is worth investigating why the focus on identity in anti-violence work is so appealing. Though social category membership plays a role in all forms of violence, so do many other factors, including aspects that foster violence, such as high rates of poverty and economic inequality.[10] However, these factors rarely receive the same attention in current anti-violence struggles, so we must examine why some explanations (e.g., identity-based) are more politically effective than others (e.g., economic inequality). The current social problems marketplace values identity-based explanations, as they relieve both the victim and those hearing about the violence of potential accusations of the situation being "their fault."[11] By attending to identity-based causes, activists are able to elicit sympathy for the victim by attributing the violence to factors outside of the victim's and the audience's control. The perpetrator of the violence is characterized as a bigoted villain, and the audiences that activists appeal to can distinguish themselves from the perpetrator by declaring their support for the identity group. By contrast, explanations such as economic inequality implicate the audience as potentially perpetuating the factors that resulted in acts of violence. Moreover, US cultural values of autonomy and individualism celebrate the ability to determine one's own life course and abhor restrictions on being one's "true self." As such, highlighting the role of identity in violence and arguing, as trans activists did, that victims were killed for being "their true selves" or "because of who they are" is particularly effective at this historical moment in the United States.[12]

In addition to identity being a successful tactic within the current political field, anti-violence activists also focus on it because they are working to construct their group as a *valuable subjecthood*. To accomplish this, activists first need to establish that the people they are struggling to protect are all members of the same social category. As identity categories are socially constructed, as opposed to being biologically determined, their boundaries are slippery and at times hotly contested. This has been particularly true for transgender since it is a relatively new identity and one that someone adopts later in life, as opposed to being assigned it at birth.[13]

In the 1990s and 2000s, activists worked to solidify this new identity category by consistently calling victims of violence *transgender* or a variation of the term. The documents produced by transgender anti-violence activists were peppered with the word transgender as well as other trans identity terms that were common at the time they were produced, including *transgendered* and *transgenderist*. Often, descriptions of a victim's experience of violence included explicitly calling the victim transgender, such as in the "Hate Crime Portraits" compiled by GenderPAC: "Brandon Teena, a 21-year-old transgender man, died in late December 1994 after being shot execution style by two men both of whom had allegedly assaulted and raped Teena the prior week upon discovering that he had female genitalia."[14] As I discuss later, this had particular ramifications when, such as in the case of Brandon Teena, the victim had not explicitly identified as transgender. Moreover, as activists adapted their terminology to the current moment, the identity attributed to victims changed over time. For example, whereas Brandon Teena was said to be "transgender" in the quote from 2005, he was called a variety of terms between 1993 and 2009, including "transgendered," "a pre-operative transsexual," and a "transman."[15]

Activists also focused on identity in their descriptions of the causes of violence experienced by transgender people. Often, activists described a victim as being killed "simply because they are transgender" or "simply because of who they are."[16] For example, Mara Keisling, executive director for the National Center for Transgender Equality (NCTE), argued: "According to news accounts, more than one transgender person per month is killed in the United States for being transgender. The statistics are chilling: hate crimes based on sexual orientation and gender identity have risen for two straight years. Literally thousands and thousands of human beings attacked, wounded, or murdered because of who we are."[17] Likewise, Lateisha Green was described as being killed "for nothing more than being transgender" and "because she happened to be a transgender woman."[18] Similarly, in 2007 the NCTE released a transgender rights calendar. The page for August focused on violence and stated that "far too many transgender people are murdered simply because of who they are."[19] These sorts of statements are rhetorically effective in US culture, which values autonomy and individualism. These values spawned what historian Joanne Meyerowitz termed the "liberal moment" of gender, in which US society started to increasingly respect trans people's self-identities.[20] By attributing the violence to being one's "true self," trans activists were tapping into this moral moment in their efforts to gain attention for their cause. However, as I detail in this chapter, this focus on identity has unintended consequences, including creating a *homogenous subjecthood* in which all transgender people seem to be at equal risk at all times. As I demonstrate in chapter 5, this produces an unlivable life characterized by a high level of fear. Moreover, as explained in chapter 6, when activists do not attend to patterns of violence, those now vested with a homogenized, *vulnerable subjecthood* are unable to use such information to try to reduce their risk for violence.

FOCUSING ON HATE

Although trans activists regularly attributed the violence to simply being transgender, more often than not they named "hatred" of transgender people as the cause. Hatred was explicitly referenced in more than half of the documents I examined. All of the murders on the most famous website focused on violence experienced by transgender people were said to have been caused by hatred: "The Remembering Our Dead project exists to honor individuals murdered as a result of anti-transgender hatred and prejudice, and draw attention to the issue of anti-transgendered violence."[21] Widely distributed documents also focused on hatred. For example, every annual National Coalition of Anti-Violence Programs (NCAVP) report attributed the documented violence to hate.

Trans activists argued that the violence was caused by hatred of trans-gender people and that actual or perceived category membership, not actions, puts people at risk for violence. All transgender people were por-trayed as being at equal risk for experiencing violence. Moreover, they argued that a person does not have to be transgender to be vulnerable to such violence; merely being seen as transgender is sufficient. As stated on the ROD website: "Although not every person represented during the Day of Remembrance self-identified as transgendered—that is, as a transsexual, crossdresser, or otherwise gender-variant—each was a victim of violence based on bias against transgendered people."[22] By claiming victims, whether or not they self-identify as trans, activists were able to increase the num-ber of people said to be affected by the violence, thus potentially increasing political focus on their cause.

Although attributing the violence to transgender status and/or to hatred of that status may not seem particularly surprising to people today, it is notable due to the likelihood that trans people who were attacked were not recognized as transgender by their attackers. Identity-based anti-violence activism rests on an assumption that perpetrators of violence know of, and despise, the identity category. This denies other explanations, and in doing so it denies possible effective responses to violence. Though transgender is becoming more well-known, it is unlikely that perpetrators in the early years of this activism had ever heard the term.[23] As such, it is improbable that they killed people for being "transgender." Moreover, it may be that a number of the assaults were motivated by the perpetrators' very inability to label the victim with a gender. Similarly, many perpetrators attack trans people because they perceive them to be gay.[24] It stands to reason that dif-ferent approaches to reducing violence are needed if perpetrators are not using the same identity categories as activists. Finally, arguing that assaults are motivated by anti-transgender hatred assumes that the trans person was read as trans before the assault began. This may cause trans people to believe that if they are perceived as cisgender, they are safe from violence. But violence can start for a variety of reasons, and the perpetrator may only realize that someone is transgender partway through the assault. It is highly likely that this "discovery" would change the style of violence. For example, criminologist Gail Mason interviewed a butch Asian lesbian who was initially attacked for being Asian. During the attack, the perpetrator realized that she was a woman and the tone of the attack changed, becom-ing more sexualized.[25] People regularly perceived as transgender may be at risk for different kinds of violence than those who are not so perceived but might be "discovered" as trans, a factor that should be acknowledged.

DENYING OTHER CAUSES

In their fight against violence, trans activists almost always argued that only one identity—transgender—motivated the violence. In their attempt to highlight the importance of transgender in the violence they discussed, activists both implicitly and explicitly denied multiple (or alternative) causes of that violence. Scholars have analyzed the slurs used during attacks on trans people and concluded that, in addition to gender, race and sexuality are also often motivations for this violence.[26] But in their struggle to ensure that people attend to the role of anti-transgender hatred, activists ignored or overtly denied these other causes.

Most documents described the victims as only transgender and offered anti-transgender hatred as the sole cause of violence. Moreover, the vast majority of the documents produced by trans anti-violence activists never even mentioned any other identity category besides transgender, even when grouping diverse victims together. For example, the popular flyer shown in figure 1 asserted: "Shown to the left are just six people who were killed simply because they were viewed as crossing the line between genders. They were murdered, along with at least 150 others in the past decade alone, simply because they were transgendered or perceived to be." What this description did not mention is both the diversity of the victims depicted and the multiple factors that might have led to their deaths. The photos show a group of people of a variety of genders and races (two were transmasculine and four transfeminine; two were black, two were white, one was Native American, and one was Latinx). However, all were said to have been killed because they were "transgender." By picturing both masculine and feminine victims together, this flyer encouraged readers to see violence against trans masculine people as similar to that perpetrated against transfeminine people. Likewise, this flyer encouraged the reader to focus on transgender status, rather than race, as the cause by showing victims from diverse racial backgrounds but portraying the violence against them as the same. The reader of the flyer was not invited to question how the violence experienced by the diversely raced or gendered bodies may have been different. Instead, the reader was told that each person was killed "simply because they were transgendered or perceived to be." It should be noted that the motivation behind the deaths of several of the pictured victims is either unknown or said to be other than anti-transgender hatred. Both Marsha P. Johnson's and Emmon Bodfish's deaths were never solved (Johnson's was, controversially, ruled a suicide, and Bodfish's may have been the result of a failed robbery attempt or a

Anti-Trans Murder: **Over One A Month**

Marsha P. Johnson
July 6, 1992

Brandon
December 31, 1993

Rita Hester
November 28, 1998

Emmon Bodfish
June 21, 1999

F.C. Martinez
June 16, 2001

Gwen Araujo
October 3, 2002

GEA02001

Shown to the left are just six people who were killed simply because they were viewed as crossing the line between genders. They were murdered, along with at least 150 others in the past decade alone, simply because they were transgendered or perceived to be.

These were not simple murders. Their killers, in displaying an especially virulent form of hatred, often went from murder to overkill, attempting to obliterate their victims, perhaps in an attempt to erase them completely, by any means necessary.

More than one new anti-transgender murder has been reported in the media every month since 1989. Countless others have been ignored.

Law enforcement and the justice system frequently regard the transgendered as disposable people, and their murders not worth investigation. Despite clear evidence of hate crimes, these cases are commonly labeled as accidents or suicides. They are quickly closed, and thus the killers are rarely apprehended. Those who are caught seldom receive sentences commensurate with their crimes. In over 200 cases, only one such murderer is currently on death row, and just two others are serving life sentences.

Violence based upon gender variance does not solely affect the transgendered. Anyone just perceived as crossing gender lines can become a victim. In one case, a non-transgendered man was murdered in a violent assault in a Tennessee department store. The reason: he was helping a blind man use a men's room, guiding him by holding his hand, while also holding his wife's purse as she tried on clothes in a fitting room.

The city with the highest incidence of transgender murders in the United States is New York, with 29 reported killings in the last 32 years. Other cities with high transgender murder rates include Atlanta, Houston, and Washington, D.C.

Laws designed to protect the transgendered from discrimination do help. San Francisco has had only one reported anti-transgender murder since 1994, when that city passed an anti-discrimination ordinance.

Data Courtesy of Remembering Our Dead
A product of Gender Education & Advocacy
http://www.rememberingourdead.org

FIGURE 1. "Anti-Trans Murder: Over One a Month." Popular flyer used to advertise Transgender Day of Remembrance events. Created by Gender Education and Advocacy, October 6, 2004. Used with permission.

dispute with his son), and F.C. Martinez's killer bragged after the fatal assault that he had "bug-smashed a joto." In their attempt to focus attention on what they identified as the "anti-transgender" motivation for violence, activists ignored other factors (e.g., homophobia, racism, sexism, and non-bias-related factors) that may have motivated the violence. This may have been in part due to a fear that if they specified which transgender people were most at risk, those who were less likely to experience violence might care less about the cause. However, not all violence experienced by trans people is solely motivated by hatred of transgender people.[27] To reduce or prevent violence experienced by trans people, other factors must be addressed.

When activists did mention other possible causes besides anti-transgender hatred, it was often in the context of denying alternative explanations, including homophobic, racist, or non-bias-based motivations, such as a disagreement. For example, a writer for *FTMi* argued in 1994 that "Brandon Teena was not killed because she was a lesbian, he was killed because he was transgendered."[28] Likewise, in a 2002 press release, the Human Rights Campaign brought up the possibility of other biases as causes and then immediately dismissed them:

> The body of Fred Martinez Jr., an openly gay, transgender, Navajo teen was found south of Cortez five days after he left home to go to a carnival. Police have arrested another teen in the murder and are investigating whether the homicide was a hate crime based on sexual orientation or race. The perpetrator allegedly bragged that he "beat up a fag." Martinez, 16, often curled his hair, plucked his eyebrows, wore make-up and carried a purse to school. His mother told the press that she firmly believes her son's slaying was a hate crime based on his gender identity or because he was transgender.[29]

A number of potential bias factors are mentioned here: race, sexual orientation, and gender. Although the police offered two explanations (sexual orientation and race), and the perpetrator used homophobic language to describe his crime, activists used Martinez's mother's words to argue that the violence was motivated by anti-transgender hatred alone, rather than any of the other causes. In making such a claim, activists assumed that the murderer both knew what transgender was and committed the violence because he hated what it meant. In this case, it seems that the perpetrator did not see Martinez as transgender but as gay. However, rather than identify the possibility of multiple, intersecting causes for violence, trans activists argued for one cause only: anti-transgender hatred.

HOMOGENEOUS SUBJECTHOOD, HOMOGENOUS RISK

In their efforts to highlight the role transgender status plays in risks for violence, trans activists did not portray the category of transgender as a diverse group of people at variable risk for a variety of forms of violence. Thus, they did not depict transgender people as full subjects existing in multiple categories.[30] Instead, transgender was portrayed as a flat, homogeneous category populated by people at equal risk of identical forms of violence. As legal scholar Sarah Lamble argued based on an analysis of Transgender Day of Remembrance, in this sort of activism "transgender bodies are universalized along a singular identity plane of victimhood and rendered visible primarily through the violence that is acted upon them."[31]

By making statements marking the violence as "anti-transgender" and claiming that "there is no safe way to be transgendered," activists portrayed all trans people as equally vulnerable to violence.[32] This approach likely encouraged people to care about this violence by making them think that they, or someone they love, would be attacked next. However, this portrayal constructed the category of transgender as a homogeneous one populated by potential victims. Although it is of course accurate to argue that being, or being perceived as, transgender was a factor in these crimes, this argument elides patterns in the violence, including of victimization, of perpetration, and in the relationships between victims and perpetrators. As I detail in chapter 6, this has had substantial consequences for proposed solutions to violence.

Eliding Patterns of Victimization

The reports, press releases, websites, and flyers produced by transgender anti-violence activists give one the impression that all transgender people are at equal risk for violence. Activists focused mainly on fatal violence and, as I have described in this chapter, both implicitly and explicitly framed murderers as solely motivated by anti-transgender hatred. This obfuscates patterns of victimization, including variations in risk related to gender, race, and age. Of the more than one thousand documents I examined, just forty-three mentioned how race, gender, age, or class shape the likelihood that a transgender person will experience violence. Almost all of these exceptions to the pattern were produced by GenderPAC and NCAVP. This is likely due to unique aspects of each organization. NCAVP collects data from its member programs about violence experienced by LGBT people, including demographic data, when known, about victims and perpetrators. In reporting that information, NCAVP highlighted other factors besides sexuality and gender in these crimes. As I describe later, GenderPAC officially rejected an identity politics model of anti-violence activism, increasing the likelihood of its focusing on more factors than just anti-transgender hatred.

In their anti-violence documents, trans activists regularly portrayed transgender men and women as at similar risks for experiencing violence. This occurred both in text and in visual representations. In their attempts to elicit sympathy for victims and to humanize the statistics they provided, activists often included photos of victims and/or short stories about their cases. Between 1990 and 2009, the victim most often shown in photographs was white and transmasculine. Brandon Teena was pictured almost four times more often than any other victim. The next most commonly photographically portrayed victims were Emmon Bodfish, a white trans man; Gwen Araujo, a Latinx trans woman; and Chanelle Picket, a black trans woman. When discussing violence, trans activists often mentioned multiple victims and tended to mention at least one trans man and one trans woman. If one was to take these visual representations and victim mentions as accurate depictions of patterns of violence, one would assume that trans men and trans women were at equal risk and that victims were often white. However, such conjectures are not reflected in the actual patterns of murders of transgender people at that time as trans men comprised less than 2 percent of murder victims and white people about 17 percent.[33]

Trans activist documents also misrepresented patterns of risk in terms of age. As demonstrated in chapter 3, because of beliefs about what makes an "ideal" victim, the most famous transgender victims of violence were very young. Although activists rarely mentioned other social categories, preferring to focus on transgender status, when they did mention something besides being transgender, it was usually a reference to the victim's age, almost always to highlight their youth. As a *Transgender Tapestry* article stated in 2008: "In the media, transgender children have been making tragic headlines. On February 12, Lawrence King, a 15 year-old student in California, was shot in school by a classmate at point blank range. On February 22, Simmie Williams, a 17 year-old student, was murdered in Fort Lauderdale Florida. They were both executed for the crime of crossing gender boundaries."[34] Notably, six transgender people were murdered in the United States in February of 2008, and their average age was 26.5 years old. However, the article only mentions the two victims who were under 18.[35] The tendency to focus on younger victims is epitomized by GenderPAC's two widely circulated reports on violence that only included younger victims. In 2006, GenderPAC released *50 under 30*, documenting the murders of fifty-one gender nonconforming people under the age of thirty. This was followed in 2008 by an updated version including sixty-eight victims under the age of thirty. The median age of transgender murder victims between 1990 and 2009 was thirty years old. By only focusing on those who were thirty or younger, the GenderPAC reports ignore half the victims. In addition to highlighting younger victims, activists also produced the impression that transgender murder victims were usually very young through inaccurate descriptions of cases. For example, a 1996 press release from GenderPAC about vigils outside the trials of the men who killed Brandon Teena stated: "In an all-to-common progression of events, as the demonstrators were leaving the courthouse that day, yet another *young* transsexual, Ms. Deborah Forte, was being violently stabbed to death back in Haverhill, MA."[36] Deborah Forte was fifty-six years old.

Eliding Patterns of Perpetration

The tendency of these identity-based anti-violence activists to focus on the transgender status of victims also disguised patterns of perpetration. One of the goals of activists was to frame victims as valuable people undeserving of violence. As such, activists tended to focus on victims and rarely discussed individual perpetrators. In the vast majority of narratives told by activists in which a victim was named, the killer was not. This was due in part to the fact that not all cases had identified accused or convicted killers. Of the 289 homicides, just 157 (54%) had a known perpetrator. However, even when someone had been convicted of the killing, activists rarely named the murderer. Instead, when they mentioned them at all, they described them in general terms such as "the perpetrator." This has the effect of deindividualizing the cause for violence. For example, a story from a list of murders published in 2002 reads:

> Amanda Milan—Throat Slashed: June 2000, New York, New York
>
> Amanda Milan, a 27-year-old transgender woman died after her throat was slashed with a knife outside the Port Authority. Witnesses say that a group of cab drivers cheered and applauded as the crime was committed and shouted transgenderphobic remarks. One of the perpetrators allegedly shouted phrases like "You're a man!" and "I know that's a dick between your legs."[37]

Not naming the perpetrators makes them faceless, a sort of villainous "everyman."[38]

More often than not, however, activists did not even mention the killer, completely removing the doer of the violence from the story and only describing the violence. This portrayed society itself as the perpetrator of the violence. Not mentioning a perpetrator was particularly common when activists listed multiple victims. For example, in 1999 activist Elizabeth Birch argued: "Compared to the murders of Matthew Shepard and Billy Jack Gaither, both openly gay men who were killed at least in part because of their sexual orientation, the murders and suspected murders of transgendered people over the last year have received far less focus and attention. Yet there has been no lack of victims; tragedies in the past year alone include Rita Hester, stabbed 20 times, near Boston; Vianna Faye Williams, murdered in Jersey City, stabbed repeatedly in the back, neck and chest; in March, Tracey Thompson was found bludgeoned to death in south Georgia."[39] By not identifying the killer at all, the violence seems to come from nowhere identifiable and thus from everywhere. The effect of the killers not always being known, combined with not naming them when they are, portrays these homicides not as individual, separate acts of violence, but as part of a larger pattern of violence performed by a population of haters of transgender people. Just as activists' narratives erased differences between victims, these sorts of tellings of violence elided patterns among perpetrators.

This trend was echoed in terms of actual mentions of patterns of perpetration. Of the more than one thousand documents produced by transgender anti-violence activists during this period, just eighteen mentioned gendered patterns of perpetration. This overlooked a very significant trend. Of the 176 homicides between 1990 and 2009 in which the perpetrator's gender was known, 167 (94.9%) were cisgender men, 6 (3.4%) were cisgender women, and 3 (1.7%) were transgender women. Despite the strikingly gendered nature of perpetration, trans activist narratives degender perpetrators, making it seem as if they could be anyone or everyone. As I detail later, given that successful anti-violence programs require knowledge of who is doing the violence, this sort of erasure is potentially detrimental to the fight against violence.

Eliding Patterns of Relationships between Perpetrators and Victims

The focus on hatred of transgender people as the sole cause for violence experienced by transgender people further obfuscated patterns in the relationship between perpetrators and victims. Moreover, the messages that "there is no 'safe way' to be transgendered" and "we are all at risk" obscured the ways in which violence tends to occur in particular situations.[40] Of the 136 homicides between 1990 and 2009 in which the relationship between the perpetrator and victim was known, 71 percent of the murders occurred in sexual interactions: 16 percent in ongoing sexual relationships, such as dating and long-term partnerships; 32 percent in new sexual relationships, such as hook-ups; and 23 percent in interactions where sex was exchanged for money or other resources. However, this pattern is not evident in activist accounts. Activists rarely acknowledged that the victim was engaged in sex work and almost never mentioned that a homicide occurred during a nonmonetary sexual encounter. The omission of these particular patterns is likely due to a fear of increasing the stigmatization of an already oppressed group. As described in an article from the Southern Poverty Law Center in 2003: "Media accounts of murders like Bella Evangelista's or Emonie Spaulding's often link the crimes to street prostitution. That infuriates transgender activists, who say it's a form of blaming the victim. 'The implication is that it's your fault for being beaten or killed,' says Jessica Xavier. 'But a lack of privilege means you don't have a choice.' Or as Mottet puts it, 'Sure, they have a choice: They can freeze and starve, or they can try to make a living.'"[41] However, successful violence-prevention practices and policies rely on knowing patterns of violence. Members of the identity group would benefit from having an accurate *geography of fear*, including knowing patterns of victimization, perpetration, and the situations in which violence is most likely to occur.[42] Moreover, if activist narratives regularly mentioned sexual interactions, they might become less stigmatized.

The tendency to elide patterns of perpetration is not unique to transgender anti-violence activism. Identity-based anti-violence activists tend to focus on victims only and downplay the interaction between victim and perpetrator in order to reduce the appearance that they are "blaming the victim."[43] By focusing only on identity, which is framed both as outside of the victim's control and as shaping the perpetrator's violence, and avoiding discussing behaviors done by the victim, activists work to tell narratives with innocent victims and villainous perpetrators. In doing so, they emphasize a single identity for victims and, when perpetrators are mentioned, a single "opposite" identity for perpetrators. Accordingly, the civil rights movement focused on white people's violence against black people, the women's rights movement highlighted men's violence against women, the gay rights movement called attention to straight people's violence against gay men and lesbians, and the transgender rights movement told narratives about cisgender people's violence against transgender people. All of these forms of violence should be attended to. However, by only highlighting a single identity for perpetrators and a single "opposite" identity for victims, identity-based anti-violence activists obscure violence within their own communities as well as important patterns of hate-based violence. For example, activists fighting to reduce violence against people of color, gay men and lesbians, and transgender people rarely emphasize the fact that most perpetrators of this violence are men.

CONSTRUCTING AN US VERSUS THEM MENTALITY

One of the widely acknowledged consequences of identity politics is that it amplifies divisions between groups while obscuring their similarities. Central to the identity politics model is a belief that the identity group members are "oppressed," while those in the "opposite" group are "oppressors."[44] We can see this in a number of political struggles, such as those around women's rights, in which men are characterized as sexist and women are seen as exempt from possessing sexist ideologies. The "us versus them" mentality that emerges from identity politics has profound consequences when coupled with anti-violence activism. As it does for all forms of identity politics, this mentality potentially obscures allies and alliances. Moreover, when combined with anti-violence activism, it also intensifies the level of vulnerability associated with the subjecthood and may, as some research has suggested, increase levels of violence. Adding "us versus them" to a conversation about violence can encourage rhetoric about how "they" are out to get "us" and that "they" will do nothing to protect "us." Such a world, particularly when "they" is the vast majority of the population, is terrifying. Reflecting this, sociologists Barbara Perry and D. Ryan Dyck found that the transgender women they interviewed lived in a constant state of fear, terrified of anyone who was not transgender. As one interviewee stated, "We don't trust anyone. We trust each other, as trans women trust each other, [but] we don't trust anyone [else] and that includes members of the queer community."[45] Identity politics highlights the differences between groups and can often make conflict between them seem inevitable, which is detrimental to anti-violence work. Moreover, this rhetoric, by exacerbating fears of "them," may encourage identity group members to avoid interactions with those who do not share their identity, fostering the very misinformation and prejudices that lead to violence.

Trans anti-violence activists regularly portrayed the world as comprised of two types of people: transgender people and haters of transgender people. Just as transness was depicted as the essence, or an essential characteristic, of trans people, hatred of transness was seen as central to most, if not all, cisgender people. Exemplifying this, a common metaphor used by activists to characterize this situation was that of "war." Activist Jessica Xavier argued in 2003 that there was "a war against transgendered women" in the United States.[46] Similarly, in its report for 2004, NCAVP argued that "the social and political forces now holding power are beyond simply opposing issues supportive to LGBT people and have now moved to open warfare against all that they hold in contempt, including and especially the LGBT community."[47] This "war," however, was almost always portrayed as one-sided, with cisgender people attacking transgender people and not the reverse. Activist Monica Helms described Texas as a "transgender killing field" in 2001 and trans people as "cannon fodder" in 2004.[48] By contrast, only two activists in the documents examined suggested that trans people should "fight back." One, Gwendolyn Smith, stated: "We have lost so many people in our community to the hand of hatred and prejudice, yet we still are not seemingly willing to fight back. Meanwhile, we die at the hands of a lover, of police, of medical practitioners, and even parents, while the news media calls us 'freaks'—and worse."[49]

Although occasionally the instigators of this "war" were named as "right-wing" politicians or "small town, working class America," usually activists using the war metaphor did not specify who was waging the war.[50] This rhetorical tactic essentialized both hatred and transgender people as hated. In these narratives, the hatred motivating the killing is not a hatred of the individual; instead, it is a hatred of an entire group motivated by what activists defined as the essence of transgender people, or violence done to people "for being their true selves." Similarly, this hatred was portrayed as society-wide, and hate was depicted as essential to much of the cisgender population, thus making all trans people appear to be at risk for violence at all times.

Framing violence as caused by hatred of difference and coupling identity politics with anti-violence activism produces the us versus them mentality across a variety of identity-based anti-violence groups. Activist narratives depict men as pitted against women, whites against blacks, and straight people against gay men and lesbians, ignoring the intersections across those categories. In their critique of the struggle for hate crime legislation, legal scholars James Jacobs and Kimberly Potter highlighted the consequences of this situation, arguing: "By redefining crime as a facet of intergroup conflict, hate crime laws encourage citizens to think of themselves as members of identity groups and encourage identity groups to think of themselves as victimized and besieged, thereby hardening each group's sense of resentment. That in turn contributes to the balkanization of American society, not to its unification."[51] Thus, combining identity politics with anti-violence activism can solidify identities, increase conflict between identity groups, and lead to misunderstandings of violence, thus making it more difficult to prevent.

Moreover, the "us versus them" mentality may actually increase levels of violence. Political scientist Ashutosh Varshney examined factors shaping ethnic conflict in various communities in India and found that places where Hindus and Muslims interacted regularly had lower levels of conflict and violence than spaces with religiously segregated social networks.[52] Thus, social networks that link potentially oppositional communities help reduce violence between those groups. By contrast, the "us versus them" mindset discourages interactions between identity groups and may increase the chances of violence between them. The tactics used by trans activists to gain attention for violence experienced by trans people often portrayed cisgender people as "fighting a war against" transgender people. As a result, transgender community members exposed to this rhetoric, as I detail in chapter 5, likely fear cisgender people. Although this fear is justified in the sense that the majority of people committing acts of violence against trans people are cis, the vast majority of cisgender people are not violent against transgender people. Though many cis people are potential allies to the trans rights movement, the language that "they are out to get us" discourages such alliances. Like the interreligious hostility Varshney studied, the violence done by cis people to trans people is likely caused by unfamiliarity. If cis and trans people interacted and got to know each other more, it is likely that violence against trans people would decrease. Indeed, research has demonstrated a significant decrease in transphobia among cisgender people given educational materials about transgender people; it has also shown that cisgender people who know a transgender person are more likely to advocate for social acceptance of transgender people.[53] In order to facilitate more connection between transgender and cisgender people, activists would need to abandon the "us versus them" lens and instead encourage members of different identity groups to join organizations together to stop violence.

THE OCCASIONAL ATTENTION TO INTERSECTIONALITY

Due to the logics of identity politics, activists engaged in identity-based anti-violence work rarely took an intersectional perspective in their statements about violence against transgender people. In the activist documents produced from 1990 to 2009, the first mention of the intersection of multiple social systems in this violence was in 2000, but such statements were incredibly rare in these documents until 2006, when GenderPAC, one of the most active organizations in the fight against "anti-transgender violence," published *50 under 30*.[54] With the exception of its typical focus on youth, this human rights report represented an alternative approach to anti-violence activism. In this document, GenderPAC identified itself as an organization that "promotes an understanding of the connection between gender stereotypes and discrimination based on characteristics such as age, race, socioeconomic status, sex, and sexual orientation."[55] In highlighting the role of multiple identities in violence, GenderPAC broke with the traditional mold of identity-based anti-violence activism. Following the release of *50 under 30*, a few other trans anti-violence activist groups also occasionally mentioned intersectionality. NCTE argued in 2007 that "patterns of age, race, class and original sex in anti-transgender violence weave intersections between marginalized groups in society."[56] Likewise, a GLAAD press release about a 2009 discussion panel on hate crimes stated: "One of the major take-aways from the conversation was that there is no one single reason for the perpetration and general tolerance of crimes motivated by anti-transgender bias. It is not simply transphobia, or sexism alone at work, but rather the way that those issues are intertwined with issues of classism and racism that have allowed crimes such as these to continue in our communities. But speaking out about these experiences and intersections will go a long way toward solving these problems."[57] Finally, for the first time in its annual reports, in 2009 NCAVP included an entire section titled "INTERSECTIONS: Transphobic, homophobic, and racist violence."[58] Moreover, the report included attending to intersectionality in its suggestions for how to address violence, recommending that activists

> engage with diverse community groups to broaden analyses, deepen tactics and strengthen movements around intersectional experiences and connections. Because LGBTQ survivors often identify with one or more additionally marginalized identities, LGBTQ anti-violence programs as well as other service providers and community groups should engage with a broad base of marginalized groups working to end violence and create safety. LGBTQ people may also identify as people of color, youth, low-income, immigrants, people living with HIV/AIDS, people living with disabilities, elders, people in the sex trade, and/or incarcerated people, among others. Each identity may present a distinct set of considerations for an LGBTQ hate violence survivor or victim. Additionally, the oppressions faced by each group mutually reinforce each other. Historically, oppressive state and societal structures have engaged in "divide and conquer" tactics, pitting the needs of one community against another and leaving each community more vulnerable to further systemic violence and trauma. In this context, the importance

of relationship-building among these communities becomes all the more clear. LGBTQ-specific anti-violence programs should work in partnership with other groups targeted for identity-based violence to expand their understanding of intersectional oppression and its impacts on LGBTQ communities.[59]

The principles expressed here were unprecedented in the materials produced by transgender anti-violence activists between 1990 and 2009. As detailed in this chapter, activists rarely ever mentioned that transgender people were diverse in terms of race, class, gender identity, and other characteristics, let alone explicitly called for attention to these factors.

Although these rare statements do indicate an alternative approach to anti-violence activism, they also echo much of the prevailing way of doing identity-based anti-violence work. Due to the logics of identity politics, when other factors besides anti-transgender hatred are mentioned, they are almost always identity categories. In a 2003 HRC press release, National Field Director Seth Kilbourn argued: "When a GLBT person of color is targeted for hate violence, it is difficult—if not impossible—to separate out race, sexual orientation or gender identity discrimination in the treatment of the victim and the victim's family and loved ones. For example, in recent years, we have seen this pattern play out in the murders of J.R. Warren in West Virginia and Fred Martinez in Colorado. In both cases, the families thought that race, sexual orientation or gender identity were factors in the murder."[60] Though the killer was convicted, investigations never revealed the motive for murdering F.C. Martinez. The murders of both J.R. Warren and Martinez were complex cases involving multiple potential factors, including some unrelated to social category membership. However, activists only highlighted identity-based causes in their discussions of the cases.

On the infrequent occasions that transgender anti-violence activists noted patterns of risk, they focused on age, gender, race, and class. As previously detailed, the attention to age tended to inaccurately identify youth as at the highest risk. By contrast, activists did note accurate patterns of risk for the other three social categories. Of the more than one thousand documents I examined, just thirty-nine mentioned racial differences in risk, all of which highlighted the disproportional level of violence experienced by transgender people of color. As Executive Director Riki Wilchins of Gender-PAC said in 2003: "With six murders in two years, it is becoming clear that minority teens who cross gender lines are increasingly at risk."[61] Similarly, the Gay Straight Alliance (GSA) issued an uncommon statement in 2005: "Over the past year, over 30 transgender people have lost their lives due to hate crimes, but this is unfortunately just the tip of the iceberg of people killed worldwide due to bias and hatred based on gender identity and expression. Most of the victims were people of color who came from working class backgrounds."[62] Twenty-seven documents attended to gendered differences in risk, twenty-three of which were among the thirty-nine that mentioned racial differences in risk. Almost all of them highlighted that transfeminine people experience more fatal violence than transmasculine people. For example, the NCAVP report for 2009 described transgender women as "among the most vulnerable communities of LGBTQ-identified people."[63] Similarly, in 2001 transgender activist Alexander John Goodrum stated: "I've learned that, perhaps right at this moment, there is a transgendered person—most likely an MTF transsexual or crossdresser, most likely a person of color—being brutally murdered."[64] Even less common than mentions of gendered patterns of violence were references to the role class played. Nine documents argued that poor transgender people were at higher risk for experiencing violence. As both of GenderPAC's reports, *50 under 30* and *70 under 30*, argued: "Poverty and gender are intertwined in many of these fatalities. Victims are disproportionately from economically-disadvantaged communities."[65] Conspicuously, however, with the exception of NCAVP and GenderPAC, organizations that highlighted these patterns of violence did not alter their proposed solutions to address issues of race, gender, age, or class.

The same documents that highlighted patterns of victimization occasionally, but less frequently, noted patterns of perpetration and patterns in the relationships between perpetrators and victims. All fourteen NCAVP reports issued between 1996 and 2009 attended to racial patterns of perpetration, and eighteen documents, mostly from NCAVP and GenderPAC, noted that most perpetrators of violence against transgender people were cisgender men. It is surprising that this was rarely attended to, given the stark gendered pattern of perpetration, in which 95 percent of murders of transgender people are cisgender men. Similarly uncommon was attention paid to patterns in the relationships between victims and perpetrators. For example, less than 2 percent of the documents mentioned that the murder occurred in a situation in which the victim was trading sex for money, despite the fact that 23 percent of homicides in this period occurred in such circumstances.

Notably, in their focus on identity, activists only attended to historically oppressed categories. As such, only the race of people of color was highlighted, and sexual orientation was only mentioned in the context of gay men and lesbians. Thus, the attention to intersectionality in these documents ignores how, due to the intersections of multiple social systems, people can experience mixtures of privilege and disadvantage. This is exemplified by *50 under 30*, which was careful to note the race of the victims of color but did not do so for the white victims. For example, on the same page that Alejandro Lucero was described as "a transgender Hopi woman" and F.C. Martinez was described as "a Two-Spirit Navajo teen," Reshae McCauley, who was white, was described just as "a cross-dresser." Similarly, two pages later Loni Kai Okaruru was described as "an Asian/Pacific-Islander cross-dresser," while Christian Paige and Lauryn Paige, who were both white, were both described simply as "a transgender woman." In this focus only on historically oppressed categories, anti-violence activists attending to intersectionality followed the dominant pattern of identity politics that emphasizes oppression and elides privilege.[66] As I detail in chapter 7, these patterns continue in current transgender anti-violence activism.

CONSEQUENCES OF REJECTING IDENTITY POLITICS: THE RISE AND FALL OF GENDERPAC

By far the most prominent transgender rights organization in the 1990s was the Gender Public Advocacy Coalition (GenderPAC), and one of the most well-known transgender rights activists was its executive director, Riki Wilchins. Dubbed "a leading activist for our community" in *Transgender Tapestry*, Wilchins united several smaller transgender rights organizations under the banner of GenderPAC in 1995.[67] Widely celebrated within the transgender community, Wilchins was often featured in the transgender press and also regularly appeared in mainstream news coverage.[68] Although GenderPAC was commonly understood to be focused solely on transgender rights and was described by many as "the national lobbying arm of the TG [transgender] community," Wilchins was opposed to an identity politics model and the initial mission of GenderPAC was to fight for "gender, affectional and racial equality."[69] As Wilchins stated in a 1997 interview with *Transgender Tapestry*:

> G-PAC itself was dedicated to gender, affectional and racial equality, to get away from identity-based politics, where an organization represents just transpeople and so on. Inevitably, if an organization is identity-based, you wind up with people saying to someone, "You don't belong, you're not our problem." TGs have been told that by everyone. The feminist organizations say, "You're not our problem." The gay and lesbian organizations say, "You're not our problem." I've seen where identity-based politics end up, and it's not someplace pleasant. The idea behind the work that I do is to get beyond identity politics and start

looking at function, and the function that I wanted to focus on was
gender-based oppression. So, I wasn't asking myself. Who's my constit-
uency?" I asked myself, "What kinds of social oppression am I trying to
overturn or contest?"[70]

In their fight for equality, GenderPAC focused heavily on violence in part
because, as Wilchins once told anthropologist David Valentine, "Violence is the
perfect issue, like motherhood. No one can be against motherhood and no one
can be for violence."[71] Following her ethos, Wilchins and GenderPAC worked
to attend to intersectionality in their anti-violence work. As stated under "Our
Mission and Vision" on the GenderPAC website in 2002:

> The Gender Public Advocacy Coalition (GenderPAC) is the national
> organization working to end discrimination and violence caused by
> gender stereotypes.
>   We are especially concerned with the way discrimination based on
> gender intersects with other kinds of discrimination, including those of
> race, class, ethnicity, and age.[72]

Although GenderPAC's breaking of identity politics norms caused
conflict from the beginning, in the 1990s, "Wilchins had been regarded
by many in the transgender community as its national spokesperson and
GenderPAC had been recognized nationally as the voice of the trans gender community."[73] That all changed in the early 2000s, as discord over
GenderPAC's refusal to focus only on "transgender issues" erupted.[74] As
GenderPAC began to more explicitly focus on how gendered beliefs shaped
a variety of inequalities, angry activists argued that, although GenderPAC
had an official mission that rejected identity politics, the actual work done
by GenderPAC had been "trans-focused."[75] Many in the trans community
felt that over time the focus had become less and less transgender centered
and, in response, several board members resigned, articles were published
in *Transgender Tapestry* blasting Wilchins, and activists formed a new
group to replace GenderPAC, the short-lived National Transgender Advocacy Coalition (NTAC).[76] Despite criticism and controversy, GenderPAC
remained very active in gender-based anti-violence work through 2006.
Wilchins's and GenderPAC's influence within the trans community diminished over time, however. With the exception of the 2008 report *70 under
30*, they did very little public work on violence experienced by trans people
after 2006 and in 2009 they officially disbanded.[77]
    Highlighting causes for discrimination and violence besides trans status
was seen as a blasphemous betrayal of the activist community because it

would deflect attention away from the role of trans status. In the social problems marketplace, reduced attention means loss of resources, and activists feared that GenderPAC would take money from the transgender community and use it in efforts that would not benefit that community.[78] By attempting to construct a more nuanced, *heterogeneous subjecthood*, Wilchins and other GenderPAC staff engaged in one of the most terrible sins imaginable within the anti-violence activism model at the time: not stressing a single identity as central to the violence one is trying to prevent.[79] GenderPAC had become the most powerful organization focused on trans issues in the nation, and at the height of its influence seemed to be turning its back on the trans community. This was seen by some as a "cold-blooded abandonment of the very community by whom and for which it was created, nurtured and financially supported."[80]

Interestingly, the conflict around GenderPAC's rejection of the identity politics model may have been exacerbated by the very tactics that have been central to identity-based anti-violence activism, tactics that Gender-PAC itself engaged in. As shown in this book, GenderPAC did take an identity-based approach to much of its activism, portraying transgender people as the most vulnerable identity group, under siege from a hate-filled cisgender population. It is likely that the construction of a vulnerable subjecthood and the "us versus them" approach to activism shaped how other activists responded to GenderPAC's apparent shift away from focusing on the transgender community. If one believes the *oppression Olympics* rhetoric, then one would see transgender people as the most oppressed and therefore the most deserving of activist attention and would experience as a betrayal a refusal to focus only on violence experienced by trans people. This can be seen in Donna Cartwright's article in *Transgender Tapestry* in 2001 explaining why she had resigned from GenderPAC, in which she stated: "I find this effort to 'mainstream' GenderPAC's message frightening and deeply painful. Transgender and other gender-transgressive people are among the most marginalized, scorned and rejected individuals in our culture. They are still often on 'the bleeding edge' of gender issues."[81] Similarly, if one accepts the premise encouraged by identity politics that it is "us versus them," any move to incorporate "them" into what was seen as a transgender rights group would be seen as abhorrent. As Cartwright argued: "As GenderPAC seeks to position itself as a group as an advocate for 'all Americans,' of necessity it will have to speak proportionately less and less about transgender and genderqueer people and issues."[82] She went on to state that if GenderPAC stopped focusing on trans people, NAACP would still focus on "non-trans African-Americans," NOW would still advocate for "non-trans feminists," and HRC would still focus on "non-trans gays and lesbians," leaving transgender people with no advocates. The use of war metaphors and other "us versus them" tactics encouraged drawing of battle lines and hoarding of resources. In the end, activists did "eat their own" in these skirmishes over which people should be focused on.[83] The construction of new organizations to replace GenderPAC thinned resources and members for all groups doing this anti-violence work. In the end, these battles over resources damaged the groups that were fighting them, resulting in the demise of the most powerful transgender rights organization at the time.

INFLUENCING UNDERSTANDINGS OF VIOLENCE AND SHAPING SOLUTIONS

There is no single form of "anti-transgender" violence. Transgender is an internally heterogeneous category, and violence experienced by transgender people is shaped by their race, gender, sexuality, and class. Violence is also influenced by non-identity factors, such as social space, witnesses to the violence, and the relationship between the people involved. Thus, understanding this violence requires an intersectional analysis. Such analysis demonstrates that gender plays a complex role in these homicides, and violence against transgender people is also shaped by race, class, and sexuality. These interlocking structures of violence come together in ways that put those who have been traditionally disadvantaged by the race and gender systems—that is, black transgender women—at substantial risk for homicide. Thus, to craft effective solutions, anti-violence activists must move beyond the "transgender people experience violence because they are transgender" line of reasoning and instead focus on the patterns of violence against transgender people.

Ignoring these patterns of violence and portraying all violence experienced by all transgender people as caused solely by their transgender status is dangerous. Denying the multiple causes of the violence transgender people experience reduces attention to all of the other causes of violence experienced by trans people, including biases against women, people of color, gay people, and sex workers, as well as non-bias-related motivations for violence. It therefore conceals from view possible solutions to such violence, such as fighting sexism, racism, and homophobia; working to end the employment discrimination that pushes people into illegal ways of earning a living; and legalizing—and therefore making safer—sex work. As I demonstrate in chapter 6, the frame of "hatred" of an identity as the cause of violence deeply influenced the solutions to violence proposed by trans activists. Because they identified only transgender status as the motivation for violence, activists focused on including "transgender" or "gender identity" in anti–hate crime legislation to the detriment of alternative solutions. Moreover, as activists tended to ignore the patterns in the violence, their solutions did not address those patterns.

In their anti-violence work, such as the Remembering Our Dead website, trans activists solidified the identity category of transgender and emphasized the role of hatred in violence experienced by trans people. But in their efforts to highlight the role transgender status plays in risks for violence, trans activists portrayed transgender as a homogeneous subjecthood populated by people at equal risk for identical forms of violence. As I demonstrate in the next chapter, in their attempt to gain attention for the issue of violence against transgender people, activists also portrayed the group as highly vulnerable to violence at all times. Combined with the construction of a homogeneous subjecthood as detailed in this chapter, transgender came to be seen as a universally imperiled, unlivable life.

5. Valuable and Vulnerable

*How Activists' Tactical Repertoires
Shape Subjecthood and Generate Fear*

On a chilly evening in San Francisco on November 28, 2000, transgender activist Jamison Green addressed the 125 people gathered in the United Nations Plaza:

> We've come here to remember: remember what it feels like to die. Remember what it feels like to fear for your life. Some of us here have felt that fear. No one should have to feel that fear. Imagine what it feels like to die at the hands of a stranger who doesn't like the way you look. Imagine what it feels like to die while others laugh. Imagine what it feels like to be so beaten down that you have no more will to live. Imagine what it feels like to be powerless. Imagine what it feels like to be an infant whose only crime was to be born with ambiguous genitals, a feature so embarrassing to your parents that all they could do was feed you broken glass and smash your head until you died. Remember.[1]

Those in the crowd held candles and signs, each with the name of a person murdered in the last year and the cause and date of their death. One sign read:

> TYRA
> HENDERSON
> BLUDGEONED TO
> DEATH & MUTILATED
> APRIL 23, 2000

Local politicians attended the event, including Supervisor Mark Leno, who stated: "Community United Against Violence tells us that of their approximately 325 incidents of violence against [the LGBT] community this last year, about 18% of those represented the transgender community.

Compare that to probably 2% of our population, of the population here in town, being represented by the transgender community. Nine times higher than the population itself."[2] Similar events occurred in thirteen other cities that day as part of the second annual Transgender Day of Remembrance (TDoR). At each location, the names of the eighteen people who had been killed that year were spoken, often followed by an action to mark their passing, such as the blowing out of a candle.

The purpose of these events, in the words of activist Monica Helms, was to "honor those victims of gender-based hate crimes. In cities across the U.S., people like us are gathering with one purpose in mind: to insure that those lives who were cut short because they appeared 'gender-different' are never forgotten. By honoring them in such a public manner, we hope to bring to the forefront of America's consciousness the tragedy that falls on one of the least understood minorities in the world—transgender individuals."[3] Activists saw these events as not only valuing the dead but also as effective in calling attention to the cause of reducing violence against transgender people. As identity-based anti-violence activists have to compete against others within the social problems marketplace, they utilize a number of tactics to garner notice. In this chapter I examine the tactical repertoires the transgender anti-violence activists utilized to gain attention within the social problems marketplace and the unintended consequences of those acts. The tactics used by activists are moments of productive power and both intentionally, and unintentionally, shape beliefs about their group.[4] In the words of philosopher Ian Hacking, activists "make up people," naming a group and influencing how the group understands itself as well as how it is seen by others.[5] This has particular consequences for identity-based anti-violence activism, which has the dual purpose of both *claiming subjecthood* (i.e., asserting that the identity group exists and is valuable) and working to stop the violence against the group.

Transgender identity-based anti-violence activism, such as TDoR, worked to mark transgender people as socially valuable and undeserving of violence ("no one should have to feel that fear"). Activists attempted to draw attention to their cause by educating people about the level and types of violence, citing statistics ("nine times higher than the population itself") and describing what was done to victims ("BLUDGEONED TO DEATH & MUTILATED"). The tactics utilized were effective, as evidenced by increased media coverage of violence experienced by trans people, inclusion of gender identity in anti–hate crime legislation, and the proliferation of TDoR events (from two locations in 1999 to hundreds worldwide in the late 2000s).

However, the same tactics that made this activism effective within the social problems marketplace also had the unintended consequence of constructing transgender as a *vulnerable subjecthood*. By this I mean that the likelihood of experiencing violence is central to beliefs about this social category. This production of trans subjectivities through narratives about violence is epitomized in statements such as "there is no 'safe way' to be transgendered."[6] As a press release from the National Center for Transgender Equality (NCTE) in 2009 stated: "Every day transgender people live with the reality and the threat of personal violence."[7] Similarly, a *Transgender Tapestry* article argued in 1999 that: "We all live with hatred and fear, whether we live in Laramie or Little Rock, in San Francisco or Washington, DC. In America's smallest towns and largest cities we live with the specter of fear over our shoulder, because we live in a society that debates whether we have a right to exist. Whether it's ignoring, killing, curing, or discriminating, the point is still erasure."[8] By claiming that violence is something all transgender people face at all times, these narratives constructed transgender as a vulnerable category populated by potential victims.

In their attempt to gain attention for their cause, trans activists utilized many tactics common in identity-based anti-violence activism. In addition to marking their group as valuable and undeserving of violence, they also (1) argued that their group was subject to more violence than other groups; (2) produced lists of victims to illustrate the level of violence against their group; (3) highlighted extreme examples of violence, such as particularly brutal murders, while implying that those forms of violence were common; (4) provided statistics about violence experienced by transgender people; (5) argued that violence was at epidemic levels; 6) dismissed evidence that violence was decreasing; and (7) asserted that no one cared about transgender victims of violence. As I detail in chapter 7, these tactics continue to be utilized in current transgender anti-violence activism. Although highly effective within the social problems marketplace, these approaches to anti-violence activism unintentionally made transgender a less livable life. Transgender people in the United States became more widely understood as valuable and worthy of protection, but in the process they were seen—and came to see themselves—as defenseless and likely to be victimized.

VALUABLE VICTIMS: "EVERY TRANSPERSON IS A REAL, VALUABLE, AND PRECIOUS HUMAN BEING"

Through their anti-violence work, trans activists attempted to do the important labor of claiming subjecthood and the right to live. They engaged in

what sociologist James Jasper called a *citizenship movement*: a social move‐
ment whose goal is to attain rights for its members and, in so doing, trans‐
form them into full subjects.[9] Philosopher Judith Butler argued that positive
social change is accomplished when a body (or group of bodies) which has
been defined as less than human "asserts a right or entitlement to a liv‐
able life when no such prior authorization exists, when no clearly enabling
convention is in place."[10] In their anti-violence activism, trans activists
endeavored to enact this form of social change, moving transgender out of
the realm of the abusable and establishing their group as a *valuable sub‐
jecthood*, equal to others and undeserving of harm. Violence, particularly
fatal violence, is an explicit denial of personhood and makes for an unliv‐
able life. Although violence is generally considered morally wrong, some
acts of violence are seen as more immoral than others. Activists engaged
in identity-based anti-violence activism fear that violence against members
of their group is seen as somewhat socially acceptable, or at least not as so
unacceptable as to be worth expending resources to reduce. They therefore
work to frame violence against their group as unacceptable and intolerable,
affirming their subjecthood and attempting to make their group a livable
social category.

In their articles, web pages, press releases, reports, and flyers trans activ‐
ists named the violence experienced by trans people as unacceptable and
asserted that they have a right to lives free of violence. Often this claim for
rights came in the form of arguing that transgender people are humans and
thus deserving of "human rights." As the conclusion of GenderPAC's 2006
publication *50 under 30* argued: "Gender expression is a human right. State
authorities' failure to adequately investigate and prosecute these murders
constitute human rights violations. Authorities must take responsibility
for ending the violence that is killing gender non-conforming youth. It is a
matter of human rights."[11] In statements such as these, activists worked to
move transgender bodies out of the realm of those perceived of as less than
human (what Butler termed *abject*) and into the realm of full subjecthood.[12]
Human societies have long defined certain individuals and groups as less
than fully human and thus undeserving of certain social protections. These
classifications as abject have been used to legitimize wars, enslavement, and
a variety of other forms of violence, ranging from lynching to rape to gay
bashing. Trans activists conceptualized the violence experienced by trans‐
gender people as similarly motivated and so included claims to complete
personhood and human rights in their anti-violence activism. As activist
Jared Miranda Stevens declared in 1996: "The tragic murder of Christian
Paige is the kind which results when a group of people are marginalized to

the point of being considered less-than-human. Each and every transperson is a real, valuable, and precious human being."[13]

Trans activists conceived of the violence as motivated by hatred of difference and disdain for a particular identity group and worked to define such violence as immoral. TDoR founder Gwendolyn Smith argued, "Too often people want to make our dead into forgotten people. Now, more than ever, we need to stand together and say that taking life from anyone is not acceptable."[14] Frequently these claims focused on arguing that everyone has a right to be who they are. As activist Beatrice Dohrn stated in 2000: "No one, regardless of labels like gay or transgendered, should be attacked or mistreated because they are perceived to be different."[15] This sentiment was echoed in 2003 by HRC's executive director, Elizabeth Birch, who said: "No person should live in fear of being attacked just because of who they are."[16]

Trans activists' anti-violence narratives regularly included statements that transgender people should be valued as much as all other people. This valuation project is key to identity-based anti-violence activism. Indeed, one of the five "guiding principles" of TDoR is that "transgendered lives are affirmed to have value."[17] Similarly, after the convictions of two of Gwen Araujo's killers in the 2005 trial, activist Julie Dorf stated: "Compared to too many other transgender murder cases, this jury clearly stated that Gwen's life was just as valued as any other human being's."[18] Through statements identifying violence against trans people as wrong and the lives of trans people as valuable, trans activists marked the violence against them as unjust and trans people as people deserving of rights. However, as I detail in the rest of this chapter, several overlapping and interdependent aspects of the particular way they fought against violence also portrayed transgender people as at high risk for exceptionally brutal forms of violence. Although they did claim a valuable subjecthood, they also produced transgender subjecthood as inherently vulnerable.

OPPRESSION OLYMPICS: VISIBILITY THROUGH VICTIMHOOD

A central project of identity-based anti-violence activists is to cultivate interest in violence experienced by their group. Although it may seem easy to get government officials, journalists, and laypeople to care about violence, the social problems marketplace is teaming with activists vying for attention for their causes. Therefore, identity-based anti-violence activists tend to utilize a number of tactics to garner notice. One common tactic used by transgender anti-violence activists was the claim that transgender people were widely hated and as a result experienced more violence than many, if not all, other identity groups. This tactic is often referred to as the *oppression Olympics*, since groups compete over which is the most socially subjugated.[19]

The argument that a group is the most oppressed is often used because it is a compelling narrative within the social problems marketplace, as it marks the danger to the group as highly important. The logic is that if a group is the most oppressed, its members are most deserving of attention, resources, and protective legislation. This was noted in GenderPAC's *50 under 30*, which stated: "Another UN human rights expert recently recognized that in the US, transgender youth deserve special protections as well because they are 'among the most vulnerable and marginalized young people in society.'"[20]

In their analysis of women's rights activism, legal scholars Mary Louise Fellows and Sherene Razack termed the phenomenon of claiming to be more oppressed than others *competing marginalities*.[21] They argued that oppression and innocence are seen as one and the same, such that claims to be the most oppressed are also claims to be the least implicated in the oppression of others.[22] This claim to innocence is highly appealing from a moral standpoint and facilitates the framing of group members who experience violence as "ideal" victims. However, it has severe consequences in terms of constructing the group as a vulnerable subjecthood and obscuring the ways in which group members participate in the oppression of others.

Trans activists often claimed that trans people are the most hated identity group and that they experience more violence than other groups. As HRC associate director of diversity Allyson Robinson, speaking in 2009 about her transition, said: "Today I diligently avoid places I never hesitated to enter before because I am a target. With little more than a change of wardrobe, I transited from one of the least vulnerable classes of people in our society to one of the most. Looking over my shoulder has become second nature."[23] Similarly, two articles published in winter 2003 by the Southern Poverty Law Center (SPLC) argued that transgender people are more hated than other groups. In one, under the subheading "The Hated," the author stated: "None are so victimized as the transgender community. These men and women—from crossdressers to those who have undergone sex change operations—may be the most despised people in America."[24] Another article quoted activist Jessica Xavier as saying that "transphobia" is "the most powerful hatred on the planet" and under the title "Disposable People" argued: "A wave of violence engulfs the transgendered, whose murder rate may outpace that of all other hate killings."[25] The claims made by the SPLC that transgender people were the most at risk for violence were likely particularly persuasive, as the organization focuses on hate violence broadly defined, as opposed to specifically on transgender experiences of violence.

Transgender anti-violence activists are not the only identity-based anti-violence activists to engage in the oppression Olympics. Jimmy Carter famously declared: "The abuse of women and girls is the most pervasive and unaddressed human rights violation on Earth."[26] Similarly, the summary of the 2013 film *I am a girl* stated: "There is a group of people in the world today who are more persecuted than anyone else. . . . They are girls. Being born a girl means you are more likely to be subjected to violence, disease, poverty and disadvantage than any other group on the planet."[27] It should be noted, however, that in the United States, cisgender men experience higher rates of violent crime than cisgender women in every category except for sexual assault, and cisgender men comprise nearly 80 percent of all homicide victims.[28]

Although it was effective in the social problems marketplace, participating in the oppression Olympics had severe consequences for transgender as a subject group. Though there is a badge of honorable innocence that may provide some emotional comfort, many feel terror when being told (or telling others) that their group is the most despised and attacked. As trans activist Carrie Davis stated in 2002: "Transpeople are 15 times more likely to be murdered than nontranspeople. . . . We have learned to be afraid to change jobs, to fall in love, to take the subway, to go into different neighborhoods, to walk to the store and to go to the emergency room. And this fear is not because of our sexual orientation. We are afraid because of the way we look and because of who we are seen as. We are afraid because we are seen, and identified, as transpeople."[29] Engaging in the oppression Olympics links identity with inherent vulnerability to violence.

This connection is particularly concerning because there is little evidence that transgender people experience more violence than cisgender people. Although this may seem astounding, one must take into account the extraordinary level of violence experienced by people of all social categories in the United States.[30] Few studies compare cisgender and transgender people's experiences of violence, but the ones that do so do not support activists' claims.[31] An innovative national study of almost three hundred transgender people and their cisgender siblings found that which group experienced the most violence differed by the type of violence. Cisgender men reported the highest levels of being punched, hit, kicked, or beaten (39%), followed by trans men (38.5%), trans women (30.0%), and cisgender women (19.3%), whereas trans men reported the highest levels of being "assaulted with a weapon" (15.4%), followed by cisgender men (12.2%), cisgender women (3.4%), and trans women (2.0%).[32] Despite the fact that scholars have long acknowledged the important role that gender plays in homicide, only one study to date has compared cisgender and transgender homicide rates. Public health scholar Alexis Dinno compiled homicide data for transgender and cisgender people from 2010 to 2014 and found that "the overall homicide rate of transgender individuals was likely to be less than that of cisgender individuals."[33]

LISTING VICTIMS:
CONVEYING VOLUME THROUGH VISUALS

In their efforts to garner notice for their cause, trans activists worked to demonstrate that their identity group experienced high levels of violence. They did this in a number of ways, including by giving raw numbers of incidents and percentages and through listing individual victims. These lists tended to focus on homicide and took two main forms: listing a series of names (often with little other information) or providing a set of short descriptions (usually including a name, the location and date of the murder, and how they were killed). Both styles ranged in length from three to hundreds of victims. Interestingly, there was almost never information about the victims' lives beyond their transgender status and usually no description of their killers. As detailed in chapter 4, this approach homogenizes transgender people and their attackers. When attempting to draw attention to a new act of violence, activists often listed past ones. For example, in a press release about the murder of Lauryn Paige in 1999, GenderPAC executive director Riki Wilchins stated: "The police description of this murder is heartbreakingly familiar. Sadistic killers, multiple stab wounds, bludgeoned and/or shot repeatedly. . . . [I]t's a familiar litany of brutally violent acts done to gender-different people: Chanelle Pickett, Brandon Teena, Christian Paige, Deborah Forte, Vianna Faye Williams, Jamaica Green, Jessy and Peggy Santiago, Tasha Dunn . . . and the list goes on."[34] Similarly, a press release issued in 2009 by GLAAD about the murder of Angie Zapata stated:

> Since 1999, over 400 people have been murdered due to anti-transgender bias. In 2008 alone, Remembering Our Dead has reported 21 murders of transgender and gender non-conforming people, including:

> *January 21, 2008:* Adolphus Simmons, 18 (Charlestown, SC), who was gunned down while taking out the trash;

February 10, 2008: Sanesha Stewart (Bronx, NY), stabbed by an acquaintance and left to die alone in her apartment;

February 12, 2008: Lawrence King, 15, (Oxnard, CA), shot in the head by a 14 year old fellow classmate at E. O. Green Junior High School;

February 22, 2008: Simmie Williams, 17, (Fort Lauderdale, FL) who was shot and killed; no arrests have been made;

July 1, 2008: Ebony Whitaker, 20, (Memphis, TN) who was shot near a daycare center; no arrests have been made;

August 20, 2008: Nakhia Williams, 29, (Louisville, KY) who died Aug. 30, 10 days after she was shot and beaten by a group of people outside her apartment;

September 21, 2008: Ruby Molina, 22, (Sacramento, CA) who was found dead in the American River by fishermen in September;

November 9, 2008: Duanna Johnson, 42, (Memphis, TN) who was shot to death just weeks ago by unidentified assailants on Nov. 9 after making news earlier this year when she was beaten by police officers in February. Johnson's lawsuit against the city of Memphis was still pending at the time of her murder;

November 14, 2008: Lateisha "Teish" Cannon, 22, (Syracuse, NY) who was shot inside her car with her brother and friend;

December 26, 2008: Taysia "Taysha" Elzy, 34, (Indianapolis, IN) who was shot and killed along with her boyfriend.[35]

Americans have become desensitized to violence; in addition to conveying the volume of violence, providing victims' names might have been an attempt to increase compassion. However, these lists also solidified the understanding that to be transgender is to be at enormous risk for violence. The inventory of homicides on the final page of GenderPAC's *50 under 30,* shown in figure 2, was intended to make these murder victims count (in all meanings of the word).[36] Listing the dead with very little information other than when and how they died is a common tactic when attempting to give a sense of the scale of violence. War memorials are often designed using this approach, and other groups engaged in identity-based anti-violence activism employ it. Although this tactic is visually arresting and likely elicits care about the cause, it also produces high levels of fear. Moreover, by reducing these victims to a name, age, year, location, and cause of death, this list unintentionally equated transgender status (which all of these victims were said to have) with death. In their attempt to get others to value the dead, activists unintentionally erased these individuals' lives and reduced them to murder victims. In doing so, they taught trans and cis people alike that experiencing fatal violence is central to being transgender. As trans activist Christian Williams put it, speaking about the impact of

IN MEMORIAM

Sakia Gunn	(15)	Murdered 2003	Newark, NJ	(stabbed to death)
Quincy Taylor	(16)	Murdered 1995	Atlanta, GA	(shot in the chest)
Fred Martinez	(16)	Murdered 2001	Cortez, CO	(beaten to death)
Allison Decatrel	(17)	Murdered 1999	Iverness, FL	(hit by car)
Gwen Araujo	(17)	Murdered 2002	Newark, CA	(beaten and strangled to death)
Nireah Johnson	(17)	Murdered 2003	Indianapolis, IN	(shot and burned)
Ukea Davis	(18)	Murdered 2002	Washington, DC	(shot multiple times)
Brandie Coleman	(18)	Murdered 2003	Indianapolis, IN	(shot and burned)
Tarayon Corbitt	(19)	Murdered 1995	Dale County, AL	(shot three times)
Jerrell Williams	(19)	Murdered 1997	Mobile, AL	(stabbed to death)
Chareka Keys	(19)	Murdered 1999	Cleveland, OH	(beaten to death)
Lauryn Paige	(19)	Murdered 1999	Austin, TX	(stabbed multiple times)
Alina Marie Barragan	(19)	Murdered 2002	San Jose, CA	(strangled)
Stephanie Thomas	(19)	Murdered 2002	Washington, DC	(shot multiple times)
Nikki Nicholas	(19)	Murdered 2003	Green Oak Township, MI	(shot to death)
Donathyn Rodgers	(19)	Murdered 2005	Cleveland, OH	(shot multiple times)
Christina Smith	(20)	Murdered 2005	Houston, TX	(shot to death)
Dion Webster	(21)	Murdered 1996	New York, NY	(stabbed to death)
Kareem Washington	(21)	Murdered 1999	Passaic, NJ	(stabbed to death)
Cinnamon Broadus	(21)	Murdered 2003	Ft. Lauderdale, FL	(shot multiple times)
Christian Paige	(22)	Murdered 1996	Chicago, IL	(beaten, strangled and stabbed)
Chanel Chandler	(22)	Murdered 1998	Clovis, CA	(throat cut)
Tyra Henderson	(22)	Murdered 2000	Washington, DC	(beaten to death)
Timothy Blair, Jr.	(22)	Murdered 2005	Louisville, KY	(shot multiple times)
Chanelle Pickett	(23)	Murdered 1995	New York, NY	(beaten to death)
James Rivers	(23)	Murdered 1995	Oakland, CA	(beaten and stabbed to death)
Michael Hurd	(23)	Murdered 2003	Houston, TX	(shot to death)
Ryan Hoskie	(23)	Murdered 2004	Albuquerque, NM	(upper body trauma)
Delilah Corrales	(23)	Murdered 2005	Yuma, AZ	(stabbed to death)
Tyra Hunter	(24)	Murdered 1995	Washington, DC	(hit by car)
Sindy Cuarda	(24)	Murdered 2003	San Pablo, CA	(shot multiple times)
Jessica Mercado	(24)	Murdered 2003	New Haven, CT	(stabbed to death)
Imani Williams	(24)	Murdered 2003	Washington, DC	(beaten and shot to death)
Amanda Milan	(25)	Murdered 2000	New York, NY	(stabbed to death)
Alejandro Lucero	(25)	Murdered 2002	Phoenix, AZ	(beaten and strangled to death)
Emonie Spaulding	(25)	Murdered 2003	Washington, DC	(shot to death)
Bella Evangelista	(25)	Murdered 2003	Washington, DC	(shot multiple times)
Feliciano Moreno	(25)	Murdered 2004	Los Angeles, CA	(shot to death)
Tamyra Michaels	(26)	Murdered 2002	Highland Park, MI	(shot to death)
Sidney Wright	(26)	Murdered 2005	Chicago, IL	(stabbed to death)
Bibi Barajas	(27)	Murdered 2002	Houston, TX	(shot multiple times)
Loni Kai Okaruru	(28)	Murdered 2001	Hillsboro, OR	(beaten to death)
Deasha Andrews	(28)	Murdered 2002	Jacksonville, FL	(shot to death)
Arlene Diaz	(28)	Murdered 2002	El Paso, TX	(shot two times)
Jacqueline Anderson	(29)	Murdered 1998	Portland, OR	(shot to death)
Francisco Luna	(29)	Murdered 2001	Houston, TX	(shot multiple times)
Robert Martin	(29)	Murdered 2001	Ashburn, GA	(beaten to death)
Joel Robles	(29)	Murdered 2004	Fresno, CA	(stabbed multiple times)
Robert H. Jones	(30)	Murdered 1997	New Castle, DE	(stabbed to death)
Reshae McCauley	(30)	Murdered 2003	Largo, FL	(stabbed to death)
Ashley Nickson	(30)	Murdered 2005	Dothan, AL	(shot multiple times)

FIGURE 2. Reproduction of last page of GenderPAC, *50 under 30: Masculinity and the War on America's Youth* (2006).

putting together a list of names to read at TDoR events: "It's a loss of innocence. As I was cataloging the victims, for the first time I understood that
there are people who would kill me, really kill me, because I chose to live
truthfully."[37] Similarly, Dan, a trans man, wrote a letter to *FTMi* describing his experience at a TDoR event: "As the names were read the world
looked a little bleaker as 28 lights were extinguished and a hush fell over
the crowd as the last woman read the name and how the person died. This
DOR I was reminded that one's light can be extinguished at a moment's
notice."[38]

Even when activists provided more details, they were often only accounts
of how the person died. Lists of homicides that included short paragraphs
about the case were common in these activist documents. For example, in
March 2002 HRC, along with the National Gay and Lesbian Task Force
(NGLTF) and the National Organization for Women (NOW), published a
short report entitled *Examples of Hate Crimes against Transgender Individuals*.[39] The report was a list of fourteen incidents, eleven fatal. All of the
descriptions focused on the violence against these individuals. Here are three:

> Loni Okaruru—Bludgeoned to Death: August 2001, Portland, Oregon
> Lorenzo "Loni" Okaruru, according to detectives, died after being sav-
> agely beaten about the head and face with a blunt instrument, most
> likely by a man who picked up someone he thought was a woman and
> was angered to find out Okarura was a biological male. Law enforce-
> ment officials have said they believe Okaruru was killed based on sexual
> orientation or gender identity. Civil rights groups and others in Portland
> are denouncing the killing and say the murder shows the misunder-
> standing and hatred directed at members of the transgender community.
> The Washington County Sheriff's Office classified Okaruru's August
> 26th beating death as a hate crime, the first such killing in the county.
> (*Associated Press State and Local Wire*, Sept. 4, 2001)

> Steve Dwayne Garcia—Shot Dead, February 1999, Houston, Texas
> Steve Dwayne Garcia died of a gunshot wound to the shoulder in a
> murder police described as a possible hate crime. At the time of his
> death, the victim was going home from a party wearing women's cloth-
> ing and shoulder length hair. None of his jewelry was taken which
> led investigators to suspect he was targeted because of the way he was
> dressed. (*The Houston Chronicle*, Feb. 7, 1999)

> Kareem Washington—Stabbed to Death: August 1999, Passaic, New
> Jersey
> Kareem Washington, a gay man who sometimes dressed in women's
> clothing, was stabbed multiple times and left to die in an industrial
> area in Passaic, New Jersey. Police were unsure of the motive for the

murder; however, the victim's wallet, with cash and identification intact, was found on his body. The victim was wearing a skirt, high-heeled shoes, and stockings. (*The Record* [Bergen County, NJ], Aug. 30, 31, 1999)

Since the activists' goal in creating such lists was to get people to care about violence experienced by transgender people, it is not surprising that the lists focused on describing violence. However, focusing on the details of deaths has unintended consequences. It is likely that lists highlighting only how a transgender person died terrified transgender people who read them. In addition, as these lists were used in educational material for cisgender people, they likely caused cisgender people to associate transgender people with high risks for fatal violence, shaping how they understand and interact with transgender people, just as narratives about violence against women shape men's understandings of women as vulnerable.[40] Thus, listing the dead does not facilitate one of the main goals of identity-based anti-violence activists: constructing the group as a valuable subjecthood with the possibility of a livable life. By only highlighting their death, activists link transgender not with value, but with vulnerability.

Occasionally these lists included information about the person's life and not just their death. However, those details almost always revolved around demonstrating that the victim was transgender—likely cementing in the reader's mind that a transgender identity is the cause of a violent death. For example, in 2005 the Gay Straight Alliance (GSA) published a three-page document explaining TDoR and offering suggestions for how to have an effective event.[41] The final page was a list of seven murder victims, including these three:

> Freddie Martinez, 16, (Cortez, Colorado) was a very striking Navajo teen who presented as female and was often harassed at school. Freddie was murdered in Cortez, Colorado.

> Nikki Nicholas, 19, (Detroit, Michigan) was an African-American transwoman making her living as a performer in clubs where she often danced and lip-synched to Beyonce songs. The youngster preferred playing with Barbie dolls rather than G.I. Joes, Nicholas' mother said, and by age 11 began experimenting with girls' clothing and makeup. Her body was discovered during a routine property check of an abandoned farmhouse.

> Stephanie Thomas, 19, and Ukea Davis, 18, (Washington, DC) were friends found shot to death together. They were a part of SMYL (Sexual Minority Youth Liaison) and were often teased for being feminine. Stephanie started wearing dresses and makeup at the age of 14. Her

mother commented that "on the school bus kids tormented her, so she would get off and walk a couple miles to the school." Through a transgender health group, Stephanie met Ukea Davis, another transgender woman. They supported one another, especially when classmates—and even teachers—harassed them about their gender identity.

Although all of these accounts included descriptions of the people's deaths, they also included some details about their lives. However, the information given was either about their trans identity or the harassment they had experienced because they were transgender. The emphasis on trans identity is the logical consequence of *identity-based* anti-violence activism. However, the emphasis on trans identity further solidified the link between the social category of transgender and experiences of violence.

EXTREME EXAMPLES

Anti-violence activists often tell narratives about particularly horrifying acts of violence in order to attract attention to their cause. The hope is that extreme examples will elicit more interest and sympathy, resulting in access to resources to reduce the violence. Sociologist Joel Best termed these *typifying examples*.[42] Although meant to represent the general problem, these typifying examples are usually atypical, as unusually dreadful and disturbing narratives are more likely to garner notice. As such, identity-based anti-violence activists almost always highlight descriptions of murders of members of their identity group, as opposed to descriptions of nonfatal violence. Lesbian and gay activists regularly centered arguments for inclusion of sexual orientation in hate crime legislation around the murder of Matthew Shepard. Similarly, the murder of James Byrd is frequently cited in discussions of race-based violence.[43] Indeed, the 2009 federal hate crime legislation was named after these two individuals. Often the fatal violence that gains the most attention includes torture or overkill. Thus, Shepard being pistol whipped, tied to a fence in freezing temperatures, and left to die, while Byrd was dragged to death behind a truck, made these incidents particularly compelling within the social problems marketplace.

Though an effective tool in anti-violence activism, the use of these extreme examples can have serious consequences when linked with identity politics. These forms of violence are relatively rare. Most violence experienced by gay and/or black men does not take the form of sadistic murder. However, when these cases dominate the public consciousness through repeated tellings, people may believe that such violence is typical and common. For example, sociologist Esther Madriz found that widespread narratives about "women being tortured [or] mutilated" caused extreme levels of fear in the women she interviewed, many of whom believed that they were at high risk of experiencing these "rare occurrences."[44] The fear elicited is what makes this tactic useful in the social problems marketplace, but when coupled with identity politics, it also shapes ideas about what it means to be a member of that social category, which can have dire consequences for the category's livability.[45]

Like many other identity-based anti-violence movements, trans activists tended to focus on fatal violence above all other forms. Moreover, in their flyers, websites, press releases, reports, and vigils, they often highlighted particularly grisly murders. For example, the Remembering Our Dead (ROD) website regularly emphasized horrifying details about the deaths. The website is minimalist in its presentation. For each victim, all that is provided is a name, the place they were killed, the cause and date of death, the source of information, and any "notes" on the murder. Often the "notes" section is left blank. When present, however, these "notes" often include gruesome details, such as the following:

Larry Venzant
Location: Chicago, Illinois
Cause of Death: Stabbed repeatedly and castrated by David Feikema
Date of Death: December 19, 1993
Source: *Windy City Times*, November 9, 1993
Notes: After Feikema stabbed and castrated Venzant, he then placed the severed penis in Venzant's mouth and shoved him in a closet. Feikema was found guilty of first degree murder.

In the summer of 1999, *Transgender Tapestry* published an issue focused on the murder of transgender people that included a two-page spread titled "Remembering Our Dead 1999." Echoing the design of the ROD website, white type listings of more than one hundred victims were printed in long columns on a black background. The article was visually striking, likely to catch the attention of someone flipping through the magazine. Looking at it, some readers probably felt a sense of inevitability, as the two TDoR attendees previously described did, that they were next. Resembling the website, this magazine piece featured depictions of overkill and grisly details:

Lauryn Paige (Donald Scott Fuller)
Location: Austin, Texas
Cause: Stabbed multiple times in the head and torso. A cut on her throat measured 9 inches long and 3 inches wide.
Died: January 9, 1999

Christian Paige
Location: Chicago, Illinois
Cause: Beaten about the head & ears, strangled, stabbed deeply in her
chest area between 15 & 2 dozen times, then burned.
Died: March 22, 1996

The detailing of the number and size of stab wounds and descriptions of victims' heads or faces as being beaten in were common features across the trans anti-violence activist documents I examined. In a press release for the National Transgender Advocacy Coalition (NTAC), anti-violence activist Ethan St. Pierre described the murder of his aunt Debbie Forte: "She was brutally murdered on Mother's day, May 15, 1995 by a 28 yr. old man named Michael Thompson who stabbed Debbie 3 times in the chest with a six inch blade, strangled her and broke every bone in her neck and beat her in the face with a blunt object until she was unrecognizable. Michael Thompson was so remorseful about what he had done that he went to work the next day and bragged to a coworker about the murder."[46] Reports on violence from SPLC also included gory details: "She had been savagely beaten, a telltale sign of a likely hate crime, then dumped in the field. 'Fingertips cut off, face smashed in—whoever did it, there certainly was a violent rage,' said Greg Miles, Okaruru's uncle."[47] Though particularly savage violence did occur in these cases, as with all narratives about violence activists had to select which aspects to include and which to leave out. As they could not include all of the parts of the person's life and death in these short descriptions, it is notable that they did include detailed descriptions of their wounds.

Extreme examples were frequently paired with statistics about violence against transgender people, implying that all the incidents were similarly gruesome. A press release from HRC opened: "Since the grisly dragging death of James Byrd Jr. on June 7, 1998, our national conscience has been shocked with wave after wave of hate-motivated violence. . . . Released in 2001, the latest FBI statistics show that as overall serious crime has continued to decrease hate crimes have continued to increase and rose 2.3 percent from 1999 to 2000." This introduction was then followed by vignettes, including the following:

September 1998, Fresno, Calif.

On Sept. 20, the apartment of transgender female Chanel Chandler was set on fire. Inside authorities discovered Chandler's body. She had been stabbed repeatedly with a broken beer bottle. According to police, the fire, which did not reach the room where Chandler's body was found, was likely a failed attempt to hide the murder.[48]

By using horror stories to illustrate the larger phenomenon of violence against transgender people, activists may have gained attention for their cause, but they also constructed an exceptionally vulnerable subjecthood, portrayed as likely to experience extreme forms of violence.

Activists often made explicit statements that argued this sort of violence is typical in cases of murder of trans people. As Riki Wilchins argued in a 1996 press release, "Transpeople are never murdered with high-powered rifles at long distances: we are always killed up close, and personal. These are crimes of immense, almost unbalanced hatred. The phrase that inevitably occurs and re-occurs in forensic reports is 'multiple stab wounds to the head and chest.'"[49] Similarly, NCTE director Mara Keisling asserted in 2007, "Trans people generally don't get stabbed once; they get stabbed 20 times, shot, burned and thrown into a dumpster."[50] Likewise, a Gender Education and Advocacy flyer often used to advertise for TDoR events (shown in figure 1 in chapter 4) stated that at least 150 people had been killed in the past ten years in anti-trans violence and that "these were not simple murders. Their killers, in displaying an especially virulent form of hatred, often went from murder to overkill, attempting to obliterate their victims, perhaps in an attempt to erase them completely, by any means necessary." Relatedly, the 1997 National Coalition of Anti-Violence Programs (NCAVP) report stated:

> In 1997 there were 18 gay-related murders reported to the 14 tracking programs of the NCAVP. That is down from 27 in 1996, which is a decrease of 33%. Even though this is a decrease in number, it is important to remember that these murders tend to be extremely violent. 39% of the murders reported were marked by a high level of violence involving "overkill." A good example of this would be a victim bludgeoned to death with a blunt object and his body was left under the Christmas tree for his parents to find on Christmas Day.[51]

Here, activists took something that is incredibly unusual (a victim intentionally left under a Christmas tree for family members to find) and contended that it is representative of the statistics they have cited. The assertion that the atypical is typical is effective in the social problems marketplace. However, the evidence from my homicide data does not support these claims. Overkill was uncommon in the 289 murders of transgender people that occurred between 1990 and 2009.

Nevertheless, activists often argued that hate-motivated violence was characterized by overkill and that overkill was evidence that violence was hate motivated. In its 2009 report, NCAVP stated: "An additional characteristic of hate violence incidents is 'overkill'—where in the course of physical violence offenders use extreme brutality. Offenders may attack their targets in close contact and with extreme force; murder victims may be stabbed or shot dozens of times (often in the face or the genitals), burned, or dismembered. . . . Anti-LGBTQ hate violence frequently involves over-kill, as a way of deeply personalizing an attack and brutally 'othering' a person of the targeted identity."[52] The belief that overkill indicates a hate-based crime becomes a circular logic. Since activists believed that most hate-based murders include overkill, any murder with aspects of overkill was assumed to be hate based. For example, in justifying its description of an unsolved murder in which two trans women were shot to death in a car as representative of a larger pattern of hate-motivated violence against trans people, the SPLC argued: "In some cases, the details remain too murky to say for certain whether these murders were hate-motivated. But all 27 have at least one of the telltale signs of a hate crime—especially the sort of extreme brutality, or 'overkill,' that was all too evident in the bullet-torn bodies of Stephanie Thomas and Ukea Davis."[53] This circular logic allowed activists to draw attention to unsolved cases—something they see as vital for making trans people socially valuable—and it increased the numbers of victims that they could list when lobbying for protection from violence. However, it also made being transgender that much more terrifying.

Focusing on cases of gruesome, fatal violence means that narratives of successful resistance get little to no attention. This has a number of unin-tended consequences. Not attending to cases where people stopped acts of violence means that activists are less likely to note factors that could be used to help prevent future acts of violence. Similarly, attention only on murder makes the world seem especially terrifying, since for most people being killed is one of the scariest and most horrible things they can imagine. As identity-based anti-violence activism tends to encourage members of the social category to *identify with the dead*, group members may internalize a sense of risk, and the risk is doubly dreadful; these narratives may teach them that not only are they highly likely to be killed, they are also likely to be murdered in particularly horrifying ways. There is a risk, then, that these narratives do not push people to stand up against the violence so much as run away and hide. One can imagine identity-based anti-violence activism that celebrated resistance narratives and worked to reduce violence by utilizing what information can be gath-ered from those cases, an alternative I take up in chapter 7. However, as I discuss later in this chapter, activists did not see success stories as effec-tive in the social problems marketplace and so tended to draw attention to horror stories instead.

JUST THE FACTS? MAKING TRANSGENDER VICTIMS "COUNT" IN THE SOCIAL PROBLEMS MARKETPLACE

Statistics, especially large ones, are another attention-grabbing tactic utilized by activists. For example, gay and lesbian activists started doing surveys to track experiences of violence in the 1970s; eventually, NCAVP was developed to merge data from various organizations and hotlines collecting information on violence experienced by gay men, lesbians, bisexuals, transgender people, and those with HIV or AIDS.[54] Gay men and lesbians also collected data about violence against their group using police records, surveys of potential or actual perpetrators, and surveys of victims.[55] In 1994, sociologists Valerie Jenness and Kendal Broad argued that "documenting antigay and lesbian violence is the most prevalent form of political action currently being undertaken by gay and lesbian communities in response to antigay and lesbian violence."[56] The data gathered about violence experienced by an identity group are often published in reports that are used to persuade the public, and especially politicians, that there are high levels of violence against the group and that something must be done to address the problem. Like all statistics, these numbers should be viewed with caution, particularly since those who gather them have a political investment in showing high levels of violence.[57]

Sociologist Joel Best has extensively detailed the persuasive power of statistics and their utilization by activists.[58] Numbers lend an aura of truth to a claim, so advocates for a diverse array of causes add statistics to their tactical repertoires. However, intentionally or not, these numbers often misrepresent the problems activists are trying to solve. Politicians and journalists are more likely to consider large problems important, and laypeople are more likely to care about problems that could affect them or their loved ones; therefore, activists tend to claim the biggest numbers possible when making their claims. They do this in multiple ways, including by (1) defining the problem broadly; (2) claiming that the problem is an "epidemic" and/or getting larger; (3) arguing that anyone can be affected by the social problem in question; (4) contending that numbers of cases of the issue in question are underreported, so the actual size of the problem is much larger than current statistics indicate; and as I described in the previous section, (5) illustrating the statistics with extreme examples. Early in claims-making around a particular issue, there is unlikely to be much information on the scope of the problem. In this situation, activists often provide statistics by guessing about the size of the problem.[59] To highlight these practices is not to argue that activists are somehow wrong in doing them; instead, it is to shine light on one of the consequences of competition within the social problems marketplace: in order to "count" in the social problems marketplace, activists must enumerate the victimization of their group and claim severe enough violence to seem worthy of public attention and resources.

Like many social movements before them, trans activists relied heavily on statistics when trying to gain attention for their cause. However, although effective in making the group they were advocating for count, these uses of statistics also construct transgender as a vulnerable subject category by making the levels of violence against them seem extraordinarily high.[60] Trans activists' flyers, press releases, reports, and websites regularly included statistics about violence experienced by trans people. The popular flyer shown in figure 3 gives counts of total number of deaths; rates of different causes; and deaths by year, month, city, and state. Numbers like these are collected and circulated in hopes that they will persuade others to care about the violence and commit resources to its reduction. As the authors of GenderPAC's report on their national survey of violence experienced by trans people explained: "Our primary objective was not to plot a scientific sample which could be published in a research journal, but rather to at least begin to document the existences of a serious problem, and establish an initial baseline. Too often we have lobbied Congress or local legislatures on trans-inclusion in Hate Crimes bills, only to be asked, 'Do you have any data? How can we be sure this is a real problem?'"[61] Although it seemed necessary to be successful within the social problems marketplace, this way of utilizing statistics, when combined with identity politics, had potentially deleterious effects for experiences of being transgender.

Statistics, depending on how they are worded, can unintentionally lend an air of inevitability to the violence. Often, trans activists made statements that murders happen at "the rate of one a month" or "one person dies every month, due to anti-transgender violence."[62] In the hopes of trying to impress upon the reader the severity of the problem, they unintentionally made it sound like this level of violence is relatively fixed. For example, Riki Wilchins stated in a 1996 press release that "every four months like clockwork another transperson is savagely killed in a fairly unambiguous hate crime."[63] Similarly, the "About This Site" page on the ROD website told visitors: "Over the last decade, more than one person per month has died due to transgender-based hate or prejudice, regardless of any other factors in their lives. This trend shows no sign of abating."[64] This style of presentation increased the sense that violence experienced by trans people is unstoppable. Rather than asking themselves how to prevent future violence, someone hearing these statements may instead ask themselves who

Trans Murder Statistics 1970 to 2004

The following statistics have been compiled from the list of murder victims on *Remembering Our Dead*, a web project dedicated to chronicling cases of anti-transgender violence and prejudice leading to death. The list contains only those deaths that are known to the transgender community or that have been reported by the media. In many cases, the victims of anti-transgender violence are not identified as such, due to the silence of their families, fear of the police among friends of the victims, and the refusal of the police to investigate these murders and/or report them as hate crimes. Despite the under-reporting of this pandemic of violence, the increase in numbers over the years shown below is most likely due to increasing awareness within the organized transgendered community, and advocacy for more accurate reporting.

Debra Forte
May 15, 1995

The complete list of names on the website includes the date, the victim's name (if known), location of the crime and cause of death. Here are some statistics derived from this list, as of October 7th, 2004:

Chanelle Pickett
November 20, 1995

321 Total Deaths   234 Domestic, 87 International
Deadliest year: 2002, with 34 reported deaths, followed by 2003 with 32
Deadliest month: December 2002 and August 2003 with 6 deaths
Averages per month: 1990 through 1994, 1.03 per month
    1995 to 1999, 1.22 per month
    1990 to September 24, 2004 - 1.37 per month
    2004 to September 24, 2004 - 1.41 per month

Chareka Keys
September 27, 1999

Causes of Death:
Shot: 128, Stabbed: 70, Beaten: 49, "Murdered" (no cause specified): 45, Strangled: 22. There are 20 additional causes. 22 individuals died from multiple causes.

Deaths by state, and number of cities reporting in that state:
California, 45, from 20 cities; New York, 41, 9 cities; Texas, 15, 6 cites; Georgia, 15, 5 cities; Pennsylvania, 13, 4 cities; Florida, 14, 10 cities; Washintgon, D.C., 11, 1 city. There are 28 other states on the full list.

Willie Houston
July 29, 2001

Deaths by city in the United States:
New York City, 30; Atlanta and Washington, D.C., 11 each; Philadelphia and San Francisco, 9 each; San Diego and Houston, 7 each; Chicago, 6; Nashville, 5; Oakland, Santa Ana, Boston, Miami, 4 each. There are 100 other U.S cities on the full list.

Nizah Morris
December 24, 2002

Additionaly, there are 25 countries on the list, with Canada topping it with 12 deaths. 7 of the Canadian deaths were in Toronto.

Statistics compiled by Gwendolyn Ann Smith and Ethan St. Pierre
Data Courtesy of Remembering Our Dead
A product of Gender Education & Advocacy
http://www.rememberingourdead.org

Bella Martinez
August 28, 2004

FIGURE 3. "Trans Murder Statistics 1970 to 2004." Flyer often used to educate the public about violence experienced by transgender people. Created by Gender Education and Advocacy, October 7, 2004. Used with permission.

will be next. This can been seen explicitly in a video by FCKH8 entitled *Potty-Mouthed Princesses Drop F-Bombs for Feminism* that went viral in 2014. In discussing sexual violence, the girls in the video stated that "one out of every five women will be sexually assaulted or raped by a man." The girls then count off. "One," says the first, "two," says the second, "three," says the third, "four" says the fourth, "five," sighs the fifth, and then the third says, "Which one of us will it be?"[65] The sense of inevitability produced by this framing of statistics is detrimental both to activism and to experiences of being a member of the identity group, as it decreases hope and increases fatalism, fostering a feeling that violence is unpreventable.

This consequence is not inescapable. To avoid fatalism, activists could present statistics in the past tense and couple them with proposed solutions. For example, a statement such as "up until this year, murders have averaged one a month, but we hope with new funding for education to lower this rate dramatically" presents a significantly different message than describing incidents of violence as happening "like clockwork." Through cultivating hope, activists can help produce a more livable life for members of their identity group.

In addition to making violence seem inevitable, the traditional usage of statistics by identity-based anti-violence activists can also be detrimental to ideas about what it means to be a member of the identity group by overstating the risk faced by individual group members. As has been well documented by scholars, including Joel Best, because statistics are numbers and we consider numbers to be facts, activists can unintentionally make false statements about the size or scope of the problem they are trying to address with minimal pushback from allies to the cause. Transgender anti-violence activism followed this trend. Activists, journalists, politicians, and academics regularly cited astronomically high levels of violence experienced by trans people, with little to no evidence supporting such claims. The most egregious of these between 1990 and 2009 was the widely cited claim, based on a misinterpretation of calculations done by Kay Brown, that "transgender individuals living in America today have a one in 12 chance of being murdered. In contrast, the average person has about a one in 18,000 chance of being murdered."[66] Given that the average number of transgender homicide victims in the United States during the time this statistic was regularly referenced was about fifteen a year, the transgender population would have to be incredibly small for the claim to be true. However, because of the widely held belief that transgender people are particularly vulnerable to violence, many people referenced this statistic without questioning it. For example, a NTAC press release stated that "according to researcher Kay Brown, transsexuals are sixteen times more likely to be murdered than the general population and three times more likely than African American males, the next highest group. Transsexual individuals, according to Brown, are more likely to be murdered than to marry."[67] Although many people have demonstrated that the statistic is false, at the time of writing this it is still commonly cited and has been joined by other false statistics.[68] Among these is this claim: "In America, trans women of color have a life expectancy of 35 years of age while that of their cisgender counterparts is around 78."[69] This inaccurate claim, which was regularly referenced by activists in the 2010s, was calculated by averaging the ages of murder victims listed on the ROD website, an erroneous way to estimate life expectancy.[70] As activist Loree Cook-Daniels argued in 2015: "Although any murder is horrible, the truth of the matter is that the vast majority of us—including transwomen of color—die of something other than murder: heart disease, cancer, dementia, accidents, etc. Scientists who have done long-term follow-up of known transgender people have not found that we are more likely to die young."[71] It is important to note that during most of the time these statistics were circulating, there was no estimate for the number of transgender people in the United States. Without the size of the population, one cannot calculate risks for murder.

Although inaccurate, these statistics take on the aura of fact because they align with the depiction of risk portrayed by anti-violence activists. Moreover, such statistics are particularly effective in garnering attention for the issue of violence experienced by trans people. However, they are also incredibly frightening for transgender people and their loved ones. To be told that you, or your family member or friend, have almost a 10 percent chance of being killed or that you won't live past age thirty-five is chilling. Illustrating this, a blog post by writer Kai Cheng Thom titled "Someone Tell Me That I'll Live" discussed the high level of fear she felt when she first heard such a statistic: "When I was 19, I read an article in Guernica magazine stating that the average life span of a transgender person is 23 years old. The article confirmed what I had already known for about a decade: I was doomed to a nasty, short, and miserable life . . . and then I was going to die, probably brutally murdered."[72] Similarly, Cook-Daniels argued about such statistics: "We are scaring ourselves to death. I can't count how many times my Facebook feed has included responses like, 'I feel hopeless' or 'I feel suicidal' from someone reacting to the 35-year 'statistic' or the seemingly endless repetition of the details of every single trans death that has been identified this year."[73] Thus, these inaccurate statistics, as well as claims that transgender people have "the highest murder rate for any subpopulation," serve only to terrify, not to teach.[74]

Moreover, such statistics may encourage some transgender people to engage in behaviors that increase their risk of experiencing violence. As transgender activist Janet Mock argued in 2013: "I also know that the intense focus on the publicizing of murder, violence, death and victimhood becomes a self-fulfilling prophecy for the young women I share space with. I've borne witness to young women and girls nonchalantly telling me that they're not going to make it to 30 (a benchmark I just surpassed) so they're going to 'get their life' at all costs. This 'get my life' mentality breeds an urgency in my younger sisters, pushing them to live a hard and fast life with little protections and resources, with little care or regard."[75] Combined with the potential to produce suicidal feelings mentioned by Cook-Daniels, it is possible that the circulation of these statistics, which was intended to reduce transgender deaths, may actually have increased them. Notably, voices criticizing the use of these false statistics, such as those of Thom, Cook-Daniels, and Mock, were exceptionally rare and did not come from national anti-violence organizations.

Though some statistics used a comparison to other groups for their impact, more often than not the statistics cited by trans anti-violence activists were stated without comparisons or context, which made them challenging to evaluate. By simply stating a rate such as one murder a month, without comparing it to the larger population, activists left the audience to assume that the rate was higher than for cisgender people. Similarly, activists often gave a raw count of deaths in a given year without explaining how the number was obtained. Statements such as "Gwen's death marks the 25th reported death of a transgendered individual since October of last year" were common.[76] What was usually not mentioned in such reports was that this was a global count. Between October 2001 and October 2002, the ROD website received information about twenty-five murders from around the world. Without that context, though, the audience was left to assume that there were twenty-five murders in the United States, more than twice the actual number.

Defining a problem broadly when gathering statistics is common in identity-based anti-violence activism. For example, some activists collecting data on violence have defined "antigay/lesbian victimization" to include "incidents of same sex incest, child abuse/neglect, unwarranted HIV testing, and domestic abuse/violence."[77] Similarly, those working to reduce sexual assaults often claim that women have a one in four chance of being raped in their lifetimes. This statistic is so widely cited that it was the name of an anti-violence organization (One in Four[78]). What they usually do not say is that the one in four figure was calculated by adding together attempted and completed sexual assaults.[79] This means that a number of the women counted either fought off their attackers or the assault was "uncompleted" for some other reason (the assailant changed their mind, was talked out of it, etc.). Rather than separate out attempted and completed assaults (and then analyze what occurred to make some of them uncompleted), activists lump them together, effectively increasing the perceived rate of violence and thus presumably both the level of concern about the issue and the level of terror among women. This lumping together also implies that attempted and completed assaults are one and the same. Though being attacked in any way is terrible and we should work to reduce all forms of violence, research demonstrates that the emotional experience of an uncompleted assault is significantly different.[80]

Trans activists engaged in a number of other practices that made levels of violence seem larger than they actually were. In producing statistics or generating lists of victims of hate-motivated violence, most of the groups I examined included unsolved crimes. NCAVP made this explicit in its 1999 report, stating that it counts "unsolved murders of LGBT individuals generally, if these seem to have been committed by strangers without any apparent motivation" or if they include "abduction and kidnapping; beating; torture; [and/or] 'overkill.'"[81] Although it is impossible to know if an unsolved murder was motivated by anti-transgender sentiments, activists seemed to assume that almost all violence experienced by transgender people was motivated by hatred of trans people, so they were comfortable including these crimes in their counts. However, this practice obscures other potential causes and further reinforces vulnerable subjecthood.

Activists sometimes also included victims who were not transgender in statistics and lists. For example, Jacqueline Julita Anderson, a cisgender woman who happened to have facial hair and was killed by her jealous ex-boyfriend, was named on the ROD website, where she was called a trans man. Similarly, Logan Smith, a cisgender man who was beaten by police and died when an organ weakened by an intersex condition ruptured, was regularly included by activists, including *Transgender Tapestry* calling him transsexual.[82] These were likely honest mistakes, as gender nonconforming and intersex people have been included in some definitions of transgender. However, neither victim identified as trans, nor were they read as such by the perpetrators of these crimes. Although these deaths should be highlighted and relationship violence and police brutality must be addressed, including people who neither identified as, nor were perceived as, transgender in counts of transgender victims of violence falsely increases violence statistics, furthering the construction of transgender as a vulnerable subjecthood.

Many cases are more ambiguous than those of Anderson and Smith. In cases of fatal violence, activists cannot ask the victims whether or not they identified as transgender. Therefore, they must guess. As a result, many activists labeled victims as "transgender" when they, themselves, never claimed that label.[83] For example, when there was a male-bodied homicide victim who had not yet been identified but was wearing one or more items of "women's" clothing, GenderPAC referred to that individual as "Jane Doe," indicating an assumed transgender identity.[84]

Trans activists also regularly argued that their estimates of violence were low and that real rates were higher. Usually, activists simply stated that this violence is underreported. However, they occasionally cited statistics for how falsely low they are. For example, in a 2003 publication, GLAAD claimed that "upwards of 50% of hate incidents are unreported."[85] This statistic, like all the claims that violence is underreported, is impossible to verify due to the very nature of the claim. By implying that real levels of violence are twice as high as current counts indicate, activists gained attention for their cause. However, like the other tactics discussed, this one also likely increased fear and thus vulnerable subjecthood. Activists also regularly claimed that the actual levels of fatal violence are higher than is thought because police officers falsely consider homicides to be suicides. This assertion appears in the flyer in figure 1 (see chapter 4): "Despite clear evidence of hate crimes, these cases are commonly labeled as accidents or suicides." It should be noted that of all the murders activists referenced in the documents I examined, just three—Marsha P. Johnson (1992), Mara Duvouw (1995), and Aimee Wilcoxons (2008)—were ruled suicides by police.

These activists are, of course, faced with a challenge, as they are positioned in a social problems marketplace in which everyone must compete for resources and most actors are working to paint a picture of their problem that is as large as possible. To refuse to play this game runs the risk of losing access to the little attention they have garnered for their cause. However, numbers are powerful and should be used with caution, as embracing this tactic may falsely heighten the fear and unlivability of the very lives they are working to protect.

EXAGGERATED EPIDEMICS

Since Americans tend to be more concerned by social problems that are getting worse, activists often speak of violence as being at epidemic levels and/or increasing dramatically, even when that is not the case.[86] Frequently, activists interpret a rise in reporting of violence as a sign of increased violence, when the rise is probably actually caused by the success of the social movement in educating people about the crime and encouraging those who experience it to report it.[87] These tactics, although they unintentionally misrepresent the violence, help social movements succeed in the social problems marketplace. Highlighting an increase in violence is effective in gaining attention for the cause, as it makes people think that not only is the problem large, but it is getting worse, and they or someone they care about may become a victim if it is not solved.

Activists working to reduce violence against transgender people regularly spoke of the violence as "on the rise," "escalating," "skyrocketing," "surging," a "wave," a "murderous tide," a "plague," a "pandemic," or an "epidemic." Activists utilizing this "epidemic" framing argued that they did so in order to highlight the patterns of violence, to dispel the myth that such violence is "a collection of random and isolated events," and to encourage people to see this violence as worthy of the same attention as "epidemics of actual disease."[88] Claims of increases were sometimes illustrated with metaphors even more terrifying than that of an epidemic, such as Riki Wilchins stating that "this country has turned into a meat-grinder" or that "it's open season for gender killings."[89] Although these descriptions make excellent sound bites, like extreme examples and fatalistic statistics, they are also likely to produce enormous levels of fear, which is antithetical to the goal of increasing the livability of the category transgender. Moreover, by suggesting that cisgender people are hunting transgender people, these sorts of statements are likely to encourage distrust of potential allies, hampering anti-violence efforts by furthering the "us versus them" perspective discussed in chapter 4.

In addition to the social costs of such a rhetorical tactic, the claim that fatal violence is increasing or is an epidemic is concerning because during most of the time this claim was made, it was simply not true. Epidemics are highly contagious diseases that quickly spread through the population. Though the fatal violence against transgender people was high (since any violence experienced by a group should be considered high and unacceptable), it did not increase dramatically over time (see figure 4). Although fatal violence levels from 2002 to 2009 appear higher than those from 1994 to 2001, they are not higher than the levels from 1990 to 1993. Considering that the transgender population in the United States was likely larger in the 2000s than in the early 1990s, there is no evidence of an epidemic. Of course, it should be noted that many of the anti-violence activists began their focus on violence in 1994. Given that vantage point, it may have appeared that violence was on the rise. However, when levels of fatal

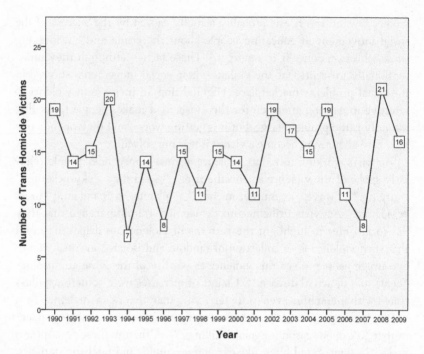

FIGURE 4. Number of murders of transgender people per year in the United States, 1990–2009. Counts are based on the dataset described in appendix B.

violence hit comparably low points in 2001, 2006, and 2007, these dips were not highlighted by most activists or interrogated for factors that could help reduce violence.

The focus on "escalating" or "epidemic" violence is concerning for another reason: it fosters the belief that only large and growing levels of violence are worthy of attention. Thus, this tactic perpetuates the very norms within the social problems marketplace that push activists to high-light large numbers of victims and unintentionally suggests that smaller levels of violence would be acceptable. By only attending to increases in violence, activists make it more challenging to get attention for their cause in the future if they were to succeed in reducing violence. Moreover, as I detail in the next section, this approach encourages them to ignore actual decreases in violence, missing an opportunity to gain knowledge useful in the struggle to reduce violence.

Of course, trans activists are not the only group who use the metaphor of an epidemic to try to gain attention for their anti-violence cause. Those advocating on behalf of gay men, lesbians, Jewish people, women, black people, Asian Americans, and people with disabilities have all claimed that violence against their group is at epidemic levels, even when reports have shown that violence experienced by the group is decreasing.[90] Legal scholars James Jacobs and Jessica Henry detailed how, in their attempt to gather proponents for inclusion of sexual orientation in hate crime legislation, gay and lesbian activists regularly stated that violence against their group was at epidemic levels. The researchers found that this occurred even when levels of violence were known to be declining. This understanding of violence has not stayed contained within these social movements. Instead, "the media have accepted, reinforced, and amplified the image of a nation engulfed by hate crime," "criminal justice scholars have accepted the hate crime epidemic hypothesis with hardly a raised eyebrow," and "politicians have enthusiastically climbed aboard the hate crime epidemic bandwagon."[91]

ACCENTUATING THE NEGATIVE

In 2000 NCAVP received data from participating organizations showing an 8 percent decline in hate-motivated violence against LGBT people. In reporting these numbers, the authors noted that "in releasing the . . . finding, NCAVP is aware that some who oppose any civil and legal protections for the LGTB community will use it to suggest that bias violence is no longer a vital concern."[92] With the competition for attention within the current social problems marketplace, any acknowledgment of improvement on a particular issue is seen as potentially ruinous for activist groups, as they fear that people will deem the problem solved and divert resources to other concerns.[93] This situation, which I term the *irony of social movement success*, encourages activists to accentuate the negative and decrease focus on the positive. Indeed, the report's authors immediately followed the preceding statement with this one: "NCAVP would like nothing more than to agree with them, but sadly, even the most cursory review of a national Internet mailing list to which most NCAVP members subscribed in 2000 reveals there were an exceptional number of brutal acts (many more than in 1999) committed against LGTB individuals in parts of the country where community-based anti-violence services are minimal or nonexistent."[94]

The practice of *accentuating the negative* is detrimental to all social movements, but potentially disastrous for those engaged in identity-based anti-violence activism. Focusing on the positive (such as decreasing levels of violence) can help social movement actors identify potential causes for the improvement and use those to generate solutions to the problem. By contrast, deemphasizing those moments of success can cause movements to miss opportunities to learn from them. In cases of identity-based anti-violence activism, there is also the component of fear. When activists highlight increases in hatred and violence and deemphasize reductions in violence, fear among identity group members grows and hope dwindles. As I discuss later, this can also affect activists, leading to burnout.

Focusing on the negative, even in moments when violence levels were decreasing, was common among trans activists, particularly NCAVP. It should be noted that the reports issued by NCAVP receive substantial news coverage each year, as trends from year to year interest journalists; thus the group's tactics for success within the social problems marketplace have especially extensive consequences. Since NCAVP tracks violence levels from year to year, it was in the best position to notice, and feel required to report, reductions in violence. However, competition within the social problems marketplace also encouraged NCAVP to then dismiss such evidence. When reporting on a decrease in violence, activists tended to lead with the decline and then immediately explain why the reduction did not actually represent an improvement. For example, in 2004, NCAVP reported a decline in attacks on trans people, only to then dismiss it:

> In looking more in-depth at victim-related data collected for 2004, it was also found that the number of people of transgender experience reporting incidents decreased (11%) for the first time in recent memory. Though this decline could be viewed as a positive trend, there is anecdotal evidence to suggest that it may in fact be an unfortunate byproduct of the transgender community's attempt to remain "under the radar" while lesbians and gay men and same-sex marriage became such targets during 2004 in general and the federal election cycle in particular.[95]

In 2005, the organization once again found a decrease and once again attributed the drop to trans people being more closeted.[96] Moreover, the activists argued that cultural forces would likely cause an increase in violence in the future: "The current virulently anti-LGBT environment, along with strong religious, ethnic and racial dynamics increase the likelihood that the level of hate crimes will rise again after the decline described in this report."[97] Overall, in the documents I examined a decrease in violence was mentioned and then dismissed more than fifty times. By contrast, reductions in violence were noted and not dismissed fewer than five times. Fearing loss of interest and resources, activists neglected the opportunity to give identity group members and allies hope for a better future. Such hope is necessary for a livable life and for empowered activism. In addition, they failed to note what may have caused such decreases: patterns that, if attended to, could be utilized in crafting better solutions and ensuring a more permanent reduction in violence.

The rare instances in which activists did not dismiss decreases in violence and treated the findings as authentic allow readers a moment of hope for the future. For example, the 2001 NCAVP report stated: "In a significant change, and perhaps one of the true bright spots in this report (programs may struggle to obtain reports on bias-related incidents short of murder, but murders are generally easily quantifiable), anti-LGBT murders decreased 40%. NCAVP officially documented 12 murders in 2001, compared with 17 that occurred in the same regions in 2000."[98] However, during the period studied, these infrequent acknowledgments of decreases in violence were not paired with investigations into the potential causes for the decreases. As such, though they provided an opportunity for celebration, they could not be utilized to generate policies to facilitate future declines.

CLAIMING INATTENTION TO THE CAUSE: "NO ONE CRIES FOR DEAD TRANSGENDERS"

In their attempts to gain notice in the social problems marketplace, trans activists frequently stated that "no one" cares about violence against trans people. The argument that trans people are treated as "disposable people" was very common among activists in the 1990s and 2000s. In an editorial in 1999, Riki Wilchins argued that murders of trans people are "rendered mute and invisible because certain kinds of bodies and certain kinds of hate don't matter as much. . . . Within the queer community and certainly within the straight press, we are disposable people."[99] This way of describing what it means to be transgender was quickly taken up by other trans activists and became so popular that it was the headline for both an article in *Transgender Tapestry* and a report published by the SPLC.[100] Similarly, Gwendolyn Smith was quoted in a *Transgender Tapestry* article as saying, "I have always told my 'significant other' that 'no one cries for dead transgenders.'"[101] These sorts of statements were often accompanied by evidence to the contrary. After describing 110 TDoR events that occurred in 2003, *Transgender Tapestry* author Monica Helms argued that "the murders of transgendered people have become an epidemic no one cares about."[102]

Although this was a highly effective rhetorical strategy, one must ask what being told that they were "disposable" and "no one cares about" them did to trans people reading these statements. Similar to extreme examples and claiming that violence was at epidemic levels, the suggestion that no one cares whether you live or die increases the feeling of vulnerability associated with transgender subjecthood. There is also a sense of hopelessness and fatalism associated with these accounts. If "no one cares," what possibility do activists have of bringing about social change? Moreover, these declarations are self-defeating because, like many forms of identity politics, they make activists unlikely to recognize potential allies. TDoR events are usually attended by both transgender and cisgender people and often include a speech from a local politician. If there are 110 cities in which people publicly mourned murdered trans people, clearly someone cares.

The argument that cisgender people do not care about murders of transgender people was often accompanied by claims that the mainstream news media did not cover these crimes. For example, on the "about" page for ROD, Smith stated that "the media's reluctance to cover our deaths lies near the heart of this project," arguing that the lack of mainstream news coverage was a key motivation for starting the web page.[103] Similarly, *70 under 30* asserted: "It is difficult to imagine another youth population subject to so much violence and so little public attention. The deaths documented in this report have gone largely unpublicized by mainstream media, as has the epidemic as a whole."[104] However, when gathering the homicide dataset, I utilized mainstream news stories, and of the 289 murders between 1990 and 2009, 267 (92%) were covered in a newspaper at least once. These claims of inattention have a compounding effect in terms of feelings of vulnerability, as transgender people were told that they were likely to be killed and their deaths would not even be reported in the media.

A similar compounding of feelings of vulnerability occurred when activists worked to increase awareness of the lack of investigation and prosecution of violence against trans people. Activists regularly highlighted murder cases that were still unsolved, as opposed to those for which the perpetrator had been caught and prosecuted. The statements made on the poster in figure 1 are a good example of this: "Law enforcement and the justice system frequently regard the transgendered as disposable people, and their murders not worth investigation. . . . They are quickly closed, and thus the killers are rarely apprehended." This sentiment was echoed throughout the documents I examined, such as an article in *Transgender Tapestry* that claimed, "Not only are we being slaughtered at an alarming rate, most transgender murder cases gather dust in the cold case files. On top of that, those caught and convicted of murdering a transgendered person usually get light sentences."[105]

Like the statement that "no one cares" about murdered transgender people, the statement that perpetrators are rarely apprehended is also inaccurate. Of the 289 murders of transgender people between 1990 and 2009, 132 (46%) did not result in an arrest. This clearance rate of 54 percent is below the national average at the time of about 64 percent, but it is not as low as activists claimed.[106] It is possible that the nature of these activists' work helped fuel the impression that many more cases were unsolved. Activists were often notified of a murder soon after it occurred but might not receive follow-up information. For example, GenderPAC's widely read 2006 report on violence against trans youth included the following statement: "On March 4, 2001, in Houston, TX. Francisco Luna (29), a transgender Latina woman, was shot multiple times in the face, stomach and shoulder. Her case remains unsolved."[107] However, the case had been solved. The perpetrator was arrested within days of the murder and was convicted within a year.

The goal of this rhetoric was to educate the audience and encourage them to fight for increased law enforcement attention to these crimes. Like many of the tactics described in this chapter, the activists' intention was to increase the value of trans lives by critiquing moments when they are not treated as full subjects. However, there was also a worrying unintended consequence: although meant to increase the value of trans lives, these statements told trans people that many believe their lives do not matter. The message that if someone kills you, not only will you be dead, but your murder will not be reported on and your killer will not be caught because your life has no social significance, is potentially highly damaging. Telling trans people that their lives are worthless in the eyes of mainstream society increases vulnerable subjecthood.

VULNERABLE SUBJECTHOOD

In the process of attempting to gain attention for their cause, identity-based anti-violence activists shape beliefs about who is vulnerable to violence. Activists working between 1990 and 2009 to reduce violence against transgender people utilized a number of tactics intended to both (1) mark transgender people as valuable and undeserving of violence; and (2) get those outside their activist circles, including journalists, politicians, and everyday transgender and cisgender people, to care about the issue of violence against transgender people. These tactics ranged from TDoR vigils to arguments that transgender people experience more violence than other groups. By naming victims, memorializing the dead, and arguing that the violence should never have occurred, activists constructed transgender as a *valuable subjecthood.* However, competition within the social problems marketplace also encouraged the use of tactics that shaped transgender into a *vulnerable subjecthood,* portraying transgender people as universally hated, at constant risk of violence, and unable to protect themselves. Moreover, trans activists told narratives that suggested transgender people were highly likely to be murdered in particularly horrifying ways, and that if they were killed, they would be ignored by journalists and the perpetrators would go unpunished. As such, risk of violence has become central to beliefs about what it is to be transgender.[108] This association has become so strong that when a transgender person dies, many people assume they were murdered. For example, when trans woman Quona Clark was found dead in Chicago in 1993, rumors spread through the trans community that she had been "bludgeoned to death in a hotel room" and "struck in the head with a hammer or a brick and stuffed between [her] mattress and box spring"; that her "throat was slit, or that [her] genitals had been mutilated"; and that "the body was so badly mutilated that [she] had to be cremated."[109] However, Quona had actually died of pneumonia.

The fact that activists linked being transgender with vulnerability had particular consequences due to its construction as a *homogeneous subjecthood.* One of the tenets of homogeneous subjecthood is that one member of an identity group is seen as interchangeable with any other member. As such, transgender people were encouraged to *identify with the dead,* seeing themselves as similar to the murder victims described in activist documents and likely to experience similar violence. Occasionally this was explicit, such as when Jamison Green told the crowd at the second Transgender Day of Remembrance, "We've come here to remember: remember what it feels like to die," or when Miqqi Alicia Gilbert, after describing the deaths of Brandon Teena, Tyra Hunter, and Joan d'Arc, told readers of *Transgender Tapestry* in 1999 that "they all died because they were transgendered. No one cared whether or not they were heterosexual, no one cared if they were out for one evening or lived full time, whether they were TS [transsexual] or CD [cross-dresser] or TG [transgender]. It could have been one of us, it could have been you."[110] The thought that they could be next produced high levels of fear in transgender people exposed to this message. As Allyson Robinson said in her speech at a 2008 TDoR event:

> The Day of Remembrance reminds me that I'm one of the lucky ones, one of the privileged few in our community. . . . And yet despite my good fortune, like many of you, I'm afraid. With the faces of those whose lives we commemorate tonight, and the sheer inhuman brutality they faced constantly in my mind, I look at strangers on the street

differently. I worry when I notice someone staring at me on the subway. I get scared when I hear footsteps behind me in a dark parking lot. I hug my wife and children tight when I get home each night and thank God I've made it. The Day of Remembrance reminds me that in spite of the privilege that I have been given, I could be next.[111]

Similarly, Diego Miguel Sanchez stated: "For some, it's a day on the calendar. For me, it's a day of vivid, visceral feeling because I know one thing: that on any day of any year, as a transsexual Latino man, I could be among those killed. I could, like too many others—remembered or forgotten—be attacked by someone with no regard for my life, someone who may not face responsibility for his or her brutal act of violence."[112] This pattern of identifying with the dead is also seen outside the activist community. In her interviews with transgender men, sociologist Miriam Abelson found that nearly half spontaneously mentioned the murder of Brandon Teena, many expressing fear that they could face a similar fate. As one interviewee stated, seeing a documentary about Brandon Teena was traumatizing "because I remember looking at pictures and thinking that that's me, that that could be me."[113] Similarly, in a poem published in 2010 by Miles Walser titled "Nebraska," the author talks to Brandon Teena:

We are walking obituaries.
Your hate crime had lines already carved across my forehead.
People look at me
and see your delicate hands
and absent Adam's apple.
. . .
I see you on the movie screen and wonder if it's my reflection.
I watch them push you into the dirt
and drag me into their car
as they break our body from between our thighs.
. . .
Sometimes, I imagine the phone call my mother would get,
can almost hear my sobbing friends,
smell the lilies on my casket[114]

It is notable that these statements of fear often come from transgender people who are white and/or transgender men, two groups at relatively low risk for fatal violence. This is a direct consequence of identity politics treating the social category as homogeneous. As they share an identity (or at least a perceived identity category) with the dead, it is not surprising that they would experience a high level of empathy. An unintended consequence, though, is feelings of fear and powerlessness. Rather than seeing the shared identity as a source of strength or community, it becomes a source of terror.

This consequence of the construction of a vulnerable subjecthood is not limited to anti-violence activism done on behalf of transgender people. Indeed, identity-based anti-violence activism has constructed a vulnerable subjecthood for a number of groups, including women and gay men and lesbians. In her analysis of debates in Australia over discussions of homosexuality in school, education scholar Valerie Harwood found that those advocating for lesbian and gay rights told what she terms *wounded truths* about queer youth, including being at risk for "suicide, increased drug use, homelessness, and violence" (467). In order to be effective within the social problems marketplace, rights advocates focused on the harm done to queer youth and not on the "happiness or pleasure" of queerness (471).[115] Similarly, in their interview research into sexual identity and feelings of safety, legal scholar Leslie Moran and sociologist Beverley Skeggs found that although they had personally experienced little violence, gay men and lesbians from Manchester had high levels of fear of violence, particularly violence from "straights." The researchers detailed a number of possible causes of this fear, including "discourses of danger and safety" produced by anti-violence activists campaigning around hate crimes.[116]

Correspondingly, many scholars have noted that women fear violence at a higher rate than men and have called this fear "paradoxical" because men experience more violence than women.[117] This paradox may be partially attributable to activism done to try to reduce violence against women.[118] Some activists have promoted an idea that women are inherently rapable, an idea that is not universal and is, in fact, baffling in some cultures.[119] As discussed in chapter 2, the linking of womanhood with assaultability can produce a feeling of inherent vulnerability.[120]

Although activists are attempting to reduce violence and mark group members as valuable, in constructing a vulnerable subjecthood activists produce the lives of identity group members as unlivable. An *unlivable life* is one filled with constant fear and without hope for stopping the violence. As such, although a vulnerable subjecthood is a subjecthood, it can be conceptualized as a second-class one. That many transgender people, women, and gay men and lesbians live in fear of violence has been well documented by scholars. Academics who have interviewed transgender people have found that very few of their interviewees had experienced violence, but almost all were terrified that they might be attacked in the near future.[121] Similarly, cisgender women also experience high levels of fear, and men and women alike tend to believe that women are more vulnerable to violence, despite the fact that men are more likely to be victims of violent crimes.[122] People who are members of multiple social categories that have been vested with vulnerable subjecthood have been shown to experience particularly high levels of fear of violence. For example, sociologists Jill Yavorsky and Liana Sayer found that although few of the transgender women they interviewed had experienced violence, almost all of the interviewees said they had substantial fears of being attacked because they were women, and the majority also feared being targeted because they were transgender.[123] Similarly, sociologists Eric Anthony Grollman and Doug Meyer have demonstrated that women, "sexual minorities," and people of color all demonstrate higher levels of fear of walking alone at night than do men, heterosexuals, and white people, respectively. Moreover, "sexual minority" women express higher levels of fear than heterosexual women, and women of color experience more fear than white women.[124]

Beyond the emotional consequences, the construction of a vulnerable subjecthood has practical consequences. Those who have been vested with a vulnerable subjecthood often constrict their behaviors to try to prevent attack. For example, activism aimed at keeping women from experiencing violence has caused women to experience high levels of fear and as a result change their behaviors in hopes of avoiding violence, particularly rape.[125] This *rape avoidance labor* severely reduces the livability of women's lives, limiting the places they can go, the time of day that they can go to them, with whom they can interact, and their clothing options. Indeed, sociologist Esther Madriz argued that "fear of crime is one of the most oppressive and deceitful sources of informal social control of women."[126]

Just as the construction of vulnerable subjecthood has influenced women's behavior, so too has it shaped how transgender people live their lives, including whether they identify as transgender at all. In order to avoid violence, many transgender men are careful to conform to gender norms, avoid particular spaces, and not challenge "systems of domination such as white supremacy."[127] Similarly, due to "a constant fear of assault," trans women engage in "hyper-vigilance," being wary of anyone outside of the "queer community" and limiting the places they go and what time of day they are in public.[128] As a respondent to the Transgender Discrimination Survey stated: "The fear of being the victim of a hate crime has also meant that I haven't lived completely freely; I know that if people on the street knew that I was born female, I'd be at risk of violence or harassment."[129] Moreover, fear of violence has pushed some transgender people to engage in body modifications that they might not have otherwise done in an attempt to reduce the risk of violence and has caused some trans people to be closeted when they might not have been so otherwise. As philosopher Jacob Hale argued:

> Transsexual activists' construction of the rape and murder of ftm "Brandon Teena" as emblematic of transphobic violence has led some ftms to seek vaginectomies for fear of being treated as women by being raped and revictimized if they report the crime. The hegemonic transsexual construction of "Brandon Teena" has seemed to provide compelling reasons for some ftms not only to stay closeted themselves but to decry other's openness for fear that increased ftm visibility will increase the chances that their own transsexual status will be discovered and that they will meet the same fate as "Brandon Teena."[130]

Similarly, an anonymous contributor to the ROD website poignantly detailed how the murder of his friend John by his fiancée's jealous ex-husband encouraged him to be closeted: "I felt if this could happen to him, it could easily happen to me as well. The only defense I had was to withdraw. I had to live with the secret, as did whomever would be my partner, but no one else need know. I had to hide, blend in as thoroughly as possible, deny part of what made me the man I am and maybe, just maybe, I would be safe, able to find a modicum of peace."[131] The author focused on his shared trans identity with John when assessing his own risk of violence instead of on other factors involved in the crime. Notably, the man who killed John was recently released from jail, murdered a woman so that he could steal her van, shot John in the shower, kidnapped John's fiancée, and then drew a gun on a police officer when he was pulled over for a broken taillight. However, rather than see the murderer as highly dissimilar from most people the author was likely to encounter, the author instead feared for his life. Thus, the coupling of identity with risk for violence that occurs in identity-based anti-violence activism may encourage people to disassociate from the identity category.

The construction of a vulnerable subjecthood has a number of other unintended consequences, including increasing risk of violence and death and negatively affecting activism and proposed solutions to violence. It has been well documented that high levels of stress increase mortality.[132] As such, the argument that the construction of a vulnerable subjecthood produces an *unlivable life* is quite literal, as the stress from constantly fearing violence increases one's risk of death. In addition, feminist scholars have argued that the production of the idea of women as inherently rapable actually increases their risk of rape because they are then seen as appropriate targets for sexual assault and, due to fear, are unlikely to fight back.[133] As such, tactics utilized by identity-based anti-violence activists in hope of reducing risk of violence and death may actually increase such risks.

Seeing a group as inherently vulnerable to violence may also impair activism. The messages about violence discussed in this chapter are discouraging and potentially disempowering. Living in constant fear likely makes it challenging to do effective activism, and the message that this violence is increasing, rather than decreasing, may lead to a feeling of hopelessness. As activist Monica Helms wrote after attending TDoR in 2005, "the 38 names that had to be read this Day of Remembrance drained the energy from my soul," causing what she described as "burnout."[134] As I detail in the next chapter, the construction of a vulnerable subjecthood also shaped proposed solutions to the violence. Due to a focus on vulnerability, activists emphasized vigils and other forms of remembering the dead, education of trans and cis people about levels of violence experienced by transgender people, and hate crime legislation. These responses almost always functioned as after-the-fact "solutions," marking an individual victim as valuable but doing little to prevent future violence.

6. Shaping Solutions

How Identity Politics Influences
Violence-Prevention Efforts

On July 16, 2008, after meeting online and exchanging numerous texts and emails, Angie Zapata went on a date with Allen Andrade. Allen spent the night in Angie's apartment in Greeley, Colorado, sleeping in a separate room. The next morning, after looking at photos of Angie and her family around Angie's apartment, Allen questioned her sex, grabbed her genitals, and then beat her to death with his fists and a fire extinguisher.[1] Activist organizations, including GLAAD, HRC, NCTE, and the Colorado Anti-Violence Program, one of NCAVP's contributing members, responded quickly. They issued press releases; functioned as liaisons between Angie's family and the media; and worked with local media to ensure respectful reporting, including the use of Angie's name and pronouns.[2] Together with Angie's family, they organized a vigil to celebrate her life and grieve her death. The more than two hundred attendees lit candles and held them high to memorialize her.[3] Activists continued to update their organizations' members and the press about the case, including when an arrest was made, when the trial occurred, and when a verdict was issued.[4] Their press releases regularly labeled the murder a hate crime, likened it to other murders of transgender people, and provided statistics on violence experienced by transgender people.[5] Arguing that the murder of Angie was reflective of the larger problem of violence against transgender people, organizations contended that the case was further evidence of the need for transgender inclusive hate crime legislation.[6] A GLAAD press release argued: "The past few months have offered Greeley residents, as well as people throughout Colorado and across the nation, an opportunity to better understand transgender lives and the horrifying reality of anti-transgender violence. Media coverage of this case has played a vital role in broadening that understanding, and it has helped more people understand the importance of a fully inclusive hate crime law like Colorado's."[7] That November, Angie's name was read at Transgender Day of Remembrance events and was regularly mentioned in press releases about those events.[8] In April 2009, Allen Andrade was found guilty of first-degree murder and hate crime charges.[9] This was the first successful prosecution of a murderer of a transgender person under a hate crimes statute in the United States and was widely celebrated by transgender anti-violence activists.[10] As one press release said: "The National Center for Transgender Equality is pleased that this horrendous crime against Angie Zapata and her loved ones was taken very seriously by local authorities, and that they treated Angie with the respect she deserves. The prosecution did a skilled and caring job of refuting the absurd and inhumane stereotype that transgender people are somehow being deceptive by being themselves and deserving of such horrific treatment. We hope that Angie's family can find some measure of peace and healing."[11]

Anti-violence activists could have responded to this murder in a wide variety of ways. What factors made advocating for hate crime legislation, holding vigils, and educating the public about levels of violence experienced by transgender people the seemingly logical approaches? The previous two chapters examined how combining identity politics with anti-violence activism shapes beliefs about the identity group, constructing a homogeneous and vulnerable subjecthood. In this chapter I examine how the logics of identity politics influence violence-prevention efforts. How has the merging of identity politics with anti-violence activism, along with the pressures of the social problems marketplace, shaped responses to and proposed solutions for violence against transgender people? Moreover, although the identity politics model and the forces of the political field make these appear to be rational responses to violence experienced by transgender people, do they have negative unintended consequences?

Between 1990 and 2009, trans activists proposed three main approaches to reduce violence against transgender people: education about levels of violence, memorializing the dead, and working to add gender identity as a protected category to hate crime legislation. These responses to violence tended to focus on marking transgender as a valuable subjecthood, as they were seen as ways to make victims "count." Activists hoped that labeling trans lives as valuable in these ways would reduce violence against them. In taking these approaches, they adopted proposed solutions from other identity-based anti-violence movements, including the movements to reduce violence against people of color, women, and gay men and lesbians. They differed from other movements, however, in that they did not regularly advocate "pride" as a solution, focus on "fighting back," or provide services for violence survivors. As I detail in chapter 7, solutions proposed by transgender anti-violence activists have not changed dramatically in recent years. Since federal transgender-inclusive hate crime legislation was enacted in 2009, activists no longer need to advocate for such laws. However, they continue to focus their efforts on memorializing victims and educating the public about levels of violence.

The tactics activists use to get attention for their movement, as well as what activists say causes the violence, can greatly impact proposed violence-prevention efforts.[12] The logics of identity politics encouraged trans anti-violence activists to ignore patterns of violence, focusing on "hatred" of transgender people as the sole cause for violence. This portrayal had important consequences for anti-violence work. With no other explanation than hatred, trans activists focused on inclusion of gender identity in hate crime legislation. However, there is little evidence that hate crime legislation reduces hate-based homicide. Murder is already illegal, and legislation outlawing it has not yet deterred people from doing it. Thus, it is unlikely that the extra prohibition of hate crime legislation will prevent the crimes from happening.[13] Moreover, although outlawing hate-motivated actions, including violence, seems like a logical solution within the current political field, hate crime legislation has notable ramifications, including expanding the power of the criminal justice system, an institution known to disproportionately criminalize transgender people.[14]

Similarly, as activists regularly argued that "no one" cared about violence against transgender people and that transgender people were treated as "disposable people," they concentrated on responses intended to increase sympathy for, and valuation of, transgender people. They did so not through celebrating the living but through mourning the dead. Activists focused on educating the transgender community and the general public about levels of violence against transgender people and on holding vigils and engaging in other practices to remember the dead. Although effective within the social problems marketplace, these tactics also furthered the construction of transgender as a vulnerable and homogenous subjecthood and, like hate crime legislation, they did little to reduce actual levels of violence or make trans lives more livable.

EDUCATION ABOUT LEVELS OF VIOLENCE

In my opinion, education is the best tool to stop the bullets.

—MONICA HELMS, "And That's the Way It Is!,"
Transgender Tapestry, no. 95 (2001): 13

Trans activists regularly mentioned education as a way to address violence against transgender people, including antibias and anti-violence education and education about what it means to be transgender. By far the most common form of education that activists advocated for was about the levels of violence experienced by transgender people. Activists argued that both the transgender community and the general public were underinformed about how much violence transgender people experienced and that it was necessary to educate people about the violence. As activist Crystal Middlestadt stated in 2008: "Whenever there is a high-profile incident in the media, many people refer back to Matthew Shepard, believing that hate crimes and murders have not happened since 1998. Unfortunately, this violence is an everyday occurrence for some."[15] Similarly, a 1996 *Transgender Tapestry* article discussing a proposed movie about the murder of Brandon Teena noted: "This film will hopefully paint an accurate picture of just how evil and demented hate crimes against TG people can be and that such a crime can happen and does."[16] Activists referred to violence experienced by transgender people as an "invisible massacre" and a "silent wave of violence."[17] Arguing that "it's time to break the silence," activists said that it was necessary to "educate the public . . . and ourselves to the fact that anti-transgender hate and discrimination continues to this day without abatement. With each passing month, at least one of us is murdered."[18]

The education about violence advocated by activists took many forms, including press releases, vigils, published reports on violence, and Transgender Day of Remembrance (TDoR). As the National Coalition of Anti-Violence Programs explained in its yearly report on violence: "Part of NCAVP's mission is to educate the public at large about the extent and brutality of anti-LGBT violence including through the distribution of this annual report."[19] Similarly, TDoR, an event honoring all murder victims in that year, was seen as a way to inform people about violence experienced by transgender people. As a GLAAD press release stated: "On Wednesday, Nov. 20, more than 35 cities nationwide will mark the third annual Transgender Day of Remembrance with vigils honoring the victims of anti-transgender violence. These events also are intended to raise public awareness of and spark discussion about violence against transgender people."[20] Activists hoped that increased awareness of violence experienced by transgender people would elicit sympathy, gain allies, and prevent violence by labeling it as morally wrong. As a 2001 National Transgender Advocacy Coalition (NTAC) press release about TDoR stated: "With each non-trans person, with each supporting ally, with each sensitive politician who hears and listens to our services and who remembers our dead, we gain support. With each successful service, we gain friends and allies."[21] Similarly, TDoR founder Gwendolyn Smith argued: "Remember, it is up to us to bring attention to anti-transgender violence, and let others know that this sort of treatment is unacceptable."[22]

Occasionally, activists went so far as to argue that education about levels of violence against transgender people would prevent violence by teaching potential perpetrators that such violence is wrong. The Gay Straight Alliance (GSA) stated:

> The Transgender Day of Remembrance serves several purposes. It raises public awareness of hate crimes against transgender people, an action that current media doesn't perform. Day of Remembrance publicly mourns and honors the lives of transgender people who might otherwise be forgotten. Through the vigil, we express love and respect in the face of national indifference and hatred. Day of Remembrance gives transgender people and their allies a chance to step forward and stand in vigil, memorializing those who've died by anti-transgender violence. Putting on the Day of Remembrance in schools can also be used as a way to educate students, teachers, and administrators about transgender issues, so we can try to prevent anti-transgender hatred and violence from continuing.[23]

Likewise, Smith argued about TDoR: "It is critical that this event be present in our schools. Maybe if Gwen Araujo's killers had seen this in their own school, she would be alive today."[24]

Activists also argued that education about levels of violence would help reduce violence by facilitating the inclusion of gender identity in hate crime legislation. In explaining the importance of a survey on violence administered by sociologist Emilia Lombardi, activist Riki Wilchins stated: "Everyone suspects the incidence of violence is high, but no one has any systematic data enabling us to call on government agencies and representatives for action. Bashing and assault against this community has to stop, and establishing solid evidence is a first step down that road."[25] The results from the survey, as well as other summaries of violence experienced by transgender people, were used at the 1997 National Gender Lobby Day, an event at which trans activists met with members of Congress to try to convince them to include gender identity in hate crime legislation.[26] Similar tactics were utilized at subsequent lobby days, and activists implored transgender community members to notify anti-violence organizations of all experiences of violence so that they could be recorded.[27] For example, in 1998 a bold headline across a page of *Transgender Tapestry* read: "IF

YOU THOUGHT YOUR SILENCE WOULD PROTECT YOU . . . THINK AGAIN." The article beseeched readers to "report the incident, even if you think nothing can be done about it or if you think it is not 'important enough' to prosecute. What's most important is that we establish a pattern of hate crimes against transgender and other gender-variant people, so that we can effect legislative change."[28]

The merging of identity politics and anti-violence activism, as well as the pressures of the social problems marketplace, encouraged education about levels of violence as a suggested solution. One claim activists commonly made in order to gain attention for their cause was that "no one" cared about violence experienced by transgender people. That framing spurred activists to try to get people to care in hopes that increasing compassion would reduce violence. A key means by which they hoped to do that was through education about levels of violence. The type of education that they advocated was similarly influenced by the logics of identity politics. Because they were focused on only one identity, as described in chapter 4, they did not educate the public about how the murders were patterned by race, gender, or sexuality. This style of education about violence is exemplified by the flyers in figures 1 and 3 (see chapters 4 and 5). Both are intended to increase awareness about violence experienced by transgender people, and they do so through focusing on the volume of violence, including details on murders per year and month, as well as the states and cities with the largest known number of transgender homicides.

Although learning about levels of violence is widely touted as a way to reduce violence, one must ask how, exactly, this education functions as a violence-prevention effort. Statistics and extreme examples are common tactics in getting politicians to care about an issue, so it is clear how education about the volume of violence would influence legislation. However, the argument activists made was that education alone would reduce violence and that it was necessary to educate both the trans community and the general public, not just politicians. The hope, it seems, was that large statistics and horrifying cases would elicit sympathy and help people see that the violence was wrong. However, one could argue for the possibility of the opposite effect. By describing the violence as very common, activists may have unintentionally portrayed violence against transgender people as more, rather than less, socially acceptable. Scholars studying rape-prevention efforts have argued that depicting women as at high risk for sexual assault has unintentionally portrayed them as "vulnerable and suitable target[s]," increasing sexual violence against them.[29] Thus, there is a risk that activist efforts to gain attention within the social problems marketplace by highlighting large statistics and particularly horrifying homicides normalized violence against transgender people.

Moreover, educational campaigns emphasizing high levels of violence against transgender people taught another lesson: that to be transgender is to be vulnerable to violence. Activists often lamented that transgender community members were ignorant about levels of violence against the group and worked to inform them. Thus, transgender community publications such as *Transgender Tapestry* and *FTMi* regularly highlighted both statistics and individual cases. As such, transgender people were frequently exposed to the message that they were at high risk for experiencing this violence. The lesson of vulnerable subjecthood was also taught to the general public through press releases and reports on violence, furthering the belief that to be transgender is to be inherently vulnerable to violence.

Though an effective tactic in the political field in terms of encouraging the inclusion of gender identity in hate crime legislation, education about levels rather than patterns of violence influenced proposed solutions in unintended ways. By treating transgender as a homogenous subjecthood, this tactic encouraged a one-size-fits-all approach to violence-prevention efforts that did not account for the diverse causes of violence against trans people. Moreover, when activists envision an identity category as homogeneous, their proposed solutions to violence tend to benefit the most privileged of the identity group.[30] As I discuss in chapter 7, attending to patterns of violence reveals a number of possible ways to reduce violence that were rarely mentioned by activists, including reducing poverty, making sex work safer through legalization, and encouraging media portrayals of transgender people as desirable romantic partners. However, because activists did not focus on factors that increased risk for certain transgender people, they instead focused on educating people about the volume of violence, memorializing the dead, and including gender identity in hate crime legislation.

REMEMBERING THE DEAD

Activists commonly advocated for remembering the dead as a response to violence experienced by transgender people. This took the form of written memorials, vigils for individual victims, and the annual TDoR. As described in *Responding to Hate Crimes: A Community Resource Manual*, published by the National Center for Transgender Equality (NCTE) in 2006, vigils were a standard response to violence experienced by transgender people: "Vigils are memorials for people that have been victims of hate crimes.

They are often held at the site of the crime or some place that was important to the victim. The purpose of a vigil is to provide a space for people to grieve the loss of a friend, family member, or community member."[31] The vigils organized by transgender anti-violence activists occurred directly after murders, at courthouses during trials, in response to verdicts, and on anniversaries of murders.[32] Remembering the dead took other forms as well, such as setting up altars memorializing murder victims at the end of the annual Trans March in San Francisco and the Remembering Our Dead (ROD) website, described in detail at the beginning of chapter 4.[33]

Vigils and other forms of remembering the dead were often described as honoring the life and condemning the death of a transgender person who was murdered. They have a dual purpose: to label the person's life as valuable and to denounce the killing. In addition, modes of remembering the dead were seen as opportunities to educate the public about the violence experienced by trans people and to bring the community together. Moreover, vigils and TDoR events were seen as chances to put pressure on law enforcement and politicians to ensure "justice" was served for victims and to call for an end to the violence. Vigils can achieve these latter goals because of the logics of democracy. Those who are elected to office must work to keep their constituents happy, and vigils were used to signal dissatisfaction. In addition, vigils that occurred at scheduled times and places were effective ways of getting news coverage for the anti-violence cause. However, these forms of remembering the dead were also moments that placed a hefty symbolic weight on the group, marking transgender people as inherently vulnerable to violence.

Vigils were much more common responses to violence than protests. *Responding to Hate Crimes* does not even use the word *protest*, instead describing the benefits of "rallies" thus: "A well-organized, energetic public rally can make it clear to the media, local officials, and the general public that a large number of people are actively concerned about hate crimes and are demanding change. Both the size and the content of a rally are important. Rallies can generate a great deal of excitement about fighting for social and political change. The purpose of a rally is to send a targeted message to the public by drawing many people and media attention."[34] Despite these tangible advantages, such responses were rare. Just 37 of the more than 1,000 documents I analyzed mentioned protests, marches, or rallies, compared to 132 documents explicitly mentioning vigils and 326 documents stating that the proper response to violence was to remember the dead, including by attending TDoR events and supporting the ROD website. Compared to protests, memorializing events are relatively passive.

It may be that activists felt that being less confrontational and speaking in *wounded truths* was a more effective way to be heard within the social problems marketplace, as it is often seen as inappropriate for marginalized groups to be "aggressive" and demand rights through events like protests.[35]

According to activist documents, one of the main purposes of the various forms of remembering the dead was to label transgender lives as valuable, in hopes that increasing the social worth of transgender people would reduce the violence against them. As stated on the TDoR website, the first four "guiding principles of the Day of Remembrance" were as follows:

- "Those who cannot remember the past are doomed to repeat it." (Santayana)

- All who die due to anti-transgendered violence are to be remembered.

- It is up to us to remember these people, as their killers, law enforcement, and the media often seek to erase their existence.

- Transgendered lives are affirmed to have value.[36]

The website further explained that TDoR "publicly mourns and honors the lives of our brothers and sisters who might otherwise be forgotten. Through the vigil, we express love and respect for our people in the face of national indifference and hatred. Day of Remembrance reminds non-transgendered people that we are their sons, daughters, parents, friends and lovers. Day of Remembrance gives our allies a chance to step forward with us and stand in vigil, memorializing those of us who've died by anti-transgender violence."[37] One of the ways the valuing of transgender people was accomplished was through particular rituals at TDoR events, including holding pictures of victims, reading their names, and following each name with the chant "We remember."[38] Activist accounts of vigils and TDoR events often highlighted the number of people in attendance and the number of cities in which events occurred. For example, a *Transgender Tapestry* story about the murder of Gwen Araujo in 2002 noted that "some 500 people" attended a candlelight vigil on the day of her funeral, followed by three more vigils in the following days.[39] The numbers of vigils and attendees were seen as evidence of the victim's value.

Another benefit of various forms of remembering the dead noted by activists was how vigils and TDoRs helped unify the transgender community. For example, an article in *FTMi* about a TDoR event in 2002 described that in addition to mourning the dead, "We sang and recited poems and read testimonies and told tales of our determination and dignity and triumphs too. I realized then that the trans community and all who have minds and hearts large enough to embrace people of all kinds are my family. We who have died in more ways than we remember can be there for each other."[40] Similarly, a GLAAD press release about Gwen Araujo's funeral, subsequent vigils, and the following TDoR event stated: "I hope I never lose my sense of horror at terrible, heinous crimes like Gwen's murder. But I am glad to know that tragedy and mourning are not the only outcomes of such crimes. They can empower and bring a community together."[41]

Activists also utilized moments of remembering the dead to educate people about the levels of violence experienced by transgender people and to emphasize their framing that the violence was motivated by hate. As described in a 2007 statement on the HRC website, TDoR:

> Is an opportunity for communities to come together and mark the passing of transgender or those perceived to be transgender individuals who have been murdered because of hate. Although the primary focus of the events is on memorializing those lost to hate crimes, the day also serves as a forum for transgender communities and allies to raise awareness around the threat of violence faced by gender variant people and the persistence of prejudice felt by the transgender community. Activities also make anti-transgender violence and bigotry visible to such key community groups as police and medical services, the media and elected officials.[42]

Similarly, a press release about the ROD website in 2005 said that it "exists to honor individuals murdered as a result of anti-transgender violence and prejudice, and draw attention to the issue of anti-transgendered violence."[43] Like these larger memorials, individual vigils, such as one for Chanelle Pickett, were "designed to heighten awareness of transgender violence."[44] For example, after a screening of the documentary *The Brandon Teena Story*, the San Francisco activist group TG RAGE held a candlelight vigil "to show others how many transgendered individuals have been murdered since Brandon."[45]

As mentioned in the HRC description of TDoR, the vigils and the annual event were also seen as opportunities to gain media coverage for the issue of violence experienced by transgender people. Annual events with fixed dates facilitate coverage because journalists can plan to attend them in advance. Moreover, events involving large numbers of people and compelling images and quotes are often seen as worthy of news coverage. Speaking about a series of vigils in response to recent murders in 1996, Riki Wilchins said: "One thing coming out of these Memorial Vigils is that they are finally forcing the media to cover these terrible crimes like they deserve. And this is one small step in stopping the toll of gender-based violence."[46] Activists often held press conferences before or after vigils.[47] To further help gain coverage, the TDoR website urged event organizers to prepare press materials to distribute to attending journalists.[48] In addition, GLAAD issued press releases and press resource kits in advance "encouraging journalists to mark the occasion with stories about the pervasive problem of hate crimes against transgender people."[49] In its request to journalists, GLAAD stated: "Media coverage of Transgender Day of Remembrance events often includes documenting lives lost to hate crimes, as well as the routine harassment, discrimination and violence that members of the transgender community encounter on a regular basis." Other activist statements echoed this, indicating that the main purpose of gaining press coverage was to educate the public about levels of violence experienced by transgender people.

Finally, vigils and other forms of remembering the dead occasionally included explicit denouncements of violence experienced by transgender people and calls for social change. Both HRC and GLAAD described vigils for Tyli'a "NaNa Boo" Mack in 2009 as chances to "bring the community together to condemn the recent violence" as well as to "denounce the ongoing violence against transgender people."[50] Similarly, a few explanations of TDoR described it as a way to take "a stand against anti-transgender violence."[51] However, the condemnation of the violence and the call for social change were usually more implicit. This is notable, considering the final guiding principle listed on the TDoR website: "We can make a difference: by being visible and speaking out about anti-transgender violence, we can effect change."[52]

A number of forces within the political field, mixed with the logic of identity politics, encouraged activists to support remembering the dead as one of the main "solutions" to violence. In order to gain attention for their cause in the social problems marketplace, activists often focused on extreme examples of violence experienced by transgender people. As such, almost all of the cases highlighted by activists were of fatal violence. This focus on homicide shaped proposed solutions, encouraging rituals that remembered the dead, as opposed to celebrating the living or highlighting resistance to violence. In addition, tactics often used to get others to care about the issue made violence against transgender people seem unstoppable. Year after year, activists described the violence as at "epidemic" levels and presented statistics in a way that made it seem as if the same numbers of transgender people were killed each month, regardless of the actions of activists. In moments when violence appears unpreventable, remembering the dead may seem to be one of the few possible responses. Finally, activists regularly utilized war metaphors, resulting in an "us versus them" portrayal of violence experienced by transgender people. Memorializing the dead is a common practice in times of war, and it is likely that the use of this metaphor shaped activists' proposed violence-prevention efforts. Notably, the response to violence of remembering the dead is an after-the-fact "solution." Although some activists indicated that they hoped that memorials would help prevent future violence, like the "solution" of education about levels of violence, it is unclear how they could do so except in the very long term.[53]

Activists' advocacy for remembering the dead had several unintended consequences. Until 2009, Transgender Day of Remembrance was the only annual national event specifically related to trans people.[54] It was also "the largest multi-venue transgender event in the world."[55] Sociologists Elizabeth Armstrong and Suzanna Crage argued that practices of commemoration are particularly important in forming a collective identity and giving meaning to that identity through the formation of shared memories.[56] They contended that activists select which events to observe and turn into collective memories through commemoration. Those events from a group's history that are memorialized are more likely to be remembered than those that are not. Given the importance of annual commemorative events to producing an idea of group membership and the meaning of that group, it is significant that trans activists chose to memorialize events of murder. Like other aspects of this form of identity-based anti-violence activism, memorials functioned to name transgender people as valuable subjects deserving of life. However, such practices, which sociologist Miriam Abelson termed *vulnerability rituals*, have unintended consequences.[57] Through the annual meaning-making event of TDoR, activists defined transgender as a perpetually imperiled identity group.

TDoR has effects well beyond transgender communities. These well-publicized and -attended memorial events happen in high schools, on college campuses, in towns and cities throughout the United States, and in a number of other countries. Moreover, the events receive substantial news coverage. For many cisgender people in the late 1990s and early 2000s, news coverage of TDoR was their first encounter with the idea of transgender people. The fact that this first encounter was a memorial for the dead likely had profound effects on their understanding of what it means to be transgender. Furthermore, the practices of remembering the dead likely affected those who would potentially identify as transgender in the future by shaping both their own understandings of transgender lives and the beliefs held by their friends and family.

The "solution" of remembering the dead has further unintended consequences, as it is focused on valuing the dead rather than protecting the living. Due to the prevalence of memorializing practices, the transgender rights movement's most famous figures were murder victims. As such, the movement had martyrs, not heroes. These representations shaped ideas of what it is to be transgender, marking transgender people as "always already" dead. This sense of fatalism can be seen in comments made by some activists about these memorializing events. Despite advocating for them, several activists indicated that they did not think remembering the dead would decrease violence experienced by transgender people. As activist Monica Helms described a 2004 TDoR event: "We had an emotional event, as we had in the past. My words and the words of those speaking that night did nothing but echo off the walls of the buildings downtown, but we cried nevertheless. The people spoke beautifully about the 58 victims. Heaven knows how many names we will read next year."[58] Surprisingly, Gwendolyn Smith, the founder of the ROD website and TDoR, shared this sentiment, stating:

> So maybe Web sites like "Remembering Our Dead," and events like the "Day of Remembrance" will help build visibility, leading to a better understanding that transgender people sometimes pay very dearly for being who we are. Perhaps, as time goes by, paving the way for a shift in the way society treats those who are presenting in a "gender-variant" manner. But I must admit being a little pessimistic. Whether it is 13 cities or 300, I know that there will still be transgendered people who will be killed simply because of the clothes they wear, or the way they act. Maybe it will be you—or me.[59]

The conception of transgender people as always already dead was also reflected in the types of solutions rarely advocated for by these identity-based anti-violence activists. Whereas they regularly called for memorial services, trans activists seldom suggested victim services. Of all the organizations I examined, just two—NCAVP and NCTE—mentioned the need to provide services for survivors, and only one—NCAVP—actually did so. As NCTE argued: "Transgender victims of hate crimes need support on a number of levels, including reestablishing a sense of physical safety and control, being listened to and emotionally validated, and knowing that they are supported by their community. Assistance from the transgender community can help a victim of a hate crime feel less isolated and regain a sense of power and safety."[60] Despite the benefits such services would provide, due to their focus on fatal violence, national trans activist organizations almost never focused on the needs of violence survivors.

HATE CRIME LEGISLATION

Just as "hatred" was the most commonly cited cause for violence experienced by transgender people, hate crime legislation was the most mentioned solution to the violence. More than one of every four documents I
examined from activists engaged in transgender anti-violence work called
for hate crime legislation. Such legal action was seen as so important that
in addition to regularly publishing articles calling for hate crime legislation,
Transgender Tapestry printed the full text of the Matthew Shepard Local
Law Enforcement Hate Crimes Prevention Act, which had been introduced
in the US Senate, in its Summer 2007 issue.[61]

Despite the focus on hate crime legislation, activist documents often did
not include explanations of how this legal approach would reduce violence.
As in their calls for education about levels of violence and remembering
the dead, activists regularly treated the benefits of hate crime legislation as
obvious. Vague statements abounded, such as saying that "[what is] needed
is comprehensive hate crime legislation in every state to stem this horrible
epidemic of crime" or "legislation currently pending in Congress, the Hate
Crimes Prevention Act (HCPA), would provide some basic protections and
federal resources to address this wave of violence."[62] Often these statements
argued that hate crime legislation would "protect" transgender people but
did not explain how this legal remedy would do so.[63] As HRC president
Joe Solmonese stated in 2005: "There's an insufficient and narrow patch-
work of laws now that leave millions of GLBT Americans unprotected. It's
past time for a meaningful and comprehensive hate crimes law at the federal level."[64] Similarly, an NCTE press release in 2009 called the Matthew
Shepard and James Byrd, Jr. Hate Crimes Prevention Act "the first federal
law to protect transgender people."[65] Occasionally, however, activists did
specify why hate crime legislation would be beneficial. Most commonly
they mentioned mandatory counting of hate crimes, having hate crime legislation as a way to mark transgender lives as valuable, the belief that stiffer
penalties would function as a deterrent, and the benefits of legislation that
included resources to assist in investigation of hate crimes.

The History of "Hate Crimes"

In the United States, identity-based anti-violence activists have assumed
that legal action is the most appropriate response to discrimination, and as
a result they have focused on hate crime legislation above other potential
solutions.[66] The concept of "hate crimes" was invented and began to circulate in the United States in the 1980s and became institutionalized and

widely recognized as a legitimate social problem by the end of the decade.[67] Although bias-motivated violence, including symbolic and physical violence, has a long history in the United States, such actions only became recognized as a distinct form of crime in the 1980s. The idea of the "hate crime" was constructed, popularized, and institutionalized by four key types of social actors: activists, government workers (including politicians and those involved in the criminal justice system), the mainstream news media, and experts, including academics.[68] Social movement actors have been central to this development. In the United States, the process of making hate a crime started with a coalition of activists working in the interests of people of color and Jewish people, who lobbied the US Congress for policies to reduce violence against their groups. This alliance was soon joined by gay men and lesbians. They used testimony from victims of violence as well as statistics gathered from gay and lesbian anti-violence organizations to make their case.[69] The activism that constructed "hate crimes" was part of a larger set of identity-based projects fighting for rights for particular groups. Borrowing narratives from these larger movements, activists framed hate crimes as "an expression of discrimination."[70] Notably, hate crime laws are written in a "neutral" way in which any form of hatred associated with a larger category is included. Although in the popular understanding, hate crimes are those committed against historically oppressed groups, the actual laws prohibit crimes based on any form of bias related to race, religion, sexual orientation, and so forth. Thus, violent acts motivated by hatred of whites, Christians, and straight people are also crimes subject to increased penalties.[71]

An early form of federal hate crime law was the Hate Crimes Statistics Act of 1990; this piece of legislation mandated the collection of data on bias-motivated crimes by the Department of Justice. Although race and sexual orientation were included in this first federal law, gender was not. There was opposition to the inclusion of gender because it was thought that violence against women was so common it would be difficult to enforce the law and the focus on other forms of hate crime would be diluted.[72] Rather than include women in hate crime legislation, a separate law, the Violence Against Women Act, was created.[73] In addition, transgender people were not included in the initial legislation because they were less socially accepted than gay men and lesbians. Scholars have detailed how, although many groups experience bias-motivated crimes, it is difficult for more stigmatized groups to be included in hate crime legislation. When less-accepted groups are included, there is sometimes an insistence by others to explicitly state that the law does not endorse the practices of the group. For example, the inclusion of sexual orientation in the Hate Crime Statistics Act of 1990 required the addition of language that the law "disclaims any intent to promote homosexuality."[74]

Since the passage of the Hate Crimes Statistics Act of 1990, legal responses to violence against certain identity groups have proliferated. These laws include (1) mandating the counting of crimes motivated by hatred of specific groups of people (e.g., the Hate Crimes Statistics Act itself); (2) providing funds for education of law enforcement officials about the identity group (both to train officers in how to spot and respond to violence experienced by the group and to reduce police harassment of, and violence against, the group); (3) authorizing the federal government to step in if local law enforcement is unable or unwilling to investigate or prosecute crimes against a member of a particular group; and (4) increasing penalties for crimes when they are committed based on hatred of a specific group (e.g., the Violent Crime Control and Law Enforcement Act of 1994 and the Mathew Shepard and James Byrd, Jr. Hate Crimes Prevention Act of 2009).

Message Legislation

Although the majority of the hate crime literature focuses on explaining why hate crimes occur, some scholars have examined both the positive and negative outcomes of hate crime legislation.[75] In their analysis, both proponents and opponents of hate crime legislation have focused mostly on its symbolic consequences. Hate crimes are widely considered "message crimes," meaning they are acts intended to send a message to the target group's members that they are hated and subordinate. Similarly, scholars detailing the positive outcomes of hate crime legislation have argued that it is message legislation, meaning that these laws are intended to communicate that this form of violence is wrong and that the groups named in the legislation are socially valuable.[76] Hate crime legislation is seen as defining who and what are and are not socially acceptable. Sociologists Valerie Jenness and Ryken Grattet argued that hate crime politics "are designed to transmit the symbolic message to society that criminal acts based upon hatred will not be tolerated."[77] In addition, these laws "affirm principles of tolerance and . . . reassure the actual and potential victims of bias-motivated violence that their safety will be protected."[78] Thus, one of the functions of hate crime legislation, according to current literature, is to encourage "compassion for victims and contempt or disgust for perpetrators."[79] Moreover, scholars have argued that through anti–hate crime activism, social acceptance of bias crimes has decreased.[80] This change may, over time, reduce this form of violence.

Trans activists have echoed these sentiments. Much of their focus on hate crime legislation was about demanding that the government codify the value of transgender lives. Trans activists saw violence against trans people as evidence of devaluing their identity category to the point of death, so they worked to label those lives as valuable. They envisioned hate crime legislation as able to do this in a number of ways. Early in the period studied much of the focus was on the counting aspect of hate crime legislation. One of the reasons trans activists wanted violence against trans people to be included in national counts of hate crimes is that this designated them as worthy of notice. In addition, activists often fought for enhanced penalties for crimes against their group. Though they generally argued that this enhancement was desirable because it would function as a deterrent, it should also be noted that greater penalties also were seen as marking trans lives as valuable. Often activists expressed outrage about shorter prison sentences and celebrated longer ones, showing that they believed that sending people to prison for more time indicates the life of the person killed is more valuable.[81] Finally, activists also fought to include crimes against trans people in legislation that would provide extra resources for investigation, either in the form of resources for local law enforcement or by giving federal agencies the right to take over an investigation when they consider local law enforcement unable or unwilling—due to their own biases—to investigate the crime properly. These extra resources above and beyond what is provided for crimes against nonprotected classes again define the identity group as worthy of protection and socially valued.

Making Transgender People "Count"

The first form of hate crime legislation in the United States, the Hate Crimes Statistics Act of 1990, mandated counting of crimes designated as hate crimes. It is notable that this initial legislation was not explicitly about prevention and instead combined the common identity-based anti-violence activist responses of educating about the level of violence and memorializing the dead. Like most trans activists' documents advocating hate crime legislation, those documents pushing for mandatory counting rarely explained why such enumeration would be beneficial. However, when they did, they usually pointed to the utility of knowing the volume of violence against transgender people as well as highlighting counting as a way to mark transgender people as valuable. As the report issued by GenderPAC in 1997 on its national survey of transgender violence argued: "An initial step toward understanding the extent of hate violence against transgendered

Americans would be to add 'gender' to the HCSA [Hate Crimes Statistics Act], with the understanding that gender should be construed to include gender characteristics, expression or identity."[82] Notably, the calls for this sort of information about hate crimes, like the calls for education about the volume of violence, almost never suggested that the data could be used to discern patterns of violence experienced by transgender people, such as those related to race, gender, or sexuality. Thus, the focus appears to have been less on prevention and more on demonstrating that there was a problem as a way to facilitate a legislative response. As activist Nancy Nangeroni argued in 1996: "Inclusion in the Hate Crimes Act will start the gathering of figures on violence and harassment of TGs [transgender people], whether CD [cross-dresser], TS [transsexual], DQ [drag queen], DK [drag king], or anywhere between. It's the first step towards obtaining legislative protection against discrimination for all TGs."[83] In addition, counting victims was seen as an important way to label transgender people as valuable. For example, in a press release in 1996 about a piece of hate crime legislation that did not include trans people in the list of protected groups, activists stated: "So we're also frustrated that our coalition partners and elected representatives don't recognize it's past time to include transgendered people in HCSA. And we're outraged by the knowledge more transgendered people will be harassed, attacked, and killed because of their gender identities and these crimes will go unrecorded and unrecognized for the hate crimes they are."[84] Thus, trans activists argued that hate crime legislation was important because it would highlight that violence against transgender people was a particularly egregious crime.

Marking Transgender Lives as Valuable

A number of other aspects of hate crime legislation were seen as important because they would construct transgender as a valuable subjecthood. In their documents calling for hate crime legislation, trans activists explicitly declared both that transgender people are deserving of full personhood and that achieving inclusion in hate crime legislation is a way to be valued and counted by society. Trans activists often argued that such laws are important because hate crime laws would legally legitimate their claim to trans subjecthood through the government officially declaring that the violence is morally wrong and trans people are valuable and worthy of "protection." In this way, the call for hate crime legislation was an extension of trans activists' goal of producing transgender as a valued category populated with people who have a right to live. Activists saw hate crime legislation as a way to accomplish this goal through two aspects in addition to mandatory counting of hate crimes: legal recognition of their identity group and enhanced penalties for perpetrators.

Trans activists perceived hate crime legislation as a way to write the value of their identity group into law. As NCTE executive director Mara Keisling stated about the passage in 2009 of the Matthew Shepard and James Byrd, Jr. Hate Crimes Prevention Act, "It's the first time that transgender people will be in federal code in a positive way. That's a really important historical moment for the country—certainly for transgender people, but really also for the country."[85] Another press release from NCTE echoed this sentiment, arguing: "In the past, federal law has only mentioned gender identity in a negative context, such as explicitly excluding transgender people from the Americans with Disabilities Act. The passage of the hate crimes bill marks a significant turning point from the days in which the federal government contributed to the oppression of transgender people to today when federal law takes action to protect our lives."[86] This form of legal recognition was seen as a way to label transgender lives as valuable through marking them as worthy of protection.[87] As stated by NCAVP: "People of trans experience . . . are often more frequently targets for violence because offenders believe that their actions against these communities will be condoned by society and by government. It is our hope that passage of this Act will send a message to the contrary."[88] This sentiment was also expressed when activists objected to the failure to pass inclusive hate crime legislation. For example, NTAC described this as "signaling that transgender, intersex, gay, and lesbian lives don't count."[89] Similarly, activist Li Anne Taft argued that this "put forth a message: the legislation, the police and the court system do not value TG people."[90]

Activists argued that hate crime legislation also marked transgender people as valuable by labeling the violence against them as wrong. For example, in a statement on the introduction of hate crime legislation to the US Congress, Keisling described two murders of transgender people and then argued: "Everyday we hear about people like these and the message that these crimes are meant to send to all of us. But today we send a message in return. A message that violence against anyone is not acceptable. And hate violence can be and will be investigated and prosecuted vigorously. Today the message from hate violence is met face to face with the message that these members of Congress send here—it is not acceptable in our society to attack people, to kill people, because of who they are."[91] Similarly, in response to the hate crime conviction of the murderer of Lateisha Green, a press release from GLAAD stated, "Today's sentencing sends a clear message that violence motivated by anti-transgender bias is unacceptable and wrong"; one from HRC asserted, "By ensuring the maximum sentence, this case sends a message in return: hate will not be tolerated, and we will fight it wherever it appears until all are safe to live their lives authentically and without fear."[92]

Many transgender anti-violence activist groups advocated for enhanced penalties as part of hate crime legislation, arguing that enhanced penalties were necessary to label transgender lives as valuable and that they would function as a deterrent to violence against transgender people. As a Gender-PAC publication explained, "Penalty-enhancement legislation is enacted so that those who commit such violence are singled out for particularly severe treatment."[93] Similarly, activist Alison Laing argued, "Unless the maximum sentence is given, we will devalue the lives of people of difference everywhere."[94] Until 2003, NCAVP regularly advocated for enhanced penalties in its annual report on violence. The organization argued that laws should "further penalize violence against lesbians, gay men and other targets of hate crimes at the state level by passing hate crimes bills to deter such acts and to provide stiffer penalties for those who commit them."[95] Likewise, NTAC argued for legislation that would "provide for enhanced penalties to help deter bias-motivated crimes."[96] However, the ability of enhanced penalties to prevent violence is highly debatable, a point I return to later in this chapter.

By contrast, one aspect of hate crime legislation that might actually function as a deterrent was mentioned by activists much less often: assisted investigation. Activists noted that the solve rates for murders of transgender people were lower than the national average for homicide and that there was a need for hate crime legislation that would provide additional resources for investigating such crimes.[97] In 2003 NCAVP reversed its stance on enhanced penalties, arguing instead:

> Ideal federal legislation would both authorize the U.S. Attorney General to investigate and prosecute anti-LGBT hate incidents—particularly those cases in which it is determined that local law enforcement does not have the adequate resources, mandate or will to do so. A primary piece of any federal hate crimes legislation should provide additional resources for enhanced law enforcement agencies, criminal justice personnel and community education, training and assistance programs actively addressing hate crimes, and in fact, it is our belief that such resources should be the primary goal of hate crimes legislation rather than the more typical or popular element of penalty enhancements.[98]

Similarly, a 2008 HRC press release stated: "Federal legislation is crucial to ensuring local law enforcement is given the tools they need to combat hate violence in our communities. If signed into law, the Local Law Enforcement Hate Crimes Prevention Act/Matthew Shepard Act would give the federal government expanded jurisdiction to investigate and prosecute violent crimes based on a person's race, color, religion or national origin as well as their sexual orientation, gender identity, gender, and disability. The Act also provides assistance to local law enforcement to investigate and prosecute bias-motivated violence."[99] Research has shown that unlike enhanced penalties, legislation that makes it more likely perpetrators will be arrested, prosecuted, and punished may work to deter crime.[100]

Factors Encouraging Hate Crime Legislation as a Proposed Solution

Hate crime legislation became the "obvious" solution to the problem of violence experienced by trans people due to the logic of identity politics and competition within the social problems marketplace. Trans activists were following in the footsteps of other groups who engaged in identity-based anti-violence activism. These previous groups had centered much of their efforts on hate crime legislation, encouraging trans activists to do the same. Indeed, trans activists' focus on violence and inclusion in hate crime legislation was caused in part by mainstream gay and lesbian advocacy organizations, such as HRC, refusing in the early years of this activism to support inclusion of transgender people in employment nondiscrimination legislation, but being willing to support their inclusion in hate crime laws.[101]

Although there are many paths to social legitimacy and valuation, trans activists, like identity-based anti-violence activists before them, including those working to reduce violence against people of color, women, and gay men and lesbians, turned to hate crime legislation. Within the belief system created by identity-based anti-violence activism, the world is composed of (a) the identity group and its allies and (b) haters of the identity group. This "us versus them" mentality encourages a focus on violence done by those outside of the identity group, particularly strangers, rather than violence occurring within the identity group or committed by people known to the victim. By saying that hatred of transgender people caused the violence, trans activists produced ideas about appropriate anti-violence practices, narrowly constructing hate crime legislation as one of the only possible response to these murders. The focus on hatred of a single identity as the cause of violence caused identity-based anti-violence activists to ignore patterns of violence, including those related to race, gender, class, and sexuality, as well as factors not related to identity group membership. By discouraging attention to intersectionality, the identity politics model encourages a focus on protecting just a single identity group from violence, as opposed to working to prevent violence against everyone.

The Other Message of Hate Crime Legislation: Vulnerable Subjecthood

Activists often point to the symbolic aspects of hate crime legislation, indicating that they hope inclusion of their identity group in these laws will "send a message" that their group is socially valued. However, another highly important message is sent with hate crime legislation, as the groups' vulnerability, hated status, and need to be protected by the state are literally written into law.[102] Historically, the disadvantaged status of particular groups has been included in legislation, such as the enslaving of African Americans and denying women suffrage.[103] In order to ameliorate this situation, the US legal system has subsequently included specific protections for historically oppressed groups, such as antidiscrimination legislation. These laws, intended to undo inequalities, unintentionally reproduce them. Though no longer legislating oppression, they instead codify a group's vulnerability. Thus, although hate crime legislation labels trans bodies as worthy of state protection, they also mark them as hated and hateable.

These symbolic consequences result from both the legislation itself and the process of fighting to be included in the legislation.[104] As I have discussed throughout this book, in their campaigns for inclusion in hate crime legislation, trans activists emphasized the vulnerability of their group and portrayed transgender people as widely hated. In this process, "transgender" became synonymous with "hated." This conceptual transfer was so prevalent that activists often did not name a cause for violence beyond "being transgender." In addition, activists argued that the failure to label a particular crime a hate crime or to include transgender people in hate crime legislation indicated that the government did not care about transgender people. For example, activists regularly said that the lack of inclusion meant that transgender people were "second class citizens."[105] Similarly, a GLAAD press release argued: "Neither New York State law nor federal law includes gender identity or expression as hate crime categories and that sends a dangerous message that it is acceptable to leave part of our community vulnerable to hateful acts of violence simply because of who they are. We call upon our state and federal lawmakers to ensure adoption of transgender-inclusive legislation that will protect everyone regardless of their gender identity and gender expression."[106] Activists made these arguments in order to gain attention for their cause. However, such claims had dangerous unintended consequences. Hate crime legislation was supposed to send a message that such violence is morally wrong. Through these statements, activists sent a different message: as long as there was no trans-inclusive hate crime legislation, violence against transgender people was socially acceptable.

The Ineffectiveness of Hate Crime Legislation

The symbolic consequences of inclusion in hate crime legislation might be a tolerable trade-off if the laws actually reduced violence. However, there is little evidence that hate crime legislation is effective.[107] Instead, such legislation is a Band-Aid solution to deep cultural problems. Inequality is built into social structures, and outlawing hate will not remedy that situation.[108] However, such legislation has the appearance of addressing the problem, is relatively inexpensive, and serves a symbolic purpose, increasing support for it. Yet that symbolic function is double edged, as it marks those included as a "protected class" as both valuable and vulnerable.

Numerous scholars of hate crimes disagree with some or all of the claimed positive effects of hate crime legislation. They argue that since these crimes are already illegal and outlawing them has not deterred people from doing them, it is unlikely that the extra prohibition of hate crime legislation will prevent the crimes from happening.[109] By contrast, activists regularly claimed that hate crime legislation "will help educate the public that violence against anyone, including transgender people, is unacceptable and illegal."[110] In her testimony to the Maryland Senate about the benefits of hate crime legislation, Mara Keisling stated: "Transgender Marylanders want to feel safe going to a restaurant with friends, walking around in large and small cities, engaging in everyday life without fear of attack. If someone dislikes how I dress or act, I want to know that the law protects me and will punish those who would hurt me because of it. Please be clear of what we are asking. We are simply asking that you help protect us. That you tell would-be criminals, 'do not hurt us, do not kill us.'"[111] Similarly, in a statement celebrating the signing of the 2009 hate crimes act, HRC associate director of diversity Allyson Robinson said: "Yesterday, my own federal government had not yet embraced its responsibility to guarantee my right to life by protecting me, and those like me, from acts of senseless violence."[112] These claims, though rhetorically effective, are highly inaccurate. Violence, particularly fatal violence, is illegal in the United States, regardless of the identity of the victim.[113] Thus, even without hate crime legislation, the law "protects" transgender people as much as it does any other group. One could even argue that not being included in hate crime legislation provides extra symbolic protection, as one's difference from the norm and resulting vulnerability is not written into law.

Claims that hate crime legislation will deter violence through added penalties, such as increased sentences or fines, have been thoroughly discredited.[114] For enhanced penalties to be effective, perpetrators would have to be perfectly rational.[115] As it is unlikely that a murderer carefully considers the consequences before committing the crime, increased punishment of perpetrators is likely to have little effect on the level of violence. Moreover, the consequences for committing acts of violence, especially homicide, are substantial in the United States. If a perpetrator was already willing to risk those penalties, enhanced punishment is unlikely to deter them. Finally, potential perpetrators would have to be aware of the laws and must think that they apply in those circumstances. It is highly unlikely that potential perpetrators have extensive knowledge of hate crime legislation, and it is very possible that those who have done violence to transgender people did not recognize them as transgender, particularly in the 1990s. Such ignorance would eliminate any protective effect enhanced penalties could provide. As extra punishment is unlikely to deter crime, this form of hate crime legislation becomes an after-the-fact "solution" focused on valuing trans victims through vengeance. As Lateisha Green's family stated after the conviction of her murderer for a hate crime: "Justice has been done. But we will never get to see Teish ever again."[116]

An additional challenge with hate crime legislation is that "hate" is difficult to prove in court.[117] Crimes such as homicide are complex, involving numerous factors. Unlike a motivation such as "robbery," it is hard to present evidence of feelings such as "hatred."[118] Demonstrating this, despite some states having transgender-inclusive hate crime legislation since the 1990s, just 2 of the 289 murders of transgender people in the United States between 1990 and 2009 resulted in hate crime convictions, and only 1 of those convictions still stands.[119] Due to the challenge of proving hate, attempts at prosecuting cases as hate crimes have resulted in mistrials. Even with extensive evidence against the four cisgender men accused of killing Gwen Araujo, the attempt to prosecute them under California's hate crime legislation resulted in two mistrials before two of the perpetrators were convicted of second-degree murder and two pled guilty to voluntary manslaughter. None received hate crime–related enhanced penalties.

Transgender anti-violence activists regularly either ignored the ways in which hate crime legislation was not effective or noted the challenges but argued that such laws should be advocated for anyway. For example, when Latisha King was murdered in an Oxnard, California, classroom in

2008, the state had had hate crime legislation that included sexual orientation since 1984 and gender identity since 1998. Despite the fact that such legislation did not prevent Latisha's murder, activists regularly used the case as evidence of the need for federal hate crime legislation. As Joe Solmonese stated: "While California's residents are fortunate to have state laws that provide some protection against hate crimes and school bullying, this pattern of violence against gay, lesbian, bisexual and transgender students is repeated too often in schools and communities across America each day. This tragedy illustrates the need to pass a federal hate crimes law to ensure everyone is protected against violent, bias-motivated crimes, wherever they reside."[120] Similar statements referencing hate crime legislation's power to "protect" transgender people from violence were made after the murder of Angie Zapata, even though the hate crime laws in place in both California and Colorado at the times of these murders did not shield either Latisha or Angie from fatal violence. Acknowledging this fact, activists occasionally stated that hate crime legislation would not reduce violence but should still be fought for. As an NCTE press release urging passage of the 2009 hate crime legislation stated: "We all know that hate crimes will still happen even if this bill becomes a law. But the words create a path for action that our government can take in response to future hate crimes."[121] An HRC statement celebrating the signing of the same legislation echoed this: "Let's be realistic: this law will not prevent the next anti-trans or anti-gay hate crime from happening, nor the one after that. Hate will hurt and kill again, and again."[122]

The Risk of Hate Crime Legislation: Increased Violence

Although hate crimes do not appear to deter violence, there is evidence that they can actually increase it, both by intensifying conflict between identity groups and through expanding the carceral state. A widely publicized crime attributed to hatred may escalate intragroup hostility, thus causing retaliatory crimes.[123] Similarly, forensic psychologist Karen Franklin found that punishing offenders under hate crime laws actually increased their level of bias because they blamed their punishment on the group against whom they had committed the crime.[124] Finally, scholars have argued that the concept of "hate crimes" encourages a "pessimistic and alarmist portrayal of a divided conflict-ridden community [which] may create a self-fulfilling prophecy and exacerbate social divisions."[125] Indeed, NCAVP noted the possibility of such a trend in its violence report for 2009, issued after the passage of the Matthew Shepard and James Byrd, Jr. Hate Crimes Prevention Act:

Monthly incident trends in 2009 indicate a possible correlation between the attention generated by the law's passage and reported incidents of hate violence. Historically, reported monthly incidents of anti-LGBTQ hate violence have peaked in May, June, or July, when LGBTQ Pride events increase visibility of LGBTQ communities. However, as indicated in the following graph, the peak in monthly incidents occurred in October of 2009, in the same month as the bill's passage. The causality behind this temporal correlation is uncertain. Frustration with increased media attention and heightened LGBTQ visibility at this time could have incited hate violence offenders to action. Alternatively, LGBTQ people could have felt empowered to report violence directed against them in the wake of recognition under federal hate crimes law. While causality is difficult to determine, it is clear that reports of violence increased around the time of this law's passage.[126]

Although unsure of whether news coverage of hate crime legislation increased violence, NCAVP was much clearer about another way hate crime legislation increases violence: by expanding the power of a law enforcement system that utilizes violence as punishment. The NCAVP report continued:

> Though many of the changes to the law were significant, NCAVP remains concerned that, as with all laws, the implementation of the Hate Crimes Prevention Act occurs in a criminal legal system that perpetuates racism, classism, anti-immigrant bias and homophobia, leaving LGBTQ people more vulnerable to prosecution under the laws meant to protect these communities against hate violence. Incarcerated people face substantial violence in the prison system, as Just Detention International's supplement to this report attests. As well, there was little emphasis on community-based education and prevention efforts in the law. Further, it was unclear within the legislation if any funding will be dedicated to these approaches, which are critical to the eradication of anti-LGBTQ hate violence. . . . NCAVP member organizations are engaging in a critical dialogue to reflect upon, challenge and expand the definitions of safety and violence. All people have the right to safety and freedom from violence, but criminalization and incarceration can yield increased vulnerability to violence. All people, including LGBTQ communities, should be encouraged to understand and validate the underlying needs of LGBTQ survivors and victims while also holding the larger picture of the short and long-term impacts of prison, policing, and criminalization strategies on all communities.[127]

Notably, NCAVP was the only organization I examined that took a strong stance against enhanced penalties due to their potential to increase inequality and violence.[128] NCAVP's perspective reflects hate crime scholarship, which has pointed to how hate crime legislation increases policing and punishment of socially marginalized people and communities.[129]

HOW MERGING IDENTITY POLITICS WITH
ANTI-VIOLENCE ACTIVISM SHAPES SOLUTIONS

The patterns I have described are not unique to transgender anti-violence activism. They occur in a number of other identity-based anti-violence movements. Most identity-based anti-violence organizations have turned to the government for protections and have lobbied politicians for laws designed to reduce violence against them. A central component of much modern-day identity-based anti-violence activism has been a fight for inclusion of their identity group in hate crime legislation. Due to a shared narrative that violence experienced by members of the group is caused by hatred of their identity, many identity groups fought for inclusion in hate crime legislation, including gay men and lesbians, people of color, and Jewish people.[130] Similarly, women's rights organizations were at the forefront of successful lobbying efforts to secure the passage of the Violence Against Women Act.[131]

Similarly, many identity-based anti-violence organizations speak about the importance of educating the public as part of their activism. Like in transgender rights activism, this "education" is often focused on teaching people about the levels of violence experienced by the group, rather than being aimed at ending the biases that are seen as fueling violence. As sociologists Valerie Jenness and Kendal Broad have noted, gay and lesbian "education efforts aimed at the general public involved highlighting the scope of antigay and lesbian violence in both local communities and throughout the country."[132] Similarly, activism around violence experienced by women has been criticized for focusing on "breaking the silence around rape" rather than on "strategies of prevention."[133]

Finally, like transgender anti-violence activists, other identity-based anti-violence groups have also emphasized vigils and other forms of memorializing the dead as responses to violence. The civil rights movement and Black Lives Matter have regularly held vigils in response to the murders of people of color. Gay and lesbian anti-violence activists have also held a number of vigils and regularly commemorate the deaths of famous gay murder victims, such as Harvey Milk and Matthew Shepard. Notably, however, neither movement has a memorial similar to the ROD website or a national event like TDoR.

Although similar in many ways, there are important differences in the responses to violence advocated by other identity-based anti-violence groups. Unlike transgender anti-violence groups, women's groups have regularly worked to provide victim services and self-defense classes. Other groups have advocated fighting back in a more direct way and have tended toward more active forms of protest rather than the vigils utilized by trans activists. Each of these differences comes from the unique way the identity group in question has been conceptualized, the tactics the movement has used to gain attention in the social problems marketplace, the time period in question, and the type of perpetrator (e.g., activists are often able to mobilize protests around violence done by police officers more easily than around that committed by private citizens).

Unlike trans activists, one of the first ways that women's groups addressed issues of violence experienced by women was to provide victim services. They hoped that domestic violence shelters would prevent future violence by providing battered women a temporary place to live apart from their abusers, as well as counseling to help them avoid future abuse. Because of the combination of identity politics and anti-violence activism, such services are usually explicitly designated for members of particular social categories, such as women. This means that victims of violence who are not part of an identity group currently being advocated for, such as men who experience domestic violence, do not have access to similar services. This also applies to those who are not seen as legitimate members of the group. Many anti-violence services for "women" either officially or unofficially exclude transgender women, due to the misguided notion that they are "really" men.

In the past, some identity-based anti-violence groups have responded to violence against their group by forming organizations to physically fight back.[134] The Black Panther Party was originally named the Black Panther Party for Self-Defense, and it took up arms in response to police brutality and lack of police protection from other forms of violence.[135] In the 1970s, lesbians and gay men formed numerous "street patrol" organizations that intervened in violence against members of their identity group, including the Society to Make America Safe for Homosexuals (SMASH) in New York and the Lavender Panthers and the Butterfly Brigade in San Francisco.[136] Similarly, in the 1990s Queer Nation activists, using the slogan "Queers Bash Back," started the San Francisco Street Patrol and, in New York, the Pink Panthers.[137] In more recent years, identity groups have rarely created organizations to physically fight violence.

It is notable that transgender anti-violence groups did not advocate fighting back. This may be due to their relative integration with those who are seen as doing violence against them. Both black and queer people often partner with, and live with, other black and/or queer people. Similarly, black people throughout the United States and queer people in both New York and San Francisco, the two cities that have produced such groups, live in segregated neighborhoods occupied mostly by other black and/ or queer people. These neighborhoods have been targeted by racists and homophobes, making an organized response to fight back logical. By contrast, most transgender people and women partner and live with cisgender people and men, respectively. Taking up arms against those who may be violent against you might be more palatable when those people are not your partners or neighbors. As such, the focus on "fighting back" in the women's movement has been on learning self-defense to protect oneself from strangers.

Unlike trans anti-violence activists, women's organizations have provided training in avoiding situations perceived as dangerous as well as how to escape or fight off an attacker.[138] Like victim services, violence avoidance and self-defense educational pamphlets and workshops are usually designated as only for particular identity groups. These divergences in proposed solutions from transgender anti-violence activism may be due to which forms of violence these movements have focused on. Whereas trans activists have focused on fatal violence as a way to gain attention for their cause, women's rights activists have concentrated on domestic violence and rape, which they portray as "a fate worse than, or tantamount to, death."[139] Identity-based anti-violence groups that focus less on murder and more on nonfatal violence may be more likely to suggest victim services and self-defense as solutions.

Finally, transgender anti-violence activism has diverged from some other forms of identity-based anti-violence activism in its focus on vigils rather than protests or marches. Women's anti-violence activism has included events such as Take Back the Night and SlutWalk. Although Take Back the Night can include vigils, it is often run as rallies or marches with a substantially different tone than TDoR. Again, this may be due to the differences between anti-violence movements that focus on murder as opposed to nonfatal violence. However, even movements that tend to highlight homicide also have one component historically missing from the transgender rights movement: a pride narrative. Whether in the form of a Pride Parade, as held by the gay rights movement, or other annual pride events such as Black History Month and Women's History Month, most identity-based movements with an anti-violence focus also highlight pride. I address potential reasons for the lack of a pride narrative in the transgender rights movement in the following chapter.

As of the time of this writing, at least 247 transgender people have been killed in the United States since the death of Angie Zapata in 2008. Almost all of those homicides occurred after the passage in 2009 of transgender-inclusive federal hate crime legislation. Each of those deaths has been mourned at TDoR events and has been included in statistics used to educate the public about levels of violence against transgender people. Unfortunately, it is clear that the most common solutions proposed by transgender anti-violence activists have not succeeded in substantially reducing violence experienced by transgender people or made trans lives more livable. Therefore we must explore alternative approaches to violence prevention. I do so in the following chapter.

7. Facilitating Livable Lives

Alternative Approaches to Anti-Violence Activism

> The quintessentially political question—the question that is both
> politically relevant and politically responsible—is not "What do
> you believe in?" but "What is to be done given a certain ensemble
> of political values, given a certain set of hopes or aims, and given
> who and where we are in history and culture?" While belief by itself
> takes no measure of history, context or effect, the question of what is
> to be done dwells only in these elements.
>
> —WENDY BROWN (2001, 94)

> But perhaps there is some other way to live in such a way that one
> is neither fearing death, becoming socially dead from fear of being
> killed, or becoming violent, and killing others, or subjecting them
> to live a life of social death predicted upon the fear of literal death.
> Perhaps this other way to live requires a world in which collective
> means are found to protect bodily vulnerability without precisely
> eradicating it. Surely, some norms will be useful for the building
> of such a world, but they will be norms that no one will own,
> norms that will have to work not through normalization or racial
> and ethnic assimilation, but through becoming collective sites of
> continuous political labor.
>
> —JUDITH BUTLER (2004, 231)

The narratives we tell about what happens in the world affect our views of
that world and how we act in it. Our ideas shape the way we tell narratives,
and the narratives we tell shape our ideas and actions. In this discursive
cycle, life-determining structures and practices are constructed, circulated, and reinforced. In the interactive process that is discursive production, meanings and practices are negotiated and changed as well as reified
and reproduced. This is particularly true in terms of narratives about, and
frames applied to, acts of violence. In the tellings and retellings of violent
encounters, ideas about victims and perpetrators are constructed as well

as beliefs about how to best prevent violence. In this book I have detailed some of the unintended consequences of the ways that frames and narratives are often used by identity-based anti-violence activists in the current social problems marketplace. It is vital to attend to these forms of identity-based anti-violence activism because they are both ubiquitous and, unfortunately, ineffective. Blending identity politics with anti-violence work too often constructs vulnerable, homogenous subjecthoods and proposed "solutions" that both do not substantially reduce the violence and can actually further harm members of the identity group. Activism that promotes the value of an identity group by emphasizing their victim status does not produce a livable life.

The merging of identity politics with anti-violence activism often results in an attempt to construct the identity group as valuable and undeserving of violence. At the same time, however, the group is frequently portrayed as vulnerable and without internal diversity. This form of activism also shapes beliefs about violence, encouraging an understanding that all violence the group experiences is motivated solely by hatred of one identity category. These beliefs shape practices of subjecthood. Those vested with a vulnerable subjecthood live in fear and expend substantial time, money, and energy in *violence avoidance labor*, detracting from their ability to make positive social change. The circulation of the belief that all those "opposite" to your identity group intend to harm you may discourage people from being open about being a member of that group and may even cause people to refuse to adopt that identity. The beliefs constructed in the melding of identity politics and anti-violence activism also shape the practices of violence prevention, encouraging such responses as hate crime legislation, education about levels of violence, and mourning the dead.

In the period from 1990 to 2009, transgender anti-violence activists were highly successful in portraying transgender as a *valuable subjecthood* and conveying that violence against this group is morally wrong. Activists were also effectual in achieving their proposed solutions to violence. On October 28, 2009, one of the main goals of transgender anti-violence activism was achieved: gender identity was added to federal hate crime legislation. But at what cost? Unintentionally, through the narratives they told about the violence and the framings of the cause of violence, they produced trans lives as unlivable lives. Moreover, as I detail in this chapter, these successes did not result in a discernible reduction in the form of violence most focused on by activists: murder of transgender people. Thus, some forms of activism may detrimentally impact the very lives they are trying to save.

The goal of this book is to improve trans lives and the lives of all the other groups that have been shaped by identity-based anti-violence activism, including women, people of color, and lesbians and gay men. I hope for a future in which no one, regardless of social category membership, fears for their life. To that end, this chapter explores alternative ways of reducing violence against historically oppressed people. To accomplish this, we must (1) reduce violence and (2) construct *multifaceted subjecthoods*. Such moves are vital for transgender people, women, gay men and lesbians, and people of color to have access to livable lives. I offer suggestions within the identity politics model as well as options that move beyond identity politics. Key to these alternative approaches to anti-violence activism is the argument that in order to reduce violence against one group, we have to reduce violence against everyone. All social structures are intertwined and mutually reinforcing. In challenging inequality, we cannot just focus on one structure; we must address the whole tangled web. Paradoxically, in the end, identity-politics is not the correct tool for decreasing violence against a particular group. Instead, we must work together across identity categories to reduce violence.

THE INERTIA OF TACTICAL REPERTOIRES

The frames, narratives, and other tactics utilized by transgender anti-violence activists have changed little in the decade since 2009. Trans activists in the early 1990s inherited many of these tactical repertoires from previously established identity-based anti-violence activists, including those working on behalf of women, people of color, and gay men and lesbians. They then passed on those tactics as new members joined the transgender anti-violence movement. To examine changes over time, I collected all of the web pages, reports, press releases, and flyers produced in 2018 by the activist groups from my original data collection that were still active.[1] I analyzed the more than forty transgender anti-violence documents produced by those organizations in 2018 using the same codes from my 1990–2009 analysis, as well as new ones as appropriate. That analysis revealed that since they continued to blend identity politics with anti-violence activism, the tactical repertoires of activists in 2018 looked much like those from 1990 to 2009. These tactics included the use of approaches that construct transgender as a both a vulnerable and homogeneous subjecthood and the focus on education about levels of violence and remembering the dead as solutions to the violence. There were a few differences, however. Most of the organizations produced fewer documents in 2018 than in 2009 that mentioned violence experienced by transgender people. Moreover, the 2018 materials did not focus on hate crime legislation as a solution to this violence. These two differences are likely related. The passage of transgender-inclusive federal hate crime legislation in 2009 caused many organizations to turn their attention toward other issues besides violence experienced by transgender people. Moreover, those still attending to that violence did not see the hoped for subsequent reduction in violence, so they were unlikely to continue to advocate for hate crime legislation as a solution.

In 2018, trans activists still regularly utilized the tactics discussed in chapter 5, which although intended to mark victims as valuable and gain attention for their cause, also produced transgender as a vulnerable subjecthood. Activists continued to focus on extreme examples of violence experienced by transgender people; almost every incident of violence highlighted by activists in 2018 was a homicide.[2] Emblematic of this focus on the least common, but most attention-grabbing, form of violence were two reports published in 2018 that focused exclusively on murder. For the fourth year in a row, HRC published a report titled *A National Epidemic: Fatal Anti-Transgender Violence in America*.[3] The 2018 edition was a daunting seventy-eight pages long. Similarly, NCAVP published a separate report from its annual report titled *A Crisis of Hate: A Report on Lesbian, Gay, Bisexual, Transgender and Queer Hate Violence Homicides in 2017*.[4] In press releases and reports on violence, activist groups included long lists of homicide victims. Often these lists contained no information other than the victim's name, that the victim was transgender, their age, and the date of their death.[5]

Further reinforcing the construction of transgender as a vulnerable subjecthood were the regular references to murders of transgender people being an "epidemic." Indeed, this violence was explicitly called an "epidemic" much more frequently in 2018 than in the 1990 to 2009 period. As an HRC press release stated: "We must . . . address the factors that continue to foster an epidemic of violence targeting transgender people, particularly transgender women of color."[6] In addition, when there were discernible drops in reports of violence, activists in 2018, like those from 1990 to 2009, dismissed those drops. NCAVP argued in its annual report: "Reports of hate violence decreased 20% and have been on a gradual decline since 2010. NCAVP does not believe this decrease in hate violence incidents reports to be reflective of an actual decrease of hate violence against LGBTQ and HIV affected peoples."[7] Finally, as in the previous period, transgender anti-violence activists in 2018 regularly stated that "the public doesn't care about trans victims."[8]

In 2018, trans anti-violence activists also engaged in the framing practices described in chapter 4, which produced transgender as a homogeneous subjecthood. At the same time, they continued the practice which became popular in 2006 of attending to particular forms of intersectionality. Throughout the documents produced in 2018, activists regularly called victims transgender and attributed the violence against them to anti-transgender hatred. For example, an NCAVP report described JoJo Striker as a "transgender woman" and included these details about the case: "JoJo Striker was killed in Toledo, Ohio on February 8th, 2017. Initial media reports misgendered JoJo, but trans activists and allies spoke out in support of JoJo as the news of her death has emerged, helping to correct her narrative. JoJo's mother spoke to press saying she believed her daughter's death was motivated by hate."[9] Similarly, HRC described Transgender Day of Remembrance (TDoR) as "an opportunity for communities to come together and remember transgender people, gender-variant individuals, and those perceived to be transgender who have been murdered because of hate."[10] In their lists of murders, activists grouped diverse victims together under headlines calling them all "transgender."[11] However, this homogenizing took a twist when combined with an increased focus on the particular risks faced by transgender women of color.

Unlike in the pre-2006 era of activism, most of the organizations active in 2018 highlighted both the race and gender of victims, especially when victims were transgender women of color. Indeed, the phrase "transgender women of color" and variations on it appeared in almost half of the trans anti-violence documents produced in 2018. These moments of focusing on the multiply oppressed differ from most identity-based anti-violence activism, which takes as the "model victim" the person who was singularly oppressed, such as the model woman victim being white and middle class and the model black victim being a cisgender man.[12] Although accurate, the way in which activists focused on the increased risk faced by trans women of color reproduced some of the unintended consequences of activism between 1990 and 2009. As in the earlier wave of activism, documents in 2018 often highlighted when a victim was of color but did not note when the victim was white. For example, the HRC report on fatal violence described each white victim only as a "transgender woman," but labeled victims of color as a "Black transgender woman," "transgender Latina woman," or "transgender woman of color."[13]

The focus on transgender women of color functioned as a new form of oppression Olympics. Activists described transgender women of color as "the most vulnerable people in our country today."[14] Press releases depicted "an epidemic of violence targeting transgender people, particularly transgender women of color" and argued that "it is clear that fatal violence disproportionately affects transgender women of color, and that the intersections of racism, sexism, homophobia, biphobia and transphobia conspire to deprive them of employment, housing, healthcare and other necessities, barriers that make them vulnerable."[15] By focusing on "the most vulnerable people" within the community, activists upheld their claim that their cause deserved the most attention, as their community was the most oppressed.[16] Notably, activists only highlighted danger and did not utilize these moments to note the relative safety of white transgender people and transgender men. The political field discourages mentioning that certain identity group members are safer than others, for fear that those less at risk will then lose interest in the cause. However, noting relative safety could potentially be empowering and provide an avenue for those least likely to experience violence to fight to protect those more at risk.[17] Furthermore, although this focus on particular patterns of violence was attention grabbing and likely highly effective within the social problems marketplace, it did not result in proposed solutions that attended to specifically reducing violence against trans women of color. Thus, though activists noted patterns more frequently in 2018 than they did from 1990 to 2009, due to the logics of identity-based anti-violence activism, that did not alter their responses to violence and instead functioned as a sort of shibboleth to signal allyship. As sociologist Salvador Vidal-Ortiz noted about academic usages of the phrase, "the transwoman of color becomes a singular figure in those moments, a utensil to reference at will."[18]

As they did from 1990 to 2009, activists in 2018 most commonly suggested education about levels of violence and remembering the dead as ways to respond to violence experienced by transgender people. Often these two responses were merged together, particularly when activists described the purpose of TDoR. As a GLAAD blog entry stated: "Transgender Day of Remembrance (TDOR) occurs on November 20th each year to observe the lives of transgender individuals who have been lost to anti-transgender violence. On this day, LGBTQ+ people and allies across the world hold marches, vigils, or other events to bring attention to anti-trans violence and the increasing rates of violence towards transgender people of color."[19] Similarly, activist Sawyer Stephenson described TDoR as "a beautiful and powerful way to honor those that we have lost to horrific, targeted violence. Inviting guest speakers is another way to honor victims and educate the public about the staggering rates of violence that trans people face on a daily basis."[20] Unfortunately these responses, as well as the transgender-inclusive federal hate crime legislation enacted in 2009, did not result in a discernible reduction in murders of transgender people.

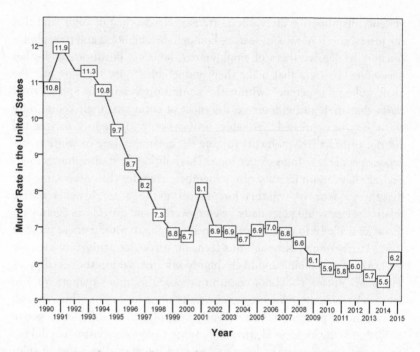

FIGURE 5.   Murder rate in the United States, 1990–2015. Murder rates are
calculated by taking the number of homicides and dividing them by the total
population in that year, then multiplying by 100,000. Counts of murders and
population size come from the CDC's National Vital Statistics System (NVSS).

THE LACK OF REDUCTION IN FATAL VIOLENCE
AGAINST TRANSGENDER PEOPLE

Homicide rates have dropped dramatically in the United States since the
early 1990s but increased slightly in 2015, as illustrated in figure 5.[21] The
drop occurred for both cisgender men and women and "across all racial and
ethnic groups, across all regions, and across all socioeconomic groups."[22]
However, despite nearly three decades of transgender anti-violence activism, levels of violence experienced by trans people are still high (see figure 6). It is impossible to calculate murder rates for transgender people
from 1990 to 2015, since national transgender population estimates were
not available until 2016.[23] Thus, figure 6 presents counts of homicides
based on my original dataset.[24] As the US population size increased during
this period, and it is possible that due to increased acceptance of transgender people the proportion of the population that is trans may have also

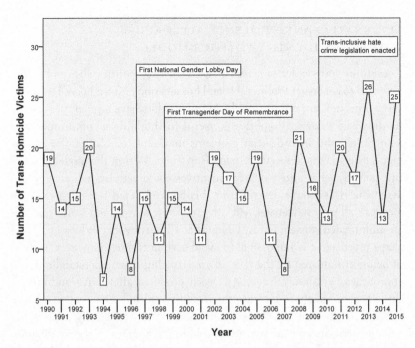

FIGURE 6. Number of murders of transgender people per year in the United States, 1990–2015. Counts are based on the dataset described in appendix B.

increased, figures 5 and 6 are not directly comparable. Nevertheless, it is clear that rates of homicide did not decrease for transgender people in the way that they did for other Americans.

During this period, activists were highly successful in achieving the most commonly suggested responses to violence. In the mid-1990s, activists began an educational campaign using events like Gender Lobby Days to educate politicians and the general public about levels of violence. Transgender Day of Remembrance began in 1998 as a way to ensure memorialization of the dead and is now an international event that is widely attended and receives substantial news coverage. Finally, transgender-inclusive hate crime legislation was enacted in 2009. However these accomplishments, which are highlighted in figure 6, do not appear to have reduced fatal violence experienced by trans people. Moreover, as I have detailed throughout this book, the responses to violence and the tactics used to achieve these accomplishments have resulted in numerous unintended consequences. Therefore, we must seek new approaches to reducing violence experienced by transgender people.

ALTERNATIVE ANTI-VIOLENCE APPROACHES
WITHIN THE IDENTITY POLITICS MODEL

Combining anti-violence activism with identity politics always has the potential to construct a vulnerable and homogenous subjecthood. However, these outcomes are not inevitable. Many scholars have argued that despite its drawbacks, identity politics is useful for building a community and being successful in the social problems marketplace.[25] Given the advantages, it seems that a rescue mission is in order. Within the model of identity politics, what anti-violence narratives could activists tell that would avoid the risks I have described in this book? I detail several here, with a caveat: all new narratives will construct new norms, and those can create unintended consequences. Given that all narratives produce ideas and shape practices, it is impossible to avoid such outcomes. However, instead of being intimidated by the risks of constructing new understandings and approaches, we should interrogate each proposed alternative and pursue those that are likely to increase the livability of life.[26] One way to achieve this is through what I term *conscientious narrative telling*. The frames utilized by activists and the narratives told in the attempt to reduce violence have substantial consequences, many of which are unintended. As such, we must pursue alternative narratives and framings of violence experienced by transgender people that would both construct transgender as a livable life and reduce the violence experienced by trans people. Possible ways to achieve this include telling narratives about successful resistance to violence, attending to all victims of violence rather than a famous few, refusing to participate in oppression Olympics, highlighting patterns of violence and crafting solutions to address those patterns, and constructing a multifaceted subjecthood through narratives of transgender joy.

Highlight Successful Resistance

In order to gain attention within the social problems marketplace, identity-based anti-violence activists have focused on the most extreme forms of violence against members of their identity group, including murders and completed sexual assaults. Although effective in the political field, such narratives are disempowering, as they terrify group members and teach them that violence is unpreventable. An alternative is to tell narratives about nonfatal violence and uncompleted sexual assaults, particularly about people who were attacked and responded in a way that stopped the violence against them. Heroic narratives about those who physically fought back against oppression are central to American culture; such a story is at the

heart of the country's origin narrative as well as many of its books and films. Thus, it is surprising that fighting back against attacks is not often discussed by identity-based anti-violence activists. However, dominant narratives about resistance tend to be confined to history and fiction and/ or are focused on straight, cisgender, white men as the heroic resistors. By contrast, dominant US culture only valorizes leaders of marginalized groups who advocate nonviolence in the face of violent oppression, such as the heroicizing of Martin Luther King Jr. or Mahatma Gandhi, as compared to the villainization of Malcolm X.

Although such narratives are rare, scholars writing about two forms of violence—men's sexual assault and partner violence against women—have begun to advocate for the telling of stories about victims resisting violence. Psychologist Jill Cermele, following the work of theorist Sharon Marcus, argued that telling narratives of resistance shows the world that it is possible for women to resist men's violence.[27] The dominant understanding of sexual assault is that women are weak and vulnerable and men are strong and dangerous; thus fighting back is futile.[28] However, women regularly fight back against sexual assault, and when they do so they are usually effective in stopping the attack.[29] Telling narratives about this resistance may decrease men's willingness to attempt violence against women and may increase the likelihood that women will resist. Narratives about successful resistance provide a new script, one in which women can be strong and powerful and men are not invulnerable. Such narratives give women hope that their resistance will be successful and can also educate women about proven techniques for resistance that they can employ in the case of an attack.

Scholars advocating for more narratives of resistance argue that these stories need to be told in multiple forums. In addition to activists telling these narratives, they must also appear in the news and the courtroom. Sociologists Jocelyn Hollander and Katie Rodgers demonstrated that despite the fact that women regularly resist sexual assaults, newspaper narratives about rapes and attempted rapes rarely mention resistance. Thus, women reading newspapers right now "learn that they are vulnerable to sexual assault but not how to fight it off."[30] Similarly, legal scholar Leigh Goodmark argued that women who have fought back against their abusive partners are regularly counseled not to speak about their resistance in court.[31] Currently, judges expect victims of relationship violence to be passive; those who are not are not granted the same protections by law enforcement officials. Goodmark demonstrated that the origin of this passive "ideal" victim can be traced, in part, to the battered women's movement. In an attempt to gain traction in the social problems marketplace, the movement portrayed women as highly vulnerable and unable to defend themselves. By silencing narratives of resistance, activists unintentionally made it harder for women who do fight back to be seen as legitimate victims in the eyes of the law. This silencing has another important unintended consequence: rather than empowering women (the ostensible goal of the battered women's movement), it denies them self-determination by prohibiting them from telling their stories.

Until judges come to accept that victims can fight back and still be worthy of protection, those who do fight back may be treated as perpetrators.[32] For those identity-based organizations that typically focus on homicide, such as those working to reduce violence against transgender people, people of color, and gay men and lesbians, the focus on fatalities may have resulted in the dead being easily seen as victims, whereas those who fight back and live are not. Indeed, several trans people who have fought back against their attackers in recent years have been jailed for this resistance. In June 2011, CeCe McDonald, a twenty-two-year-old black trans woman, and four friends were walking home from buying groceries. They passed a bar, where they encountered three people who started shouting racist and transphobic slurs at them.[33] One smashed a glass in CeCe's face, cutting her. During the melee that followed, CeCe stabbed one of the attackers with a pair of scissors. CeCe was charged with second degree murder and "accepted" a plea deal that would result in a forty-one-month prison sentence. Like CeCe, Ky Peterson, a twenty-year-old black trans man, was also jailed for fighting back. In October 2011, Ky was propositioned by a cisgender man outside a convenience store.[34] When Ky rebuffed his advances, the man followed him, hit him in the back of the head, and raped him. Ky fought back, eventually pulling a gun from his backpack and shooting the perpetrator. Ky also "accepted" a plea deal and was sentenced to twenty years in prison.

The risk of being sent to prison for resisting an assault is particularly concerning for trans people, as they are likely to be assigned to a prison based on the sex they were labeled at birth rather than their gender identity. This increases the risk of experiencing violence in prison, and US prisons are notorious for transphobic harassment of prisoners, including denial of access to health care such as hormones.[35] These increased risks make it vital for activists and journalists to start regularly telling narratives of transgender people's resistance to violence. If such narratives cast resisting victims in a positive light and become part of the dominant narrative of violence against transgender people, judges will be less likely to see those who fight back as deserving punishment. Moreover, a key component of antiviolence activism should be implementing legislation that protects victims who fight back from legal penalties. A trans person being attacked should not be faced with a choice between going to jail or dying.

Make All Victims Matter

One of the central goals of identity-based anti-violence activism is to make the lives of identity group members socially valuable. Although advantageous within the current political field, the practice described in chapter 3 of focusing on a few famous victims goes against this goal, as it sends the message that some group members are more valuable than others— that some lives matter more and are more worthy of being mourned. By expressing outrage about murders, activists spread the message that those lives are worth protecting. If this outrage is only expressed about a few victims, particularly if those victims are not representative of most victims, the unintended message is that only a few types of lives are worth protecting. Thus, if the goal is to establish trans people as valuable, it is imperative that activists focus on all victims, both of homicides and of nonfatal violence, showing the value of all their lives. Although only focused on murders, the website Remembering Our Dead was a step in this direction, as were TDoR events. On the site and at these events, no victims were supposed to be prioritized over others. By focusing on all victims, the website and events give people a (albeit potentially overwhelming) sense of the scope of the problem. Moreover, the value of each victim is proclaimed. However, where both the website and TDoR events often fall short is in terms of humanizing victims. With the focus of including all homicide victims, the information about each is minimized, often including just their name, the date of their death, and a brief description of how they died. This is successful in terms of conveying the sheer volume of violence but is lacking in terms of valuing individual lives. Narratives about victims' lives and deaths humanize them and are effective in the social problems marketplace. However, as this book has demonstrated, how those narratives are told needs to be carefully attended to. Nevertheless, if activists engage in conscientious narrative telling, they will be able to demonstrate the value of all the lives within their identity group. Of course, the importance of focusing on all victims and not just a few holds true for more than just activists. It is also vital that academics examining these forms of violence avoid the pitfalls of focusing on famous victims and instead broaden their lens to include all victims.

Boycott the Oppression Olympics

A key tactic utilized to gain attention within the social problems marketplace is to claim that your group is more oppressed than other groups. This

166 / Chapter 7

framing is ultimately self-defeating, as it pits identity groups with overlapping membership against each other. Moreover, emphasizing oppression does not encourage resistance or help produce livable lives. Rather than argue that they are the most oppressed, identity-based anti-violence groups would likely be more effective in reducing violence if they attended to moments of success. As I detailed in chapter 5, trans activists often dismissed moments in which violence levels appeared to be decreasing. However, attention to those moments is key to reducing violence. If activists can determine what caused a downturn in levels of violence, they can utilize that information to maintain the decline and to further reduce violence.

Similarly, in the fight to claim that they are the most vulnerable, identity-based anti-violence activists often emphasize the proportion of a population that is likely to experience such violence. For example, a cover of *The Nation* in 2014 proclaimed in large, bold text: "1 IN 5 WOMEN IS SEXUALLY ASSAULTED IN COLLEGE: Are Universities Capable of Providing Justice?"[36] Such a phrasing implies that such violence is inevitable and that the only response is the after-the-fact solution of "justice." It also emphasizes those who have experienced violence, rather than those who have not. A different approach to identity-based anti-violence activism might proclaim: "4 OUT OF 5 WOMEN ARE NOT SEXUALLY ASSAULTED IN COLLEGE: What Can Be Done to Make it 5/5?" By flipping the script and highlighting moments in which violence does not occur, activists may be able to reveal patterns that can be used to help increase the number of people within the identity group who do not experience violence. Moreover, emphasizing moments in which a large majority of group members are not victims of violence may help to prevent the construction of a vulnerable subjecthood.

Craft Solutions to Address Patterns of Violence

To successfully reduce violence, identity-based anti-violence activists must attend to the patterns of violence against their group and develop solutions that address the revealed causal factors. Rather than attributing all violence experienced by transgender people to anti-transgender hatred, successful anti-violence campaigns must explore alternative causes of violence and their accompanying solutions. In order to do that, however, they must be aware of the patterns of violence.[37] Once patterns are known, activists can then engage in legal scholar Kimberlé Crenshaw's proposed "bottom-up" solution to inequality, in which addressing the needs of those who are most disadvantaged within an identity group ensures that the needs of everyone within the group are met.[38]

Currently, violence experienced by transgender people is understudied, particularly when that violence is fatal. My original dataset of murders of transgender people in the United States from 1990 to 2015 (described in appendix B) is one attempt to address this lack of knowledge. Transgender is an internally heterogeneous category, and transgender people's diverse social locations also influence the violence against them. Thus, understanding this violence requires an intersectional analysis. Such an analysis demonstrates that gender plays a multidimensional role in these homicides, and violence against transgender people is also shaped by race and sexuality. An examination of this dataset reveals that transgender women are murdered much more often than transgender men, and transgender women of color are killed at higher rates than white transgender women. Finally, trans women are often murdered in sexual interactions with cisgender men.

This raises a new set of questions around why these patterns exist and what can be done to reduce this violence. Why do black transgender women experience such high murder rates? There is substantial existing research that can help answer this question and points to promising policies for reducing violence. Black transgender women are subject to multiple types of discrimination, including inequalities related to being transgender, black, and women. The gender and racial patterns in transgender homicide appear to be caused by a complex interaction between beliefs about gender and beliefs about sexuality, as well as intersections of racial and gendered discrimination that push black transgender women into two situations strongly linked to risk for homicide: poverty and prostitution. Although there is a debate among scholars about whether relative or absolute deprivation (i.e., economic inequality or poverty) most influences homicide rates, scholars generally agree that being poor greatly increases one's risk of being murdered.[39] Moreover, as discussed in chapter 4, part of the gender disparity in murders of transgender people is related to violence in sexual relationships. Cisgender men in sexual interactions with transgender women sometimes attack their partners due to the belief that transgender women are "whores," shame about their own desires, and/or because of a belief that transgender women are "gender deceivers" who deserve to be punished.[40] These murders may be a form of what homicide scholars call *honor contests*, in which cisgender men perceive their honor to be challenged and respond with violence as a way to reclaim their social status.[41]

Though sexual situations increase the risk of murder for all transgender women, transgender women of color experience additional risks, since racial inequality combined with *transmisogyny*—a mixture of sexism and transphobia—results in a particularly precarious economic situation for transgender women of color.[42] In the United States, large levels of economic inequality combined with racial inequality have produced high poverty rates among people of color. Racial inequality then further concentrates this poverty through residential segregation, creating neighborhoods characterized by *anomie*.[43] As sociologists Judith Blau and Peter Blau argued, this "general state of disorganization, distrust, and smoldering aggression . . . easily erupts into violence."[44] Racial inequality combined with transmisogyny greatly increases the risk of transgender women of color living in racially segregated neighborhoods with concentrated levels of poverty and high levels of anomie, intensifying their risk of homicide. Though poverty alone raises the risk for experiencing violence, this risk is further magnified for transgender women due to beliefs about sexuality. As described by sociologist Elijah Anderson, neighborhoods with concentrated disadvantages are ruled by the *code of the streets*, a situation in which it is even more likely that challenges to someone's social status will be met with violence.[45] It may be that in these situations in which "respect" and "honor" must be closely guarded, heterosexual, cisgender men are particularly likely to be violent toward transgender women in sexual interactions. This risk is heightened by the fact that transgender women of color are often denied access to legal forms of employment and so turn to sex work to survive, increasing their chances of being in dangerous sexual situations with cisgender men.[46] Thus, the intersections of race, gender, sexuality, and class put trans women of color, especially black trans women, at high risk for homicide.

Though violence from heterosexual cisgender men in sexual interactions may explain a substantial part of the gender gap in these homicides, we must examine other factors to fully understand the gendered racial gap. Although transphobia damages the lives of all transgender people, intersections of race and gender cause more severe economic consequences for trans women of color. Transphobia in the form of family rejection, harassment in school, employment discrimination, and denial of social services weakens an individual's safety net. For those already facing high risks of poverty due to racial inequality and sexism, the additional economic precarity caused by transphobia can literally mean the difference between life and death.

A portion of transgender people of all races experience rejection by their families.[47] However, studies have shown that transgender youth of color are much more likely to be kicked out of the home than are whites.[48] That rejection may have more dire consequences for those trans people whose social safety net has already been damaged by racial inequality, as familial rejection of transgender people has been linked to decreased educational attainment, poverty, homelessness, and engaging in survival sex work, all factors connected to increased risk of being murdered.[49]

Schools are another site in which the intersections of race and gender are particularly detrimental to trans people of color. The mistreatment of students of color, especially black students, has been widely documented by scholars.[50] Due to associations between blackness and criminality, black students are watched more carefully by teachers and staff, increasing the chance that they will be caught breaking rules; moreover, when caught, they are punished more harshly.[51] These factors decrease educational attainment, cause higher dropout rates among black and Latinx students, and create a *school-to-prison pipeline*.[52] For transgender students of color, this discrimination based on race is then compounded by transphobia, as transgender students experience high levels of harassment due to gender and/or perceived homosexuality.[53] Experiencing transphobia and/or homophobia from both other students as well as school staff decreases transgender students' educational attainment and increases their likelihood of dropping out of school.[54] The combined factors of racial and gender inequality in schools thus increases transgender youth of color's risk for poverty and, consequently, homicide.

Similar factors combine in the job market to decrease wages of transgender women of color. Race-based employment discrimination is widespread in the United States, as is employment discrimination against transgender people.[55] Transgender people who have not obtained a legal name change and/or changed the sex marker on their official documents— processes that can be unaffordable for poor transgender people—are particularly at risk for employment discrimination.[56] Indeed, employment discrimination against transgender people is such a significant factor in the United States that needs assessments for transgender communities often list employment as the most important unmet need of transgender people.[57] The 2015 US Transgender Survey found that transgender respondents had unemployment rates three times higher than the general US population.[58] Employment discrimination does not affect all trans people equally, however. Just as cisgender people face race-based employment discrimination, so do transgender people. As a consequence, transgender people of color are much more likely than whites to be unemployed, in poverty, and homeless.[59]

Transphobia is not the only form of gender-based discrimination faced by transgender people. Gender is multidimensional and inequalities exist between transgender men and transgender women, as transgender women are discriminated against for their femininity. This transmisogyny increases employment discrimination against trans women.[60] Indeed, although earnings of trans women are reduced by almost a third following their transition, trans men sometimes find that their pay increases.[61] When these two forms of gender inequality combine with race-based employment discrimination, transgender women of color are at particularly high risk for poverty and its associated risk of experiencing violence.

Though many Americans faced with sudden job loss or homelessness will seek the assistance of the safety net of social services such as welfare and homeless shelters, these services are often not accessible to transgender people.[62] Most homeless shelters are sex segregated. Regularly, shelter staff will only accept trans people into shelters designated for members of their birth sex. As such, homeless trans people are faced with a "choice" between living on the streets or denying their gender identities, and especially in the case of trans women, potentially experiencing harassment and violence in the shelter.[63] Fearing violence in shelters, some trans people "choose" to live on the streets, increasing their risk of being murdered.[64]

For poor trans women who are denied access to both legal forms of employment and social services, one of the few remaining options is sex work. Studies have shown that experiencing familial rejection, harassment in school, employment discrimination, and homelessness substantially increases the likelihood that a transgender woman will sell sex.[65] Combined with economic inequality, social pressures to obtain body modifications also encourage participation in sex work. Although not all trans people desire body modifications, many do, as body modifications such as hormones and surgeries can help their body fit their self-identity and may increase their ability to move through the world without experiencing transphobic harassment.[66] However, body modifications are often expensive, and impoverished trans women may engage in prostitution to earn the needed funds.[67] Although potentially lucrative, prostitution, like living in neighborhoods with concentrated disadvantages, is incredibly dangerous.[68] Due to racial and gender inequality, the risk of violence associated with prostitution is not evenly distributed. Though trans men do engage in prostitution, trans women are much more likely to sell sex, and transgender women of color are much more likely than whites to have done sex work.[69]

Thus, transphobia alone cannot explain the patterns of murders of transgender people in the United States. Instead, intersections of transphobia, sexism, and racism put transgender women of color in situations that greatly increase their risk of being murdered. Beliefs about gender and sexuality put transgender women at heightened risk for violence in sexual situations, and familial rejection, harassment in school, employment discrimination, and denial of social services are particularly likely to push transgender women of color into poverty and prostitution, substantially increasing the likelihood that they will be killed.

One of the many reasons hate crime legislation fails to reduce murder rates may be the fact that these multiple intersecting factors shape risk of experiencing violence. Hatred of transgender people is not the only dynamic causing violence against transgender people. To reduce transgender homicides, we must address the factors that cause high murder rates in general in the United States, including extreme levels of racial and economic inequality.[70] Moreover, since sex work is linked to murders of transgender women, decreasing violence against sex workers should also be a priority. Studies have shown that legalizing prostitution greatly reduces violence against those who sell sex.[71] Despite this evidence, those engaged in anti-violence activism on behalf of transgender people between 1990 and 2009 never called for the legalization of sex work in their anti-violence materials. Activists were also startlingly mum on the issue in 2018. In its report on homicide, which does include analysis of the large number of victims involved in sex work, HRC came the closest to calling for legalization: "We must educate policy makers on how criminalization of sex work contributes to a higher risk of violence and hold law enforcement agencies accountable to equally serving transgender individuals regardless of their engagement in sex work."[72] However, this call falls short of demanding legalization and has not resulted in an active campaign from HRC to change government policies related to sex work.

As poverty increases the risk of being murdered, anti-violence efforts should include work to reduce employment discrimination against transgender people.[73] Historically, policy makers in the United States have proposed legislation that outlaws employment discrimination in order to address inequalities in hiring, promotion, and firing. Paradoxically, however, these laws can sometimes increase discrimination against the group they are trying to protect. For example, research on the Americans with Disabilities Act and the Age Discrimination in Employment Act has shown that these laws may have actually reduced the employment of older workers and people with disabilities, as employers avoid hiring members of protected groups for fear of being sued if they fire them later.[74] Although punitive approaches have produced mixed results, scholars have demonstrated that policies that provide employers with incentives to recruit, hire, and retain employees from groups that have historically been discriminated against are effective, especially when the program assigns responsibility for employee diversity to a particular person or team.[75] Thus, anti-violence efforts should include incentive programs for employing transgender people, particularly transgender women of color.

Though inequality in employment is one key factor increasing violence against transgender people, it is not the only one. To reduce violence against transgender people there must also be policies that work to decrease other dynamics rooted in transphobic attitudes, including familial rejection, discrimination in schools, denial of social services, and violence in sexual situations.[76] Although outlawing behavior based on biased beliefs like transphobia has proven ineffective, recent research points to other avenues for effectively reducing transphobic beliefs, including interpersonal contact with a transgender person or an LGB ally, short activities in which cisgender people are asked to take the perspective of a transgender person, and webinars and other educational programs.[77] As all of these methods are relatively short (ranging from ten minutes to an hour), they can easily be introduced in business places, schools, government agencies, churches, and parenting classes.

Trans activists did occasionally call for some of these solutions. However, they were overshadowed by the more prevalent calls for hate crime legislation and were often not framed as ways to decrease violence. Indeed, of the more than one thousand activist documents I examined from between 1990 and 2009, just seven suggested that reducing employment discrimination would lessen violence. Anti-violence causes garner widespread support within the social problems marketplace, and making an explicit argument that policies such as employment incentive programs and education programs designed to reduce anti-transgender bias would reduce violence should increase the chances of such proposals becoming a reality.

Construct a Multifaceted Subjecthood

One of the main goals of most identity-based anti-violence movements has been to highlight the violence experienced by their group and mark that violence as wrong. Many of those groups have been successful in educating the public about levels of violence, so much so that some identities have become borderline synonymous with being at risk for experiencing violence. Those vested with vulnerable subjecthood, such as women, transgender people, gay men and lesbians, and people of color, are often pitied by those outside their groups. However, there are glorious, beautiful aspects of being a member of these identities. This fact is often obscured in anti-violence work, but if attended to, it could be a powerful tool in reducing violence.

Perceived vulnerability should not be the defining aspect of any community, as it makes for an unlivable life and can actually increase violence experienced by the group.[78] As I argued in chapter 5, the construction of *vulnerable subjecthoods* has caused members of those groups to live in fear. High levels of fear can be extremely disempowering, making it less likely that group members are able to engage in activism against violence. Moreover, narratives of vulnerability can actually increase violence against the group, as they mark the group as an easy target and teach group members that they are unable to protect themselves.[79] This is not to say that experiences of violence should not be discussed; they absolutely should. However, vulnerability should not be the only factor focused on. Instead, activists should continue to work to create *valuable subjecthoods* while also attending to a third aspect: vibrancy. By portraying their group as a *vibrant subjecthood* through highlighting joy and facilitating pride, activists can better convey the complexity of their group members' lives, constructing a *multifaceted subjecthood*. Portraying this complexity and highlighting vibrancy are key to reducing violence against the group.

Highlight Transgender Joy and Celebrate the Living   In order to produce transgender as an empowered, desirable category, trans activists should tell narratives about the joyful parts of trans people's lives. When trans activists spoke of the value of "education" to reduce violence, they mainly focused on education about levels of violence and other factors relating to discrimination. However, violence reduction strategies should also include education about how amazing and wonderful it is to be transgender. As activist Janet Mock has argued, "We can't *only* celebrate trans women of color in memoriam. We must begin uplifting trans women of color, speaking their names and praises, in their lives."[80] Similarly, author Kai Cheng Thom stated: "We should be talking about the living as well as the dead. We should be offering young trans women just starting to think about themselves as such the hope that they will be able to live long and happy lives."[81]

As discussed in chapter 5, a regularly named goal of transgender antiviolence activists was to value transgender lives. Activists saw constructing a valuable subjecthood as key to decreasing violence. As an early *Tapestry* article stated: "The sad fact is that murders of transgendered persons—crossdressers and transsexual people—are all too common. And there will be more unless our society learns that transgendered persons are people, too."[82] However, because of activists' focus on fatal violence, that valuing usually concentrates on mourning the dead rather than celebrating the lives of the living. This construction of *valuable victims* often occurred through naming the dead, including a picture of the victim when one was available, and talking about how the victim was loved and missed.

Although somewhat prevalent throughout the period from 1990 to 2009, the practice of including a picture and describing the victim as widely loved and deeply missed was rampant during 2018. This was facilitated by the rise in social media use between 2009 and 2018, as victim photos and statements from loved ones included in these reports often originated in social media posts. The reports on homicides issued by HRC and NCAVP in 2018 both included lists of victims with at least one photograph per victim and a statement about how much they meant to their now griev- ing family and friends. The HRC report described individual victims as a "great person," "always trying to help somebody," a "wonderful soul," "inspirational," "fun and positive," a "very sweet, kind, lovely person," "beautiful," and as having an "incredible personality."[83] Similarly, the NCAVP report included such descriptors as "a caring person," "loved," "the sunshine of our family," a "playful spirit," "a light, always trying to make everyone around her happy," and "the sweetest, most kind, most courageous, most selfless person that would give the shirt off her back to anyone in need."[84] Both reports also highlighted how much the vic- tim was mourned, including statements of grief from family and friends and tallies of the number of attendees at vigils and memorials. These moments of highlighting the joy that the person brought to others and the extreme sadness at their death are beautiful and moving. However, to reduce violence, transgender people must be celebrated while living, not just when dead.

Within these anti-violence documents, there is a missing narrative of transgender joy. This is a common failing of identity-based anti-violence activism. Education scholar Valarie Harwood, who criticized the discourse of *wounded truths* that she found circulating in discussions of queer youth, suggested that rather than tell just wounded truths, we should also tell narratives of the joys of being queer. She argued that along with informa- tion about some of the negative portions of the lives of queer youth, there should also be discussions of "happiness or pleasure."[85] Similarly, sociolo- gist Tey Meadow argued in a blog post about teen suicide titled "Queer Children Are Dying . . . But Many More Are Living":

> The struggles and recent deaths of so many youth deserve our atten-
> tion, discussion, and deep grief. We need to hear these stories and
> acknowledge these losses. However the media's singular focus on them,
> to the exclusion of any positive coverage of LGBTQ youth, creates
> a deadly echo chamber. The repetitive tale about the inevitability of
> our collective failure to address the pain felt by many LGBTQ youth
> may translate into high readership rates, but it doesn't translate into

inspiration for the kids who are still here. . . . They need stories of teen-
agers just like them who are safe and happy *now*.[86]

Meadow extended this argument in a subsequent blog headlined "Gay
Is Great (Not Just Tolerable)": "The time has come to change the conversation. It's time for us to throw away all of our old language around
LGBTQ youth: words like tolerance, sensitivity and respect. It's time to
replace them with a language of celebration. It's time to abandon phrases
like 'it's okay to be gay' and replace them with others like 'it's great to be
gay,' 'your gender is beautiful,' and 'difference enriches all of our lives.'"[87]
There have been some moments of such celebration within trans activism. For example, in 2012 Jen Richards, frustrated by the lack of websites
that "talked about positive transgender experiences," created We Happy
Trans.[88] The project highlighted joyful aspects of being transgender on its
website and on Twitter and Facebook for several years.[89] It included a range
of content, including reposts of articles like "10 Trans Women of Color in
Love" as well as promotions of "Trans 100." This annual event, co-run by
We Happy Trans, was intended to "celebrate the living" by highlighting
trans activists.[90]

A call for a celebration of transness does not mean that activists should
ignore violence against transgender people. Instead, it is an appeal for bal-
ance in the portrayal of transgender lives. Much like anthropologist Carole
Vance's argument that discussions of "female sexuality" should focus on
both "pleasure and danger," narratives about transgender lives should
highlight gender euphoria, not just dysphoria, as well as transgender joy,
not just risk for violence.[91] Indeed, a focus on the wonderful aspects of
being transgender is likely to decrease levels of violence. Empowerment
and increased confidence have been shown to reduce the risk of experiencing violence.[92] Transgender anti-violence activists occasionally mentioned
such a benefit. As Riki Wilchins argued: "When I see transpeople, what I
see are people who feel radically disempowered, who are ashamed of their
bodies, ashamed of what they are, afraid to come out, with good reason,
afraid of violence, who often are extremely depressed about their social
position. I think just helping people, like me, to get out of that and start to
feel some sense of empowerment, is by itself one of the more radical things
that you can do."[93] Unfortunately, such a "radical" approach was rarely
advocated by anti-violence activists between 1990 and 2009. Some more
recent activist endeavors work to explicitly to blend anti-violence activism with a celebration of being transgender. The Trans Day of Resilience
art project was started in 2014 to "create visions of a world beyond fear

FIGURE 7. *Trans Power* poster by Rommy Sobrado-Torrico. Created for Trans Day of Resilience 2016 in collaboration with Translatin@ Coalition. Used with permission.

and violence."[94] It, like TDoR, occurs on November 20. The organizers explained: "Trans Day of Resilience is an expansion and reimagining of Trans Day of Remembrance, not a replacement. We need space to mourn the dead as well as celebrate, support, and defend the living. We know that trans people of color have always existed and have always used art to survive. In these times of struggle, we offer you this art as a balm for the spirit and fuel for trans resistance."[95] This art (see an example in figure 7) blends anti-violence statements with empowering messages about trans lives.

Flip the Script on the Deception Narrative In addition to empowering transgender people, a celebration of transgender identities could also reduce violence by correcting common misconceptions. A dominant narrative told by both perpetrators and journalists is that transgender women are "deceivers" who "trick" heterosexual men into same-sex sex.[96] Anti-violence activists occasionally mentioned this narrative in order to discredit it, calling it "bogus," "absurd," and "defamatory."[97] This is understandable, as such an explanation is frequently used both to blame the victim for the assault and to try to reduce the charges from homicide to manslaughter by claiming it was a "crime of passion." However, these dismissals discouraged activists from exploring the possibility that the perpetrators actually did feel deceived. If feelings of deception, however abhorrent, prompt the violence, it seems prudent to work to dispel the factors that cause those feelings. Unfortunately, the identity-based anti-violence model encourages a focus on hatred as the only cause for violence against the group and an "us versus them" mentality. Thus, activists treated claims of feeling deceived as themselves an attempt at deception. They refused the possibility that it was an actual factor that, once changed, would reduce levels of violence. For example, HRC president Cheryl Jacques argued: "Gwen's murder was motivated by hatred; to claim anything else is the only real deception."[98]

In contrast to the dismissals of narratives of deception, a celebration of transness could help eliminate such feeling by highlighting how transgender people are in no way being deceptive by living as their gender identity. Such a stance rarely occurred in anti-violence documents. An exception was a GenderPAC press release that argued: "In fact, Brandon's 'true identity' was revealed every single morning as he left his house and lived openly and publicly as a man. Each of us has the right to express our gender orientation as we see fit and to have our gender orientation respected by our family, friends, neighbors, the media, the courts, and law enforcement without fear of discrimination and violence."[99] Future anti-violence activism could go even further, highlighting the beauty of living one's truth, regardless

of dominant gender norms. Messages in mainstream culture that transgender people living as members of their gender identity rather than the
sex they were labeled at birth is a matter of *truth* rather than *deception*
would greatly reduce violence.

In chapter 4 I detailed a number of patterns obscured by activists who
focused on hatred of transgender people as the only cause for this violence.
In addition to eliding patterns of race and gender in the risk for violence,
the narrative that all transgender people are at risk at all times because of
transphobia also ignored differential risk in terms of body modification.
Transgender anti-violence activists almost never mentioned body modification. However, of the 289 homicide victims between 1990 and 2009, just 4
(1.4%) had had genital surgery. Although we do not currently have data on
what percentage of transgender people have genital surgery, it is unlikely
that it is less than 2 percent. Thus, we can conclude that those working to
reduce violence should take this pattern into account and perhaps engage
in educational campaigns about both the existence, and wonderfulness, of
women with what are traditionally considered "penises" and men with
what are often labeled "vaginas."[100] Such a celebration of bodily diversity
may greatly reduce the amount of fatal violence against transgender people
who have not had genital surgery.

Promote Pride   Feelings of pride can be empowering and are often a central
goal of movements engaged in identity politics.[101] Despite the advantages,
historically the transgender rights movement has not focused on pride in
the narratives they tell about what it means to be transgender. Transgender
groups participate in LGBT pride events and occasionally mention the need
to be proud about being transgender, but there are rarely transgender-
specific pride events or narratives. As activist Gwendolyn Smith argued in
2001: "It's June, and around here that means Pride Month. And that means
that I want to talk a bit about transgender pride. That sounds almost like an
oxymoron. While transgendered people are no stranger to guilt and shame,
pride can be very elusive."[102] Moreover, when there is a pride narrative, it
is rarely coupled with anti-violence activism. One exception was Monica
Robert's speech at the 2009 New England Transgender Pride March and
Rally, in which she proclaimed:

> It's time to stop wandering in the desert of shame and guilt. It's time
> for us to cast aside the woe is me victimhood about being transgender
> Americans and boldly stride forward towards the oasis of freedom,
> equality, justice and pride in who we are as transgender men and
> women. Our pioneering predecessors passed a torch to us. As their

successors, it's up to us to keep it lit, hold it high and not allow anyone to douse the freedom flame until we can pass that torch on to the next generation of transpeople. . . . We must act for not only the transkids that Barbara Walters profiled on 20/20 and others yet unborn, but for our fallen brothers and sisters such as Deborah Forte, Chanelle and Gabrielle Pickett, Rita Hester, Tyra Hunter, Gwen Araujo, Brandon Teena and F.C. Martinez. We must act for every transperson who fought, marched, organized, lobbied, lived a stealth life, raised hell and died so that our lives could be a little bit better than theirs. . . . Never again must we allow ourselves to sit still and allow ourselves to be victimized by friend or foe. It's past time for us to say it loud, "I'm Transgender and Proud."[103]

This rare example shows the transformative potential of a pride narrative coupled with anti-violence work. Rather than constructing a vulnerable subjecthood, such a pairing can produce empowered, vibrant subjects who, though aware of horrible acts of violence, strive to ensure that such violence never occurs again. This statement of pride is notably different from much of the anti-violence rhetoric that I have analyzed in this book, in that it does not encourage the audience to *identify with the dead* or to see violence as unstoppable. Instead of telling listening transgender people that they could be next, Monica Roberts bid them to maintain the "freedom flame" and to refuse to be victimized. Central to this was a call for "pride in who we are as transgender men and women." In making this rallying cry, Roberts referenced other identity-based anti-violence movements, particularly the civil rights movement, as well as past actions of resistance by those who lived as a gender other than the one they were labeled at birth. Roberts argued:

Nelson Mandela said a decade ago that to be free is not merely to cast off one's chains, but to live in a way that respects and enhances the lives of others. Once we cast off the chains of self-doubt, shame, and selfhatred, the first people we owe respect to are ourselves. So how do we do that? We show respect for ourselves by standing up and fighting for our rights and our basic humanity like my African-American GLBT brothers and sisters did at Philadelphia's Dewey's Lunch counter in 1965. We show respect for ourselves by standing up and fighting like our brothers and sisters did at San Francisco's Compton's Cafeteria in 1967. We show respect for ourselves like Miss Major, the late Sylvia Rivera and our brothers and sisters did almost 40 years ago this month at Stonewall in 1969. We show respect for ourselves when we stand up and loudly proclaim in one voice that we will no longer meekly accept or tolerate second-class treatment or second class citizenship. We are putting friends, foes and "frenemies" on notice that we are demanding an upgrade to first class citizenship.[104]

As I discussed in chapter 6, calls to fight back are rare in transgender anti-violence materials.

Unlike in many other social movements that have worked to replace shame with pride, pride has not become dominant within the transgender rights movement, and pride narratives are incredibly rare in anti-violence activism in general.[105] Why? I explore five possibilities here: (1) the lack of a suitable target for anger, (2) the use of a murder as a flashpoint story, (3) the first national event for the group being a memorial for the dead, (4) rhetoric that being "out" or "proud" has caused fatal violence, and (5) integration with groups portrayed as "them" in "us versus them" rhetoric.

Sociologists Lory Britt and David Heise argued that activists engaged in identity politics work to move members of their group through four stages of emotion: from shame to fear to anger to pride.[106] This *emotion work* is no easy task, in part because, as sociologist Deborah Gould discussed, anger is not seen as an appropriate feeling for marginalized people to express.[107] Despite that limitation, Gould demonstrated that members of ACT UP (the AIDS Coalition to Unleash Power) were able to transform their grief around AIDS-related deaths into anger by focusing on government actors and others with social power who they felt were not doing enough to stop the epidemic. It may be that pride is a missing discourse in many anti-violence movements because activists do not highlight a suitable target for their group's anger.[108] As such, their emotions remain stuck at the "fear" stage. As legal scholar Dean Spade argued, transgender anti-violence activists have focused on transphobic individuals as the source of violence, rather than on the larger systemic inequalities that increase transgender people's risk for violence.[109] If activists switched their attention to being angry at social structures and institutions, rather than being fearful of transphobic individuals, they might be able to develop pride as part of their anti-violence project. As Gwendolyn Smith stated about the ROD website: "When you look at the names here, remember these people. Cry for those who we have lost, and let your anger out for a society that would allow them to die."[110] Unfortunately, this anger at *trans necropolitics*—meaning a social system that facilitates trans deaths—has not become central to transgender anti-violence activism.[111]

As I discussed in chapter 3, most identity-based rights movements have a *flashpoint story*, a narrative about the event that is said to have "sparked" the movement. Unlike the civil rights movement with Rosa Parks and the gay rights movement with the Stonewall riots, the modern transgender rights movement's beginnings are often attributed to a murder, that of Brandon Teena.[112] By choosing a homicide to rally around, activists shaped conceptions of what it means to be transgender and likely influenced the development of a pride narrative. Although many flashpoint narratives include acts of violence, such as the police brutality that ignited the Stonewall riots, focusing on fatal violence by ordinary citizens may have a dampening effect on pride rhetoric due to its tendency to evoke fear and its lack of a suitable target for anger. By contrast, attention to nonfatal violence and/or violence done by social institutions and structures as well as government officials may facilitate a pride narrative.

Until 2009, TDoR was the only transgender-specific national event in the United States. As an article in *FTMi* argued in 2002, "In terms of transgender-related days, we only have one—the Day of Remembrance— to remember people who have been murdered. . . . It struck us as a shame that there was no day of celebration."[113] It is likely that the focus on, and the resources required to hold, annual TDoRs diminished activists' abilities to host additional events dedicated to more uplifting messages. To address this gap, Rachel Crandall started the Transgender Day of Visibility in 2009. As Rachel argued: "Whenever I hear about our community, it seems to be from Remembrance Day which is always so negative because it's about people who were killed. So one night I couldn't sleep and I decided why don't I try to do something about that."[114] Transgender Day of Visibility was intended to "focus on all the good things in the trans community"; however, in recent years the event has been criticized for not going far enough.[115] As the Trans Women of Color Collective (TWOCC) argued in 2019: "Visibility is not freedom. Freedom is freedom. Visibility is not liberation. Liberation is liberation."[116] Notably, activists have yet to develop a national annual event for transgender people that is focused on pride, freedom, and liberation.

An additional factor impeding a pride narrative is the regular claim in anti-violence materials that being out and proud resulted in a victim's death. Despite the fact that none of the known murders of transgender people at the time occurred after a transgender person came out to a coworker, a 2001 article in the *Journal of Homosexuality* coauthored by GenderPAC activists argued: "Working adults who disclose their transgendered experience, or request reasonable accommodation to it, are fired, harassed, intimidated or assaulted by supervisors and coworkers, have their privacy violated, have their property defaced and destroyed, or are murdered."[117] Similarly, a GLAAD press release stated that F.C. Martinez "lived his life proud of who he was and for that, his life was taken."[118] Echoing this, a Southern Poverty Law Center *Intelligence Report* described Terrianne Summers as "out and active" and stated: "Friends and family members, including

Summers' partner and two children, are left to wonder whether that visibility might have cost Summers her life."[119] This sort of rhetoric was used to solidify the claim that this violence was motivated by hatred of transgender people. However, such a tactic suppresses a pride narrative by arguing that to be out and proud is to court death. Moreover, it runs contrary to the actual statistics on risk of fatal violence for trans people. Most of the trans people killed in the United States between 1990 and 2009 were killed by people who at least claimed that they did not know that the trans person was trans, then "discovered" that fact and reacted to that discovery with violence. Thus, it is arguable that being out or otherwise visibly trans may actually decrease one's risk for fatal violence.[120]

Another deterrent to a pride narrative may be relative integration with groups defined as "them" in "us versus them" rhetoric. As discussed in chapter 6, transgender people and cisgender women often live and partner with members of the groups described as perpetrators by identity-based activists (cisgender people and men, respectively). By contrast, people of color and gay men and lesbians tend to live and partner with members of their own identity group. Notably, people of color and gay men and lesbians have been more likely, historically, to have a pride narrative. Black activists promoted black pride through the Black Power movement and through slogans such as "Black is Beautiful." Similarly, gay men and lesbians have an annual pride month.[121] By contrast, women and transgender people do not have similar pride events.

The closest mainstream efforts have come to "pride" events or slogans for women are "girl power" and Women's History Month. Notably, "girl power" is infantilizing, as it uses a gendered term for children (girl) rather than adults (woman). Moreover, it is notable that what is often celebrated during Women's History Month is women engaged in activities that have traditionally been associated with men.[122] By focusing on women who were successful in math, science, politics, and so forth, the month works to expand the range of activities seen as acceptable for women. However, it also reinforces the idea that masculine pursuits are valuable. The failure to celebrate women for doing "women's work" perpetuates the devaluing of femininity and dampens the potential of the month to reduce discrimination against women. One place in which pride in being a woman has been expressed is in feminist separatism. As opposed to mainstream heterosexual women, those practicing feminist separatism do not partner or live with men. How integration versus segregation shapes pride narratives may be due to the binary logic of identity politics, through which expressing pride in your group may be seen as implicitly denigrating "the other" group. As many trans people partner with cis people, that may make a trans pride narrative less likely, as celebrating a trans identity might be perceived as disparaging a cis one. Furthermore, if anger is a step toward expressing pride for historically oppressed groups, it may be that those who are more segregated from the "them" in the "us versus them" narrative are more likely to be angry at those groups and then express pride in their own group.

One way to encourage transgender pride would be to have an annual day celebrating transgender people. In conjunction with other pride festivities, there has been an annual Trans March in San Francisco since 2004. A number of other cities, including Los Angeles, Portland, and Seattle, also hold Trans Pride marches and festivals in June.[123] Making such events national would increase access to these empowering experiences and would encourage news coverage of the wonderful aspects of being transgender. Although some activists have argued that increased visibility, including pride events and news coverage, can heighten levels of violence, empowerment of transgender people and positive messages about what it means to be trans are likely to decrease violence over time.[124]

Improve Media Narratives   To reduce violence, transgender people should be marked as valuable and their joys should be highlighted in mainstream media narratives. Trans people are becoming increasingly visible on television, in movies, and in news coverage.[125] However, the narratives told about transgender lives are often tragic ones, including numerous news stories about murders of trans people and numerous fictional storylines in which trans people are murder victims.[126] Activists have criticized disrespectful news coverage, arguing that it facilitates violence against transgender people. As a 2009 GLAAD press report stated: "Too many times, police and media correspondents have failed to accurately identify and respect the gender identities of trans people, in spite of the commonly accepted Associated Press guidelines that clearly state that reporters should use pronouns and names in accordance with the individuals' identity. This disrespect only perpetuates the ignorance that so often fuels verbal harassment and physical violence."[127] In response, trans and LGBT activist groups have done substantial work to ensure that journalists use the correct names and pronouns of transgender victims of violence.[128]

To reduce violence experienced by trans people, the focus must extend beyond increased and respectful coverage of transgender homicides. It is detrimental when most of the trans people represented in mainstream media are murder victims. Thus, anti-violence activism must include pushing for positive representations of living transgender people, both in the news and in fictional representations. Separate from its anti-violence work, GLAAD has labored to improve depictions of trans people in the mainstream media by working directly with media producers and giving annual awards for positive representations.[129] Similarly, Vice's Broadly has recently created a free library of gender diverse stock photos in hopes of increasing the depiction of a wide variety of ways of being trans in ads and news stories.[130] Scholars have demonstrated that exposure to images of, and television story lines about, transgender people improved cisgender people's attitudes toward trans people.[131] Thus, these excellent projects and others like them will likely shift dominant understandings of what it means to be transgender and, as a result, reduce violence.

Such media representations of trans people are most likely to decrease violence and improve transgender people's lives if they include three key elements: (1) narratives of transgender joy, (2) depictions of the diversity of the trans community, and (3) portrayals of trans people as appropriate and desirable sexual partners. To counteract the construction of a vulnerable subjecthood, mainstream media should regularly tell narratives about the wonderful aspects of being transgender. This can be accomplished through news coverage of trans people's accomplishments as well as television, film, and book plots with happy transgender characters. Ideally, these representations would portray trans people as multifaceted individuals, rather than simply focus on their being transgender. It is also vital that characters not simply reproduce *transnormativity,* as these dominant understandings of the "correct" way to be transgender, including having a binary identity, understanding oneself as "trapped in the wrong body," and engaging in a medical transition, limit trans possibilities.[132] To reduce violence, transgender media representations must portray a wide variety of ways of being trans. This includes calling into question the expectation of gender conformity within one's gender identity as well as depicting transgender people as diverse in terms of race, class, age, ability, and sexuality.

As journalist Ray Filar argued in 2015, with the increased portrayals of transgender people in the media there is a serious disjuncture between "who gets seen, who gets celebrated" and "who gets murdered."[133] Since fatal violence disproportionately targets transgender women of color, it is vital that there be more positive representations of this group in the mainstream media. One outstanding move toward affirmative, diverse representations is the young adult novel *Pet.*[134] As author Akwaeke Emezi explained their choices regarding the characters and plot:

When it comes to trans characters, especially black trans girls, black trans women, when they're being amplified, it's usually because someone died. Trans people are already living their reality. So I was like, if I'm writing something for black trans kids, what spell do I want to cast? I want to cast a spell where a black trans girl is never hurt. Her parents are completely supportive. Her community is completely supportive. She's not in danger. She gets to have adventures with her best friend. And I hope that that's a useful spell for young people. I hope that's a spell where someone reads that and they're like, this is like what my life should be like. This is a possibility.[135]

This is an excellent example of a form of conscientious narrative telling, as Emezi actively worked to tell a story that would make trans lives more livable.

Since a disproportionate number of murders of transgender people occur in sexual interactions, the mainstream media should also include narratives that portray transgender people in healthy, happy romantic relationships and as desirable sexual partners. A step in this direction was the February 2018 cover of *Cosmopolitan* featuring Laverne Cox and the hashtag #SayYesToLove. The fact that Cox was the first openly trans "cover girl" and that the issue was focused on Valentine's Day, sex, and love sent a powerful message. Another example is the television show *Pose*, which in 2019 featured a romantic relationship between Angel and Lil Papi that has been described as a "healthy and loving relationship between a trans woman and cisgender man" and "one of the best representations of a romance between a trans woman and a cis [man] on TV ever."[136]

Alter Academia Finally, to reduce violence, academics must stop reproducing vulnerable subjecthood in their scholarship. A substantial number of academic publications on transgender people open with statements about levels of violence experienced by trans people, even when the piece is not about violence. This practice reproduces the cultural conflation of "transgender" and "victim" and impedes the production of transgender as a vibrant subjecthood. This is not to argue that academics should not attend to violence against trans people; they very much should. However, it is worth considering alternative ways of introducing transgender topics, such as highlighting the wonderful aspects of being transgender before then exploring factors that oppress and constrain trans lives. Traditionally, social scientists have focused on the negative, and scholarship highlighting positivity and joy has been devalued. We must examine how emphasizing vulnerability and downplaying joy can negatively impact the very communities whose oppression we decry.

UNLINKING ANTI-VIOLENCE ACTIVISM AND IDENTITY POLITICS

So far in this chapter, my suggestions for alternative models to anti-violence activism have focused on those done through identity politics. However, given the potential detrimental outcomes of combining identity politics and anti-violence activism, it is vital to explore how to do anti-violence work outside of the identity politics model. In addition to constructing vulnerable and homogeneous subjecthoods, identity-based anti-violence activism has also historically pursued "solutions" that have not resulted in a reduction of violence. Moreover, because activist organizations are generally focused on a single identity, solutions are pursued piecemeal. For example, although there has been legislation covering crimes related to race, religion, and national origin since 1968, there was no federal anti–hate crime legislation that included gender identity until 2009. In addition, when pursuing solutions in an identity-based, piecemeal fashion, more marginalized groups are frequently the last to be included. Illustrating this, transgender people have regularly not been included in laws aimed at protecting others under the LGBT umbrella. Finally, as numerous queer theorists have argued, engaging in identity politics has the detrimental effect of reifying the very categories that oppress us.[137] By emphasizing identities, we reproduce the belief that gender, race, sexuality, and so forth are important social distinctions. This facilitates future oppression. As such, we must undo this reification of identities in our activism and in our proposed solutions to violence.

I opened this chapter with quotes from political scientist Wendy Brown and philosopher Judith Butler. I turn to both of these theorists now to develop an approach to anti-violence activism outside of the identity politics model. Butler argued that we should strive for "a world in which collective means are found to protect bodily vulnerability" and that such an endeavor should "be guided by the question of what maximizes the possibilities for a livable life [and] what minimizes the possibility of unbearable life or, indeed, social or literal death."[138] One way to achieve these goals is to separate anti-violence activism from the model of identity politics. This can be accomplished through forming anti-violence organizations around the desire for the end of violence, as opposed to around identities. This divestment of identity as the reason for the movement and the cause of the violence may produce a more hopeful narrative. Brown argued that a formation of identity around an understanding of the group as oppressed or wounded is common in current forms of identity politics. She demonstrated that in the critique of power, politicized identities tend "to reproach power rather [than] to aspire to it" and, through demanding rights based on their victimized identities, become invested in their own victimhood and in their own status of oppressed outsider.[139] This also works to naturalize and perpetuate the system that constructed them as outsiders. Her solution to these problems is to encourage a move from claims of "who I am" to claims of "what I want for us."[140] This is a move away from fixed identity toward desire for change. In the case of a fight against violence experienced by trans people, this would mean a shift from a narrative of "I am transgender and I am vulnerable to violence because of *who I am*" to a call to action of "*I* (or we) *want* to end violence in order to make more lives livable." I would edit this slightly to "we demand," moving it from the realm of desires to requirements in the struggle for livable lives. This method of mobilization, which is somewhat reminiscent of some of the work described in chapter 4 that GenderPAC did outside of the identity politics model, would facilitate broad-based coalitions and would reduce the construction of vulnerable subjecthoods.

In the history of social movements, ACT UP is an example of this model outside of anti-violence activism. Although certain identity groups, such as gay men, were harder hit in the early years of the epidemic, activists quickly realized that HIV and AIDS did not follow identity boundaries and so put together a very successful movement that transcended identity categories and instead focused on a set of demands. Though many members shared identities as gay, lesbian, and queer, the group was not limited to them or solely focused on how the virus threatened people with those identities.[141] Instead, the group was organized around a set of goals related to access to health care and experimental drugs, research into the virus, and the distribution of accurate safer sex information. It is possible to take a similar approach to anti-violence activism, stating: "We demand safety in our homes and in public. We demand safety in our romantic relationships and when interacting with strangers, including the police. And, we demand these things, not just for people who share our identity or identities, but for everyone." Notably, in a political field where numbers matter, this model is more effective than an identity-based one, as the size of the group you represent is limited only by the number of people who share your goals. Though certain forms of violence may be greater threats to particular communities, by working to reduce violence for all communities we will protect the most vulnerable. This is especially true if anti-violence activists focus on the needs of the most marginalized and are attentive to any way in which they are unintentionally reproducing inequality.[142]

Traditionally, activism to reduce sexual and relationship violence has been done within the identity politics model. As such, it has mostly focused on men's violence against women, and solutions have emphasized teaching women to avoid particular behaviors seen as increasing their risk for violence.[143] *Rape avoidance labor* and *relationship violence avoidance labor* are highly constraining to women's lives, and the narratives of their necessity construct womanhood as a vulnerable subjecthood. Moreover, women who do not engage in these avoidance practices, for example those who go out alone at night or wear short skirts, are then perceived to have "deserved" or "asked for" the violence they experience. Finally, such a focus ignores other forms of sexual and relationship violence that occur, such as that against men and in same-sex relationships. As the "who I am" approach to activism against these forms of violence has substantial unintended consequences and has not markedly reduced violence, a new approach must be sought. Adopting a "we demand" tactic may produce better results. Calling for consent in all sexual interactions and an end to violence in all relationships would avoid the construction of vulnerable subjecthoods and would reduce violence for everyone. As such, schools, parents, and the mainstream media should emphasize active, affirmative consent for all sexual interactions. Lessons about affirmative consent can start very young, teaching children both to ask before touching others and that they have the right to say no when others ask to touch them.[144] Similarly, schools, parents, and the media can teach and model healthy relationships for children starting when they are very young. None of these lessons need to be gendered. Instead, they can focus on emphasizing kindness and respect of boundaries for all.

It is also possible to separate self-defense from the traditional identity politics approach. Historically, boys have been taught self-defense in an informal way, often by relatives and peers who treat boys' and men's ability to enact violence as innate. By contrast, formal self-defense classes have been taught to girls and women as well as LGBT individuals, emphasizing their vulnerability.[145] Violence avoidance and self-defense educational pamphlets and workshops are usually designated as only for particular identity groups, excluding those outside the identity group. These strategies are likely to be more effective if approached from a "we demand" perspective. By demanding that everyone be able to feel safe both in public and at home, we can improve the livability of many people's lives. Such a demand would include self-defense lessons for everyone, regardless of identity. These classes should not encourage people to do violence but should instead focus on empowering participants as well as teaching de-escalation techniques. People who know that they can defend themselves if necessary have higher confidence levels and move through the world in a way that makes them less likely to be attacked.[146] This would encourage those who have traditionally been taught to avoid either being in certain public spaces (e.g., women and people of color) or being "visible" in public (e.g., LGBT people) to openly utilize public spaces, reducing the risk of violence to a single individual. The "we demand" strategy could also shift the focus from "self-defense" to "community safety." In this model, the goal is to make a neighborhood, school, or city a safer place for everyone. Doing so could include constructing "safe spaces" where those experiencing violent threats can go to seek assistance and addressing the *bystander effect* by teaching people how to intervene to stop violence.

A "community safety" approach would be facilitated by non-identity-based anti-violence education. Currently, anti-violence or antibias education tends to focus on teaching people that it is wrong to hate or be violent toward those who are "different" from you or have been "oppressed." Such education unintentionally reifies difference and in so doing facilitates future oppression. Rather than telling children that it is wrong to hit girls or discriminate against gay people, it would be better to teach them that it is wrong to discriminate against or hit anyone. Truly effective anti-violence education would teach that all forms of violence are wrong, not just violence against certain identity groups. These lessons will only be successful if US culture stops using violence as an acceptable form of punishment. The United States is a punishment culture that tries to enforce laws and norms through threats of violence.[147] If, however, the argument was that all forms of violence are wrong, this would necessitate (and facilitate) the elimination of spanking of children, police brutality, and the death penalty. It would also require the elimination of violence as a form of entertainment, including that in sports like boxing, and violence as an acceptable way to solve problems in movies and television shows. Instead of violence and other detrimental forms of punishment, communities could pursue "restorative justice." NCAVP has advocated for this approach, arguing: "Measures such as these may decrease recidivism and minimize the harmful impacts of incarceration on the offender while helping the survivor or victim to heal and access justice."[148]

Although law enforcement officers are supposed to reduce violence in communities, they are also a source of violence. Moreover, fear of police reduces the likelihood that people will seek their protection if under attack or will cooperate with investigations of violent incidents.[149] Current approaches to reducing police brutality have followed an identity politics model, with separate organizations focusing on police violence against people of color, gay men and lesbians, and transgender people.[150] One of the dangers of focusing only on police violence against particular groups is that it obscures a broader pattern of police brutality. It is vital to note levels of inequality; however, the identity politics approach turns police brutality into a "black issue" or "LGBT issue" rather than what it is: a social justice issue. Law enforcement officials harm individuals of all races, classes, genders, sexualities, ages, and ability statuses. Rather than fight in a piecemeal way for the right to not be subject to violence, it may be more prudent at this time to take a step back and examine law enforcement violence in general and then demand change, asking: Do we want to have police officers at all? If not, how would we like to use public funds to improve safety and well-being? If we do, do we want police officers to be able to utilize violence? If so, what forms of violence and under what circumstances? If not, what tactics do we want officers to utilize when enforcing the law? What elements of policing culture currently encourage abuses of power? How can those be eliminated? The advantage of such an approach is that a reexamination of policing culture and of laws around police violence should reduce violence experienced by everyone, including those most often targeted by law enforcement officers.

Violence scholars have identified a number of factors that have led to the United States having unusually high rates of violence, particularly homicide. These include widespread gun ownership, substantial poverty, and extensive residential segregation which concentrates poverty and increases rates of violence.[151] All of these elements can—and should—be addressed outside of an identity politics model. Scholars have argued that one of the things preventing effective gun control in the United States has been a lack of an "owner" of the social problem.[152] "Owners" of social problems are activist organizations that are widely known and thus highly influential. Part of what may have prevented the development of an "owner" of the issue of gun control is the dominance of the identity politics model within the current political field. Whereas those who are opposed to gun control share an identity as "gun owners," those in favor do not. By abandoning the identity approach and instead focusing on increasing livability, a group intent on gun control could develop ownership of the issue and enact much-needed legislation. Similarly, the issues of poverty and residential segregation have mostly been addressed using the identity politics model. For example, separate activist organizations have worked to reduce employment and housing discrimination against people of color and LGBT people.

This piecemeal approach keeps the central logic of the oppression intact. Those engaged in discrimination argue that they should be able to base hiring and so forth on identity group membership. Identity-based activists counter this with the argument that discrimination against their particular identity group should be illegal. This leaves unquestioned whether one can discriminate based on identity. By contrast, activism outside of the identity politics model could focus on reducing poverty and segregation for all. This would include arguing that no identity is a justifiable criterion for hiring, promotion, firing, or access to housing.

The logics of identity politics pervade the current political field, deeply influencing what seems possible for social movements. As such, doing identity politics from a space of empowered vibrancy rather than vulnerable victimhood and unlinking identity politics from anti-violence activism may seem unattainable. However, it is through imagining new possibilities that we make more lives livable. Transgender rights activists have already accomplished what many once saw as undoable: they have substantially reduced the stigma attached to trans identities and have constructed transgender as a valuable subjecthood. There is an anti-transgender backlash currently occurring in US culture; however, general public opinion about trans people and willingness to support transgender rights have increased dramatically since the early days of this movement.[153] Although the transgender rights movement has made great strides in terms of acceptance, the constraints of the social problems marketplace have pushed anti-violence activists into practices that have linked transgender with being exceptionally vulnerable to violence. Thus, though much of the population no longer sees transgender people as cultural villains, they are now perceived as vulnerable victims. Moreover, the "solutions" generated through this approach have not noticeably reduced violence experienced by transgender people and transgender lives are still in the realm of the unlivable. Therefore, it is time to reenvision how to do anti-violence activism both within and outside of the identity politics model. As we enter a new decade, I am optimistic that we can. The alternatives I have presented in this chapter will, I hope, work to reduce violence without the devastating unintended consequences of the current approach to identity-based anti-violence activism. This will facilitate more livable lives for all.

APPENDIX A

Transgender Anti-Violence Organizations

Although all of the activist groups I analyze in this book tended to utilize similar tactics, each group has its own history. The organizations I examined are diverse in terms of their missions, including those focused specifically on transgender rights, those serving LGBT people more generally, and those focused on hate violence. They are also diverse in terms of their audience, including the mainstream media, politicians, the general public, and the trans community. That the narratives about violence and framings of the issues are so similar across groups speaks to the power of the political field in shaping how anti-violence activism is done as well as the diffusion of the narratives used successfully by the civil rights, women's rights, and gay rights movements. Here I discuss the thirteen organizations analyzed in this book chronologically by date of formation to provide a history and context for this activism.

SOUTHERN POVERTY LAW CENTER

The Southern Poverty Law Center (SPLC) started out in 1971 as a small civil rights law firm and slowly expanded its focus to include activism around numerous forms of hate crimes. Although its main focus has been on race-related violence, starting in the late 1990s it began including information on violence experienced by transgender people. In 2003 the SPLC published an intelligence report covering twenty-seven murders of trans people. The report described transphobia as "the most powerful hatred on the planet" and argued that "none are so victimized as the transgender community. These men and women—from crossdressers to those who have undergone sex change operations—may be the most despised people in America."[1]

TRANSGENDER TAPESTRY

Transgender Tapestry was first published in the late 1970s and was named *TV-TS Tapestry* until 1995. It was a quarterly magazine produced by the International Foundation for Gender Education (IFGE) "by, for, and about all things trans, including crossdressing, transsexualism, intersexuality, FTM, MTF, butch, femme, drag kings and drag queens, androgyny, female and male impersonation, and more."[2] This long-running and widely distributed publication released issues 55 through 115 between 1990 and 2009. These volumes featured regular coverage of violence experienced by trans people, including, starting in 1995, a section called "Trans-Actions: News & Notes from the Gender Frontier" that contained numerous stories about violence, particularly murder, as well as coverage of the struggle for inclusion of gender identity into hate crime legislation. In summer 1999 *Transgender Tapestry* published a special issue on violence, which featured an article on the Remembering Our Dead website. In spring 2001 Transgender Day of Remembrance was on the cover, and in spring 2003 a special "Gender Educational" issue was produced, aimed at a cisgender audience. The educational issue included eight articles that mentioned violence experienced by trans people as well as copies of the flyers shown in figures 1 and 3 (see chapters 4 and 5). *Transgender Tapestry* stopped publication in 2009 after a controversial change of leadership at IFGE.[3] The magazine reached a diverse group of people who were not necessarily involved in anti-violence activism. As violence was a regular topic in the publication, narratives about the relationship between being transgender and risk for physical harm had the potential to deeply affect its readers.

HUMAN RIGHTS CAMPAIGN

The Human Rights Campaign (HRC), which has had a variety of names and forms, started in 1980. HRC works for the rights of lesbians, gay men, bisexuals, and trans people (although whether its activism consistently includes the latter two groups has been debatable). HRC's public texts include violence experienced by trans people, beginning in 1999 with a press release written by Riki Wilchins detailing five murders. After that, it regularly issued statements about violence experienced by people whom trans activists labeled as transgender. However, when covering the violence, HRC occasionally labeled those victims, such as F.C. Martinez and Latisha King, as gay. In 2002, in cooperation with the National Gay and Lesbian Task Force (NGLTF) and the National Organization for Women

(NOW), HRC released a document titled *Examples of Hate Crimes against Transgender Individuals*. All but three of the entries were about murder. In 2005, in an effort to educate cisgender people about trans issues, HRC published *Transgender Americans: A Handbook for Understanding*, which included a section on "hate violence" and detailed descriptions of two murders.

GAY AND LESBIAN ALLIANCE AGAINST DEFAMATION

The Gay and Lesbian Alliance Against Defamation (GLAAD) was started in 1985 to advocate for positive media portrayals of gay men and lesbians, including influencing news coverage of violence experienced by those groups. GLAAD was criticized by trans activist Riki Wilchins in 1995 for not including transgender people in its activism and responded publicly, detailing its trans-inclusiveness. However, it was not until the late 1990s that GLAAD's publicly available texts began to regularly feature trans people. These texts included celebrations of news outlets using names and pronouns that reflect the identities of transgender victims of violence (as well as condemnations of those who did not) and guides published for the mainstream media detailing how to properly cover hate crimes against trans people. GLAAD regularly hosts award ceremonies recognizing media outlets that it feels are providing good coverage, and family members of murder victims have been frequent speakers at these events. Violence, and particularly murder, is central to the organization's focus. In the description of its history on the GLAAD website in 2005, shaping coverage of violence was first in the list of accomplishments: "GLAAD has . . . impacted millions through newspapers, magazines, motion pictures, television and visibility campaigns. We've focused media attention on: the hate motivated murders of Matthew Shepard, Arthur 'J.R.' Warren, Brandon Teena, Fred Martinez, Gwen Araujo and others; the anti-gay advocacy of 'Dr. Laura' Schlessinger; Eminem's hate lyrics; the openly gay heroes and victims of 9-11; the anti-gay right's fraudulent 'ex-gay' ads; and most recently, attempts by Catholic Church officials to scapegoat innocent gay priests in the growing sex-abuse crisis."[4]

FTM INTERNATIONAL

FTM International (first called simply FTM) was started in 1986 by Lou Sullivan. In 1987, the organization began to publish its popular quarterly newsletter, *FTMi*. Early in its existence, its intended audience was described as "the female-to-male crossdresser and transsexual," and by 2005 that audience had altered and expanded to "female-to-male transgender and transsexual people and allied partners, lovers, family members, friends, and professionals."[5] Starting in 1994, the newsletter regularly covered violence experienced by trans men and women, including news pieces on acts of violence and court cases, articles about the larger problem of violence experienced by the group, reviews of the documentary and film made about the murder of Brandon Teena, and coverage of Transgender Day of Remembrance events. As with all of the organizations I examined, the vast majority of the discussions of violence included at least one mention of murder. Although it has not officially disbanded, the group stopped issuing *FTMi* in 2008.

GENDER EDUCATION AND ADVOCACY

Gender Education and Advocacy (formerly the American Educational Gender Information Service or AEGIS) was founded in 1990 to distribute educational information about "gender variant" people. Members of the organization sought to educate and advocate "for all human beings who suffer from gender-based oppression in all of its many forms."[6] At the time of data collection, the website had been inactive since 2004. The organization helped run the Transgender Day of Remembrance, including producing the two influential flyers in figures 1 and 3 (see chapters 4 and 5), distributed information to the mainstream media on how to cover trans issues (including violence), and regularly issued press releases on violence experienced by trans people.

NATIONAL COALITION OF ANTI-VIOLENCE PROGRAMS

The National Coalition of Anti-Violence Programs (NCAVP) collects and analyzes data from anti-violence projects throughout the United States. It published its first report on violence experienced by gay men, lesbians, and those with HIV in 1994 and began including data on trans experiences of violence in 1995. The group's annual reports track patterns of violence from year to year, noting factors such as weapon use; the role of law enforcement; and the age, race, and gender of victims and perpetrators. Reports examined for this book (1994–2009 and 2018) highlighted murder victims and tended to focus on increases in violence. Each report since 1997 has also included detailed recommendations to reduce violence against these groups. Other activist organizations frequently cite NCAVP's data and its annual reports receive regular news coverage, shaping the public's understanding of violence experienced by LGBT people.

GENDER PUBLIC ADVOCACY COALITION

The Gender Public Advocacy Coalition (GenderPAC) was started in 1995 by Riki Wilchins. GenderPAC's original mission was to fight for "gender, affectional and racial equality."[7] Over time this mission was modified to "working to guarantee every American's civil right to express their gender orientation free of stereotypes, discrimination and violence."[8] As part of this work, GenderPAC produced numerous press releases detailing violence experienced by transgender people, condemning transphobic media coverage, berating other organizations for not supporting trans equality, and calling for inclusion of gender identity in hate crimes legislation. In the early years, those press releases were published under the name "InYourFace." GenderPAC also organized annual National Gender Lobby Days to speak with members of Congress about gender-based violence and discrimination. To better understand violence experienced by trans people and to provide statistics for lobbying, in 1997 GenderPAC produced The First National Study on Transviolence. Findings from the study were published in *The Journal of Homosexuality* in 2001. In 2006 GenderPAC produced a study of nonnormatively gendered youth murdered between 1995 and 2005 titled *50 Under 30: Masculinity and the War on America's Youth* and in 2008 extended the data for *70 Under 30*. Although GenderPAC always had a broad focus to its gender-based activism, it had traditionally focused on transgender issues. Over time, as I detail in chapter 4, the more general focus on how the gender system leads to inequality and violence became increasingly central, and many trans community members felt abandoned. GenderPAC officially disbanded in 2009.

GAY STRAIGHT ALLIANCE

The Gay Straight Alliance (GSA), founded in 1998, is a network of school-based organizations that provide support for, and fight discrimination and violence against, LGBT youth. Its website includes information on how GSA groups can work against transphobia, make schools safer spaces for trans students, and organize annual Transgender Day of Remembrance events. During the time period studied, GSA's weekly emails regularly included links to news coverage of violence experienced by trans people, including extensive coverage of the murder of Gwen Araujo and the subsequent trials of her killers.

REMEMBERING OUR DEAD

In 1998 Gwendolyn Smith created the Remembering Our Dead website as an educational memorial to murdered transgender people. While discussing a recent murder and connecting it to past homicides in the Transgender Community Forum on America Online, she was shocked to discover that many people had not heard about the deaths. In response to this lack of awareness, she started the website, which opened with a quote from George Santayana: "Those who cannot remember the past are doomed to repeat it." Clicking on the quote opened a new page with a black background, shadowy pictures of murder victims in the background, and all of the names of the murder victims in white. If the user clicked on a name, a new page opened, listing the name of the victim, the location where they were killed, cause of death, date of death, sources of the information, and notes (if any). When available, there was also a black-and-white photo of the victim and links to writings about the death. The whole page was black, gray, and white, designed to look like the Vietnam War Memorial. The "about" section of the website informed visitors: "There is no 'safe way' to be transgendered: as you look at the many names collected here, note that some of these people may have identified as drag queens, some as heterosexual crossdressers, and some as transsexuals. Some were living very out lives, and some were living fully 'stealth' lives. Some were identifying as male, and some, as female. Some lived in small towns, and some in major metropolitan areas."[9] Many groups, including Gender Education and Advocacy and GenderPAC, used the information on the Remembering Our Dead site to produce reports and other educational materials about murders of trans people. The site stopped adding new victims in 2005.

TRANSGENDER DAY OF REMEMBRANCE

Transgender Day of Remembrance was started by Gwendolyn Smith in 1998 soon after she started the Remembering Our Dead website and serves a similar purpose. Between 1990 and 2009, Transgender Day of Remembrance was the only annual national holiday-like event specifically related to trans people. Every November, people across the United States and around the world gather to memorialize "those who were killed due to anti-transgender hatred or prejudice."[10] Often Transgender Day of

Remembrance events are held in the evening, with participants holding candles in honor of the dead, reading the names of murdered trans people, and sometimes marking the deaths in other symbolic ways such as ringing a bell or blowing out a candle after each name is read. These events are frequently held on college campuses or at LGBT community centers and can include daytime educational sessions and workshops about violence experienced by trans people. Extensive flyering for the event and mainstream news coverage are common. As such, Transgender Day of Remembrance has the potential to profoundly influence cisgender people's understanding of trans people in addition to trans people's understandings of what it means to be transgender. Before it was replaced with a new site, the Transgender Day of Remembrance website featured a number of flyers that event organizers could use (including those in figures 1 and 3), recommendations on how to best run the event, and "first person narratives" for attendees to read, such as: "I'm Timothy Blair, Jr., and I was a 19 year old crossdresser living in Louisville, Kentucky. I was shot multiple times on May 22nd, possibly by someone I met in an Internet chat room." Both versions of the website also include lists of murder victims and a list of events for that year. Before and after events, activists publish a number of press releases detailing the event and the murders of trans people from that year.

NATIONAL TRANSGENDER ADVOCACY COALITION

Activists started the National Transgender Advocacy Coalition (NTAC) in 1999 in response to frustrations with other activist groups for their perceived failure to advocate for transgender rights. Much of NTAC's focus was on pushing for a transgender-inclusive Employment Non-Discrimination Act (ENDA). Its press releases and activist actions regularly targeted HRC and GenderPAC, criticizing the groups when they did not appear to support an inclusive ENDA and highlighting the shortage of transgender staff working for these organizations. Arguing that GenderPAC "has failed to represent the concerns of transgenders," NTAC dubbed itself "the nation's preeminent transgender civil rights organization."[11] Although much of its work was focused on an inclusive ENDA, NTAC described itself as a "civil rights organization working to establish and maintain the right of all transgendered, intersexed, and gender-variant people to live and work without fear of violence or discrimination."[12] In that work, NTAC released numerous press releases about violence experienced by trans people, and its main web page had a sidebar called "Transgender Death Statistics." NTAC was a relatively short-lived organization, as much of its work was subsumed by the National Center for Transgender Equality.

NATIONAL CENTER FOR TRANSGENDER EQUALITY

The National Center for Transgender Equality (NCTE) was founded in 2003. Based in Washington, D.C., NCTE regularly lobbies for legislation to promote transgender rights. NCTE's focus from 2003 to 2009 was often on violence, and it was integral to the passing of transgender-inclusive hate crime legislation in 2009. In 2006 NCTE published *Responding to Hate Crimes: A Community Resource Manual*. This twenty-eight-page document provides detailed instructions for how activists should respond in the aftermath of a hate crime in their community, including suggestions for how to interact with victims, their friends and family, perpetrators, law enforcement, the trans community, and the mainstream media. In addition, NCTE has been an active advocate for transgender-inclusive anti-discrimination legislation, including both ENDA and the Equality Act. For much of the period analyzed in this book, NCTE's website described its mission thus: "The National Center for Transgender Equality is a national social justice organization devoted to ending discrimination and violence against transgender people through education and advocacy on national issues of importance to transgender people."[13] NCTE is currently one of the most prominent national transgender-specific activist organizations in the United States. Over the years its mission has changed slightly and is now posted on the website thus: "The National Center for Transgender Equality advocates to change policies and society to increase understanding and acceptance of transgender people. In the nation's capital and throughout the country, NCTE works to replace disrespect, discrimination, and violence with empathy, opportunity, and justice."[14] Both versions highlight how central anti-violence activism is to their work.

Collecting Data on Murders of Transgender People

The best measures of homicide in the United States—the Federal Bureau of Investigation's (FBI's) *Uniform Crime Report* and the Centers for Disease Control and Prevention's (CDC's) National Vital Statistics System—do not include information about whether the victim was transgender. Moreover, official hate crime data are insufficient for the study of violence experienced by transgender people. Actual or perceived gender identity was added as a protected category to hate crime legislation in 2009 with the Matthew Shepard and James Byrd, Jr., Hate Crimes Prevention Act. However, FBI reports only started including counts of crimes stemming from gender-identity bias in 2013, making time trends difficult to assess using these data.[1] In addition, very few acts of violence against transgender people are labeled hate crimes, so examining just hate crime cases would severely undercount the problem. For example, of the sixty-four murders of transgender people that occurred between 2013 and 2015, only one was included in the FBI's *Hate Crime Statistics* reports.

To improve knowledge of violence experienced by transgender people, I collected all the available texts produced about murders of transgender people by anti-violence activists, mainstream news, and government sources in the United States between 1990 and 2015. Information from these sources was then used to create an original dataset that includes (a) the victim's birth name, chosen names(s), sex, gender, level of body modification (if any), race, and age; (b) the perpetrator's name, sex, gender, race, and age; (c) the murder date and location (the town/city, the region in the United States, and the physical location, such as the home of the victim or on the street); and (d) the primary weapon used in the homicide, the relationship between the victim and perpetrator, and the circumstances of the killing.

CRITERIA FOR INCLUSION IN THE DATASET

Cases were included in the dataset if they met two main criteria. The first was whether the victim was transgender. When dealing with homicide victims, it is not always possible to know how they identified, so for the purpose of this research, the term *transgender* is used to describe perceptions of behavior rather than the victim's self-identification. Victims were included if they were described at the time of their death (1) as either having self-identified or having been identified by others as "transsexual," "transgender," "trans," "a cross-dresser," "a transvestite," or "two-spirit"; (2) as wearing clothing, jewelry, makeup, and/or accessories associated with a gender other than the one they were labeled at birth; and/or (3) using phrases such as "a man in a dress," "a woman posing as a man," or "a man living as a woman."[2]

The second criterion for inclusion in the dataset was whether the death was a homicide. Determining whether a case was a homicide was straightforward in most instances, but a few were more complicated. Activist accounts commonly included cases in which the person died as a result of being denied medical care.[3] Although these deaths were the result of negligence, they were not homicides, so deaths that resulted from denial of medical care were not included. Activist lists also included a small number of cases in which there was evidence that the death was a homicide, but law enforcement had ruled the death an accident or suicide. In these cases (n = 10), there was sufficient evidence that these deaths were homicides and they were included in the dataset.[4] I also included one case that police ruled a justifiable homicide.[5] Including these eleven cases does not meaningfully alter the results, as these cases are reflective of the gender, race, and murder-year patterns seen in the dataset.

DATA COLLECTION PROCESS

As anti-violence activists often collect information about murders, utilizing their records is a logical first step. However, activist accounts, which rely on activists hearing about a homicide and recording that information, are likely to be incomplete.[6] Homicide data collected from newspapers has been proven to replicate official homicide data, and scholars have successfully used newspaper data to study homicide trends for populations and practices that are either undercounted or not counted at all in government homicide data, including prostitutes, LGBT people, and homicide-suicide cases.[7]

Newspaper sources are particularly useful for gathering data on the murders of transgender people because, as scholarship on journalism practices has long demonstrated, unusual occurrences receive more news coverage.[8] Thus, murders get more coverage than other forms of violent crime, and homicides that are considered sensational or unusual, criteria that murders of transgender people likely fit, receive even higher levels of coverage.[9] However, it should be noted that although unusual homicides are highly likely to be covered in newspapers, other factors also shape coverage. Level of murder coverage differs by individual newspaper, as well as by city and year.[10] Moreover, although some studies have found little to no difference in coverage based on the race and gender of the victim, others have found that homicides in which the victim is white and/or female are more likely to receive newspaper coverage.[11] Finally, the relationship between perpetrator and victim may shape the likelihood of receiving coverage. For example, criminologist Derek Paulsen found that whereas 69 percent of the murders in Houston, Texas, were covered by the *Houston Chronicle*, 75 percent of murders by intimates (i.e., spouses, dating partners, etc.) received coverage.[12] Although the differences in coverage found in studies are often slight, it seems probable that a dataset of homicides based on newspaper coverage will somewhat undercount total homicides and will overrepresent white victims, female victims, and murders by intimates.[13] Though using news reports and other "open-source" data is not a perfect way to study homicide patterns, until official sources begin tracking these subpopulations, it is an innovative and effective approach.[14]

To create the dataset, I engaged in a multistep process of data collection that included activist accounts, mainstream news coverage, and government documents. The steps taken to collect the data for this study are summarized here:

1) Collect activist accounts.
   a. Remove cases that do not fit the study's criteria.
2) Search news media search engines for cases identified in activist accounts.
   a. Compile coverage and use it to develop a set of search terms.
3) Search news media archives for cases that were not included in the activist accounts.
   a. Add to the dataset cases that fit the study criteria.
4) Acquire police reports and other government documents about the cases.

I started by collecting all the press releases, reports, flyers, lists of victims, and web pages published about murders by all the national social movement organizations engaged in anti-violence activism on behalf of transgender people in the United States between 1990 and 2015.[15] The organizations I gathered accounts of homicides from include the Anti-Defamation League, FTM International, Gay and Lesbian Alliance Against Defamation, Gay Straight Alliance, Gender Education and Advocacy, GenderPAC, Human Rights Campaign, National Center for Transgender Equality, National Coalition of Anti-Violence Programs, National LGBTQ Task Force, Remembering Our Dead, Southern Poverty Law Center, Transgender Day of Remembrance, Transgender Law Center, and Trans Murder Monitoring Project.[16] I also gathered information from national LGBT community publications including *The Advocate, Transgender Tapestry,* and *FTMi,* as these publications regularly included articles about murders of transgender people.[17] After gathering all the activist accounts of murders of transgender people between 1990 and 2015, I closely examined them to see if they fit the criteria for inclusion in the dataset. Using these criteria, I gathered and coded a total of 1,443 activist accounts about 316 murders.

The activist accounts are extensive but not exhaustive. To ensure that I accounted for all known murders of transgender people, I also searched the mainstream news media for information about both the murders that were known to activists and any cases not included in activist accounts. From the activist accounts, I compiled a list of names of people identified as either victims or perpetrators. Using those names, a research assistant (RA) and I searched two mainstream news media search engines, Access World News and LexisNexis, for stories about these murders.[18] I then read through the thousands of stories I had collected and made a list of terms and phrases used to describe transgender murder victims. Altogether, I gathered a list of ninety-eight terms and phrases, ranging from "transgender" and "transsexual" to "posed as a woman" and "true gender."

Next, an RA and I searched the news media search engines for those terms and phrases in order to find stories about murders not included in activist accounts. I then read through those stories and added to my list of names, terms, and phrases. With those lists, an RA and I did a final search of the news media search engines. Searching news media sources garnered information on 294 of the 316 homicides known to activists, as well an additional 87 transgender homicide victims not known to activists, resulting in a total of 403 victims between 1990 and 2015.

Although some scholars and activists have claimed that there is no media coverage of most murders of transgender people, that was not the case during the period studied.[19] My searches resulted in 7,554 unique news stories about these cases. Moreover, of the 403 murders, 381 (95%) were covered at least once in the mainstream news.

In the final stage of data collection, an RA and I gathered information about each case from government sources, as government documents can contain information that is missing from activist and news accounts. For example, most government documents label victims and perpetrators with a race, whereas many newspapers have policies about only mentioning a person's race if it is relevant to the story, such as if the murder was race-based.[20] Although police reports are considered public records and are available under the Freedom of Information Act, each police department has its own policy about what reports it will release. I was denied access to the police reports in sixty-eight of the cases. The most common reasons for denial included that the case was still under investigation or the report had been destroyed.[21] When a police report was unavailable or provided insufficient information, I sought information from other government sources, including court records, the Department of Corrections, Social Security records, and arrest records made public by state agencies. These official sources were helpful in acquiring information commonly not included in news and activist accounts, such as the race of the victim. Because I used all these sources, information about the race of the victim is missing in just 3 percent of the cases examined.

By triangulating information from activist, mainstream news, and government documents, I ensured that the data are the most comprehensive, detailed, and accurate available.[22] There is every indication that if a trans person is killed, the murder will be reported in at least the local paper, as transgender people are perceived as unusual enough by reporters to be considered news. Moreover, activists working to reduce violence experienced by trans people have put considerable effort into gathering as much information as they can about murders and making that information available to the public. Although a true census is not possible, by using both activist and news sources, my dataset is as close to a census as is possible at this time. My dataset includes higher per-year victim counts than any previous study of murders of transgender people. For example, my count includes twenty-five homicides in 2015, whereas the National Coalition of Anti-Violence Programs (NCAVP) report for 2015 includes sixteen and a Human Rights Campaign (HRC) report detailed twenty-one.[23] These discrepancies arise from the difference in sources; the NCAVP report only includes cases reported to its thirteen member programs, and the HRC report includes just those murders known to activists. By contrast, my dataset also includes homicides covered in the mainstream news.

That said, my dataset is not without limitations. Despite extensive searching and careful collection of cases, some murders might have been missed. The reliance on newspaper accounts means that it is possible this dataset undercounts these murders in general and particularly undercounts transfeminine and black victims, as homicides in which the victim is white and/or female are more likely to receive newspaper coverage. The news stories I gathered often labeled transgender women as male even though it was counter to their identity, particularly between 1990 and 2002 and still with some frequency from 2003 to 2015. It is possible that a different method of collecting the data would result in a larger number of cases. For example, an Italian research team read through every death report and autopsy for homicides in Milan between 1993 and 2012 and found a much higher number of murders of trans people in that city than in any city in my dataset.[24] It is unclear whether the comparably high numbers found by this research team come from a difference in murder rates between Milan and US cities, the different data collection methods, or a different definition of "transgender."[25] Future research should explore alternative data collection methods, such as the (extremely labor intensive) death and autopsy report approach, as well as including transgender status in well-respected datasets such as the FBI's *Uniform Crime Report* and the CDC's National Vital Statistics System.

VARIABLES

All descriptors (sex, gender, race, and age) about both the victims and the perpetrators of these homicides are based on the perceptions of others (activists, journalists, police officers, and other government officials) rather than self-identity. This form of coding is standard for homicide research, as self-identity is often not available for homicide victims, so researchers must rely on descriptions of the victims in police reports and other official documents.

Sex of victims was coded as male or female. No victims were described by any sources as intersex. Based on descriptions by family, friends, activists, and police officers, each victim's gender was coded as either "transmasculine" or "transfeminine." Victims were coded as transfeminine if they were said to have been labeled male at birth and identified as women or otherwise presented in ways such that they would be read as "doing gender" as a woman or as "doing transgender."[26] Similarly, victims were coded as transmasculine if they were said to have been labeled female at birth and identified as men or otherwise presented in ways such that they would be read as doing gender as a man or as doing transgender.

Victims were coded as Asian/Pacific Islander, black, Latinx, Native American, or white.[27] Government documents, such as police reports and records from the Department of Corrections, typically only list one racial category for a person, even if that person was multiracial. The same is generally true for newspaper stories and activist accounts. Just three victims were ever described as multiracial. To make my data comparable to data on cisgender homicides, I recoded the three multiracial victims into single-race categories.[28]

The relationship between the perpetrator and victim was coded with both an expanded and a condensed set of categories. For each, only one code was used per victim. Relationships of a sexual nature were coded as "partner" (romantic relationships of over two months), "dating" (romantic relationships of less than two months), "hook-up" (a first time sexual encounter), "hit on" (the perpetrator or victim had propositioned the other for a sexual relationship), "ex-partner" (there was an ongoing romantic relationship between the perpetrator and victim in the past), or "sex work" (the perpetrator gave the victim money in exchange for sex).[29] Nonsexual relationships were coded as "family member," "friend," "acquaintance," "coworker," "neighbor," "stranger," or "police officer."

Notes

PREFACE

1. For example, Burton (1998); Campbell (2005); Marcus (2002).

CHAPTER 1. UNLIVABLE LIVES

1. Barack Obama, "Remarks at the Reception Commemorating the Enactment of the Matthew Shepard and James Byrd, Jr. Hate Crimes Prevention Act," October 28, 2009, White House Archives, https://obamawhitehouse.archives.gov/the-press-office/remarks-president-reception-commemorating-enactment-matthew-shepard-and-james-byrd-.

2. Joe Biden, "Remarks at the Signing of the Violence Against Women Act," March 7, 2013, White House Archives, https://obamawhitehouse.archives.gov/the-press-office/2013/03/07/remarks-president-and-vice-president-signing-violence-against-women-act.

3. *Victim* in this book means someone who has experienced an act of violence. It is not an essentialist statement about who a person is. Throughout this book, I describe anti-violence activism on the behalf of a number of groups in addition to transgender people, including women, gay men and lesbians, and people of color. In doing so, I often list those categories. Such lists are not intended to imply that they are mutually exclusive categories; they are not. There is considerable overlap between these groups. A single individual, such as a transgender lesbian of color, can occupy all of them. However, activist groups rarely attended to those overlaps, instead focusing on a single identity at a time. My listing of categories here is thus intended to highlight the identity categories on which various activist groups focus.

4. Although this movement often uses the acronym "LGBT," it has historically ignored bisexuals, so most examples in this book related to sexuality-based identities are of activism on behalf of gay men and lesbians.

5. I draw heavily in this book from social movements scholarship on frames and narratives. My use of the terms *stories* and *narratives* here is not intended to call into question the truth of these tellings of events. Rather, this terminology highlights the ways in which all understandings of events are filtered through cultural lenses.

6. By "unlivable" Butler (2004) does not mean that it is impossible for a being to survive such conditions, but that constant fear without hope for change is a situation that does not allow for a fully human life as we understand *human* and thus is unlivable as a human. In contrast to this unlivable life is a livable one, characterized by those aspects commonly associated with subjecthood, in particular relative autonomy and freedom.

7. Bettcher (2007) and Stryker (1994) (monstrous "evil deceivers"); Stone (2019) (dangerous to children); Welch (2007) (black people as criminals).

8. Mason (2014).

9. Moran et al. (2003).

10. Gould (2009).

11. Butler (2004, 8).

12. Butler (2004, 31).

13. Butler (2004, 29).

14. Best (1990).

15. Taylor and Van Dyke (2007). Although activism increasingly occurs on the internet, effective tactical repertoires have not changed substantially (Maratea 2013).

16. Ray (1999, 7).

17. Crenshaw (1991).

18. Bernstein (1997); Weldon (2006).

19. Crenshaw (1991).

20. Crenshaw (1991); Richie (2000).

21. Spade and Willse (1999).

22. Spade and Willse (1999).

23. Butler (1993, 2004).

24. Brown (1995); Jacobs and Potter (1998).

25. Harwood (2004).

26. Rickford (2016); Zangrando (1980).

27. Berns (2004).

28. Stanko and Curry (1997).

29. Jenness and Broad (1994); Jenness and Grattet (2001); Taylor, Haider-Markel, and Lewis (2018).

30. Meyerowitz (2002).

31. Meyerowitz (2002); Stryker (2017).

32. Broad (2002); Denny (2006); Spade and Currah (2008); Stryker (2017); Westbrook (2010).

33. Denny (2006); Valentine (2007).

34. For an analysis of the controversy surrounding this labeling of a person who had never claimed "transgender" as an identity and who also may never have used the full name "Brandon Teena," see Hale (1998).

35. Inaccuracies in narratives about murders are common in these activist documents, including this misdating of the 1993 homicide.

36. For counts of homicides from 1990 to 2015, see figure 6 in chapter 7.

37. Jenness and Grattet (2001).

38. Blee (2005).

39. Davis and Martinez (1994).

40. Cisgender people identify with the same sex and gender categories to which they were assigned at birth.

41. More "professionalized" organizations, such as those at the national level, have been found to be less likely to engage in "radical" or "disruptive" tactics (Creek and Dunn 2011). As such, it is possible that local organizations are more likely to employ some of the anti-violence solutions I suggest in chapter 7. Future research should compare how identity-based anti-violence activism is done in national versus local organizations.

42. NCAVP detailed the impact of the financial crisis on LGBTQ anti-violence organizing in its report on hate violence in 2009.

43. Bourdieu (1991) ("symbolic violence").

44. Regarding the Wayback Machine, see https://archive.org/web/.

45. Shapiro (2004).

46. Strauss and Corbin (1990) (grounded theory).

47. Ferree et al. (2002, 9).

48. For example, Bourdieu (1998, 40–42).

49. Butler (1993).

50. Christie (1986) ("ideal victims"); Nichols (1997) ("landmark narratives").

51. Dinno (2017); cf. Stotzer (2017) (not more fatal violence than cisgender people); Beeghley (2003) (high homicide rate for cisgender people in the United States).

52. Westbrook (2008) (status as hated into law); Spade (2011) (criminalize transgender people).

53. Jenness and Broad (1994).

CHAPTER 2. VIOLENCE MATTERS

1. Hollander (2001); Madriz (1997); Valentine (1992).

2. Rader and Haynes (2011).

3. Here I focus on the distinctions between productive and repressive as umbrella categories of power, not on the subforms Foucault described such as "biopower." Across his body of work, Foucault vacillated between describing repressive power as a misperception or a true form that was more common in previous historical moments. I see it as an actual form of power. It should be

noted that these forms are given different names in some of Foucault's work. What is termed *repressive power* in *The History of Sexuality* is similar to the *sovereign power* described in *Discipline and Punish*; the equivalent to *productive power* in *Discipline and Punish* is *disciplinary power*.

4. Foucault (1990).

5. Foucault (1990, 85).

6. For execution as an example of sovereign/repressive power, see Foucault (1977b).

7. Foucault (1990, 93).

8. Foucault (1990).

9. Foucault (1982a, 49).

10. Butler(1993); Foucault (1990).

11. Mills (1997, 16).

12. Mills (1997, 15).

13. Mills (1997, 45).

14. For example, Eileraas (2002); Herek (1990); Witten and Eyler (1999); Wyss (2004).

15. For example, Namaste (2000).

16. For exceptions, see Abelson (2019); Lamble (2008); Snorton (2017); Snorton and Haritaworn (2013); Valentine (2007).

17. Butler (1993, 2004).

18. Foucault (1982b, 20).

19. When Foucault uses the term *power* in this essay, he means productive power.

20. Foucault (1977a, 73).

21. Foucault (1977a, 26).

22. Anderson and Umberson (2001); Berns (2001); Blee (2005); Campbell (2005); Hollander (2001); Jenkins (1994); Morash (2006); Shepherd (2007); Westbrook (2008); Wilcox (2015).

23. For example, Banerjee et al. (2004).

24. Mason (2002, 97).

25. Mason (2002, 130).

26. Mason (2002, 6).

27. Butler (1993).

28. Goffman (1986, 8).

29. Benford and Snow (2000); Best (1999); Ferree et al. (2002); Jenness and Grattet (2001).

30. Lyons (2008).

31. Benford and Snow (2000).

32. Scott (2000).

33. Scott (2000).

34. Kindt and Müller (2003).

35. Franzosi (1998).

36. That narratives about violence are not perfect tellings of fact is evidenced by the large number of discrepancies between versions of particular

homicides in the documents I analyzed for this book. These include inconsistencies in the reporting of the victim's age at death, location of the murder, circumstances of the killing, and whether the perpetrator(s) was/were convicted. This often occurs with very famous killings whose telling and retelling has become a ritual among activists; much as in a game of telephone, the version told changes over time.

37. Polletta (2006) (shaping beliefs and practices).

38. Cerulo (2002).

39. Boonzaier (2008); Burton (1998); Hollander (2001); Jacobs (1996).

40. Although these are stories about real people, in their telling, narrators select only certain aspects of the person to tell about. The use of "characterize" can remind us that these are representations of people.

41. Hollander (2001).

42. Polletta (2006).

43. Best and Horiuchi (1985).

44. Stephen Jimenez, *The Book of Matt: Hidden Truths about the Murder of Matthew Shepard* (Hanover, NH: Steerforth, 2013). I include this example not to argue that one narrative is true and another not, but to illustrate the influence of culturally resonant narratives.

45. Freddie deBoer, "Kill Your Martyrs," *New Inquiry*, January 27, 2014.

46. Stanko (2003).

47. Jenness and Broad (1997).

48. Hollander and Rodgers (2014).

49. Hollander and Rodgers (2014, 359).

50. Hollander and Rodgers (2014).

51. Best (1999); Jenness and Grattet (2001).

52. Campbell (2005).

53. Thank you to Dawne Moon, Dawn Dow, Anne Marie Champagne, Omar Lizardo, Jocelyn Hollander, and Siri Colom for helping me generate the term *rape avoidance labor*. Although the example I give here is about how women work to protect themselves from men's sexual violence, all genders engage in rape avoidance labor. See Herman (1989) and Valenti (2007) for "rape schedule."

54. Hollander (2001); Madriz (1997); Rader and Haynes (2011).

55. Hollander and Rodgers (2014).

56. D'Cruze and Rao (2004); Shepherd (2007); Snorton (2017).

57. Crenshaw (1989).

58. Collins (1998, 919) (emphasis in original).

59. Hollander and Rodgers (2014); Madriz (1997); Marcus (1992) (enforcement of gender norms); Butler (1993); Harris (2000); Hollander (2001); Rich (1993) (maintain sexual hierarchies); Correia (2008) (regulate racialized subjects).

60. Violence also shapes beliefs about, and practices of, other social categories such as age, class, and disability.

61. Marcus (1992).

62. Hollander (2001).

63. Campbell (2005, 119).

64. Anderson and Umberson (2001, 359).

65. By highlighting these parallels, I do not mean to imply that these categories are mutually exclusive. The categories transgender and cisgender each contain both women and men and vice versa.

66. Hollander (2001); Mason (2002, 108).

67. Fanon (1963).

68. Blee (2005, 602) (emphasis in original).

69. Peterson (2010).

70. Hollander (2001).

71. Westbrook (2008).

72. Rader and Haynes (2011, 291 and 299)

73. Burton (1998); Hollander (2001).

74. Marcus (1992); Mehta and Bondi (1999).

75. Madriz (1997).

76. Day (1999); Valentine (1989).

77. Marcus (1992, 437) (emphasis in original).

78. Britt and Heise (2000, 256).

79. It should be noted that most of the victims of the Pulse shooting were also of color. Despite the possibility of attributing the shooting to racism, that explanation was not common in mainstream accounts of the atrocity.

80. Glenn Greenwald and Murtaza Hussain, "As the Trial of Omar Mateen's Wife Begins, New Evidence Undermines Beliefs about the Pulse Massacre, Including Motive," *Intercept*, March 5, 2018.

81. Foucault (1990, 138).

82. Lamble (2008); Snorton and Haritaworn (2013).

83. Butler (2004, 31).

84. For example, Mason (2002).

85. Hanhardt (2013).

86. Andersson (2008).

87. Hartman (1997).

CHAPTER 3. ATYPICAL ARCHETYPES

1. Nancy Nangeroni, "Trans-Actions: News & Notes from the Gender Frontier," *Transgender Tapestry*, no. 74 (1995).

2. See appendix B for details.

3. Christie (1986).

4. Madriz (1997).

5. Carrabine et al. (2009).

6. Valier (2004).

7. Nichols (1997).

8. Chancer (2005).

9. Hale (1998, 311).

10. Although it is typical to refer to people by their last names in most academic work, within the field of transgender studies, it is more common to refer to transgender people by their chosen first names to demonstrate respect for their gender identity. Therefore, I refer to Brandon Teena as Brandon and Gwen Araujo as Gwen throughout this book. However, I use full or last names for trans academics and activists, as that is the standard way of showing respect to people in those social categories.

11. James et al. (2016).

12. Flores et al. (2016).

13. They are also representative of the majority of trans people in the United States. As numerous scholars have demonstrated (e.g., Grant et al. 2011), most trans people do not have surgeries. This pattern occurs for a number of reasons, including not desiring such body modifications (despite the normative narrative that "true" trans people want surgeries) and not being able to access these body modifications because of financial barriers and/or because of race- and gender-based inequalities in access to health care.

14. Six (3.4%) of the perpetrators were cis women and three (1.7%) were trans women. None of the perpetrators were trans men or nonbinary.

15. Hollander (2001); Madriz (1997).

16. It may be that Ruby Ordeñana was raped before being murdered in 2007; however, prosecutors did not pursue the case after convicting the perpetrator of another crime, so it is unclear whether that occured.

17. Transfeminine is an umbrella term for people who were labeled male at birth and identify and/or behave as more feminine than masculine. Transmasculine is an umbrella term for people who were labeled female at birth and identify and/or behave as more masculine than feminine. As the homicide data I collected are focused on transgender behaviors rather than identities, I use transfeminine as the adjective form of transgender woman and transmasculine as the adjective form of transgender man.

18. Twelve (4%) were Asian/Pacific Islander and six (2%) were Native American.

19. This erasure of black victims can be seen starkly in the case of the murder of Brandon Teena. In addition to Brandon, John Lotter and Tom Nissen also shot and killed the other two adults in the farmhouse that evening: Lisa Lambert, who was white, and Phillip DeVine, who was black. Both of these cisgender victims are rarely mentioned when discussing the murder, but of the two, DeVine is particularly invisible in these narratives. For example, the fictionalized retelling of this case in the film *Boys Don't Cry* includes Lambert (who is renamed Candace) but, tellingly, not DeVine (Brody 2002; Snorton 2017).

20. Of the rest, 1 percent were convicted of another murder and so were not tried, and 3.5 percent of the accused perpetrators died before they could go to trial.

21. Of course this is not always the case. The murders of Nicole Brown Simpson and JonBénet Ramsey are notable exceptions.

22. People, unlike characters in a story, are complex. As such, most people who are portrayed as "ideal" victims in activist narratives have some aspects of their lives that are counter to the criteria for "ideal" victims. However, activists downplay those, such as Brandon's arrest for check forgery and Gwen's drug and alcohol use, and emphasize the more "ideal" ones.

23. Joy Vannelia Hughes, "The Whole World Wasn't Watching," 2000, https://web.archive.org/web/20011216034929/http://www.gender.org /remember/about/core.html. (To access this specific item, go to the URL and click on "Alina Marie Barragan.")

24. Dixon and Maddox (2005); Greenwald, Oakes, and Hoffman (2003).

25. Nagel (2003).

26. Nireah and her cisgender friend Brandie Coleman were tied up with wire, put in the back seat of their car, driven to a parking lot, and shot. The perpetrators returned later and set the car on fire.

27. As demonstrated in scholarship by philosopher Talia Mae Bettcher (2007) and in my own work with sociologist Kristen Schilt (Schilt and Westbrook 2009), the "discovery" narrative is a common trope in narratives about violence against trans people. I put "discovered" in quotes to call into question the knowability of the body and to highlight that it is not really clear what is "discovered" in these moments.

28. Quoted in GenderPAC, "GenderPAC Condemns Martinez Killing," August 27, 2001, https://web.archive.org/web/20020201015045/http://www .gpac.org/archive/news/index.html?cmd=view&archive=news&msgnum= 0329.

29. Schilt and Westbrook (2009).

30. Hamermesh (2013) (associated with good character).

31. GenderPAC, "Menace Calls Off Picketing NBC," March 10, 1996, https://web.archive.org/web/20050106235750/http://www.qrd.org/qrd/trans /1996/menace.calls.off.nbc.picket-03.10.96.

32. NTAC, "Araujo Murder Trial Scheduled to Begin March 29th," March 27, 2004, https://web.archive.org/web/20041204114122/http://www.ntac.org: 80/pr/release.asp?did=91; and Monica Helms, "And That's The Way It Is," *Transgender Tapestry*, no. 87 (2003): 10.

33. David Steinberg, "Comes Naturally," *Transgender Tapestry*, no. 100 (2002): 55.

34. Armstrong and Crage (2006).

35. Stryker (2017).

36. Westbrook (2010) (recently coined term).

37. For example, see Jordy Jones, "FTM Crossdresser Murdered," *FTMi*, no. 26 (1994), and "Brandon Teena Murder Trial Demonstration," *FTMi*, no. 30 (1995).

38. Nancy Nangeroni, "Trans-Actions: News & Notes from the Gender Frontier," *Transgender Tapestry*, no. 74 (1995): D3.

39. For those wondering why this occurred when it did, I am unable to say for sure using the data I gathered. However, I believe that increased access to

the internet played a role (this has been pointed to by Stephen Whittle [1998]), as well as a new group of trans activists who had gained experience in ActUP and Queer Nation groups.

40. Nancy Nangeroni, "Hundreds Turn Out in Boston after Transexual Murder," December 22, 1995, https://web.archive.org/web/20050106233835 /http://www.qrd.org/qrd/trans/1995/boston.actions.after.murders-12.22.95. (The spelling of *transexual* in this press release follows that of the group Transexual Menace.)

41. GSA, "Transgender Day of Remembrance," June 29, 2007, https://web .archive.org/web/20090219155449/http://www.gsanetwork.org/resources/pdf /DayofRemembrance2.pdf.

42. Lack of transgender identity is likely why the others murdered with Brandon Teena are rarely mentioned by trans activists.

43. Jamison Green, "FTM-Lesbian Dialogue from PlanetOut," *FTMi*, no. 64 (2007): 6.

44. A search on Access World News shows almost three thousand stories for each between 1990 and 2009.

45. GLAAD, "Transgender Day of Remembrance 2007," November 15, 2007, https://web.archive.org/web/20081008154145/http://www.glaad.org /publications/archive_detail.php?id=4108.

46. For example, Gilchrist (2010).

47. Best (2016).

48. Schilt and Westbrook (2009).

49. Schilt and Westbrook (2009).

50. The mainstream media often report on murder trials. Thus, homicides that never go to trial receive less coverage, and those with multiple trials receive more.

51. Hale (1998).

52. Westbrook (2010) (early definitions of transgender); Garrison (2018) (the primacy of binary trans identities).

53. Abelson (2019); Yavorsky and Sayer (2013).

54. Quoted in Sam Feder and Amy Scholder, dirs., *Disclosure* (Netflix, 2020), www.disclosurethemovie.com/.

55. GLAAD, "Covering Hate Crimes," October 1, 2003, https://web.archive .org/web/20050313203850/http://www.glaad.org/media/resource_kit_detail .php?id=3495&PHPSESSID=97c8af8444c4674ba34dddb10688fab9.

56. HRC, "Transgender Basics," 2003, https://web.archive.org/web /20060103041804/http://www.hrc.org/Template.cfm?Section=Transgender _Basics.

57. Travers (2018, 133).

58. Buist and Stone (2014).

59. Jody Norton, "The Rectitude of Death," *Transgender Tapestry*, no. 87 (1999): 40.

60. GLAAD, "Transgender Day of Remembrance 2007."

61. Halberstam (2005, 25).

62. There were 48 in the Northeast, 72 in the West, and 130 in the South. Variation by region is likely affected by population size.
63. Madriz (1997).
64. Valentine (1992).

CHAPTER 4. HOMOGENEOUS SUBJECTHOOD

1. Gwendolyn Smith, "Remembering Our Dead: Behind the Website," *Transgender Tapestry*, no. 87 (1999).
2. Remembering Our Dead, "About This Site," https://web.archive.org/web /20051124173501/http://www.rememberingourdead.org/about/core.html.
3. Burton (1998, 183) (*"all* women are potential rape victims"; emphasis in original); Richie (2000, 1134) ("any woman or child").
4. Jenness and Broad (1994) (emphasis in original).
5. Crenshaw (1991).
6. Jenness and Broad (1994).
7. Crenshaw (1991); Nixon and Humphreys (2010); Richie (2000).
8. Richie (2000, 1135).
9. Crenshaw (1991); Richie (2000).
10. Beeghley (2003).
11. Richie (2000).
12. For example, Joy Vannelia Hughes, "The Whole World Wasn't Watching," 2000, https://web.archive.org/web/20011216034929/http://www.gender .org/remember/about/core.html. (To access this specific item, go to the URL and click on "Alina Marie Barragan.")
13. For excellent analysis of debates about who is or is not transgender, see Hale (1998) and Valentine (2007).
14. GenderPAC, "Hate Crime Portraits," March 10, 2005, https:// web.archive.org/web/20051110052938if_/http://www.gpac.org/violence /hatecrimes.html. Note that Brandon was actually killed in December 1993.
15. Dana Priesing, "TG & Busted! What to Do!," *Transgender Tapestry*, no. 76 (1996, 6) ("transgendered"); and It's Time, Massachusetts!, "If You Thought Your Silence Would Protect You . . . Think Again," *Transgender Tapestry*, no. 85, special insert (1998): 1 ("a pre-operative transsexual"); GenderPAC, "Supreme Court Denies Appeal of Brandon Teena's Murderer," July 6, 1999, https://web.archive.org/web/20051110111949/http://www.gpac .org/archive/news/notitle.html?cmd=view&archive=news&msgnum=0178 ("transman").
16. GLAAD, "Shannon Garcia—'What Does the Transgender Day of Remembrance Mean to You?,'" November 20, 2008, https://web.archive.org /web/20100615060952/http://glaadblog.org:80/2008/11/20/shannon-garcia -what-does-the-transgender-day-of-remembrance-mean-to-you/ ("because they are transgender"); NCTE, "It's Official: First Federal Law to Protect Transgender People," 2009, https://web.archive.org/web/20091219004618 /http://transequality.org:80/news.html ("who they are").

17. Mara Keisling, "Statement on the Introduction of the Local Law Enforcement Hate Crimes Prevention Act of 2005," NCTE, May 26, 2005, https://web.archive.org/web/20051215145321/http://nctequality.org/hate crimesintroduction.pdf.

18. Moe Macarow, "The 10th Annual Transgender Day of Remembrance," GLAAD, November 20, 2008, https://web.archive.org/web/20110804053249 /http://glaadblog.org/2008/11/20/speaking-out/ ("being transgender"); NCTE, "Verdict in Lateisha Green Court Trial," July 17, 2009, https://transequality.org /blog/verdict-in-lateisha-green-court-trial ("transgender woman"). By explicitly marking being transgender as an illegitimate reason to kill someone, statements like this unintentionally imply that there are valid motivations for murder.

19. NCTE, "Human Rights Calendar," 2007, https://web.archive.org/web /20081203184041/http://www.nctequality.org//calendar.html.

20. Meyerowitz (2002).

21. Gwendolyn Smith, "2005 Transgender Day of Remembrance Announced," June 1, 2005, https://web.archive.org/web/20060908081211 /http://www.rememberingourdead.org/day/files/dorpr_01.txt.

22. Remembering Our Dead, "About the Day of Remembrance," https:// web.archive.org/web/20050215183548/http://www.rememberingourdead.org /day/what.html.

23. Moran and Sharpe (2004).

24. Bettcher (2007); Schilt and Westbrook (2009).

25. Mason (2002).

26. Moran and Sharpe (2004); Stotzer (2008).

27. Lamble (2008).

28. Jordy Jones, "FTM Crossdresser Murdered," *FTMi*, no. 26 (1994): 3.

29. HRC, "Examples of Hate Crimes against Transgender Individuals," March 2002 (document available upon request).

30. Juang (2006).

31. Lamble (2008, 25); see also Beauchamp (2007).

32. Li Anne Taft, "There Is No Safe Way to Be Transgendered," *Transgender Tapestry*, no. 97 (2002, 11).

33. See appendix B for details on how these data were gathered.

34. Denise Leclore, "Fore Word," *Transgender Tapestry*, no. 114 (2008): 114.

35. The other victims were twenty, twenty-five, thirty-three, and forty-nine years old when killed.

36. Riki Wilchins, "Saturday Night Live: Brandon Teena & Friends '. . . Deserve to Die,'" GenderPAC, February 28, 1996, http://www.qrd.org/qrd /trans/1996/snl.slur.response-02.28.96 (emphasis added).

37. HRC, "Examples of Hate Crimes against Transgender Individuals."

38. I borrow this concept from literary theory. Although the gendered nature of the term would usually be problematic, it is appropriate here, as the murderers of trans people are usually men.

39. Quoted in GenderPAC, "HRC Issues Statement on Gender Hate Crimes," May 30, 1999, https://web.archive.org/web/20001207233800/http://

www.gpac.org/archive/news/index.html?cmd=view&archive=news&msgnum
=0201.

40. Remembering Our Dead, "About This Site" ("no 'safe way' to be trans-gendered"); Riki Wilchins, "Disposable People," *Transgender Tapestry*, no. 87 (1999): 11 ("all at risk").

41. Bob Moser, "Disposable People," *SPLC Intelligence Report* (Winter 2003), https://web.archive.org/web/20040414161146/http://www.splcenter.org/intel/intelreport/article.jsp?aid=149.

42. Valentine (1989).

43. Best (1999).

44. Brown (1995); Fellows and Razack (1998).

45. Perry and Dyck (2014, 58).

46. Moser, "Disposable People."

47. NCAVP, *Anti-Lesbian, Gay, Bisexual and Transgender Violence in 2004*, 2005, 13.

48. Monica Helms, "And That's the Way It Is!," *Transgender Tapestry*, no. 95 (2001): 13 ("transgender killing field"); Monica Helms, ". . . And That's the Way It Is," *Transgender Tapestry*, no. 105 (2004): 14 ("cannon fodder").

49. Remembering Our Dead, "About This Site."

50. For example, NCAVP, *Anti-Lesbian, Gay, Bisexual and Transgender Violence in 2004*, 14; and Mark Potok, "Rage on the Right," *SPLC Intelligence Report* (Winter 2003), https://web.archive.org/web/20040414115327/http://www.splcenter.org/intel/intelreport/article.jsp?aid=141 ("right-wing" politicians); David Steinberg, "To Be a Man: 'Boys Don't Cry' and the Story of Brandon Teena," *Transgender Tapestry*, no. 90 (2000): 48 ("working class America").

51. Jacobs and Potter (1998, 131).

52. Varshney (2008).

53. Flores et al. (2018); Tadlock et al. (2017).

54. GenderPAC, "Finally—The Full Story of the Killing of PFC. Barry Winchell," May 30, 2000, https://web.archive.org/web/20050322195837/http://www.gpac.org/archive/action/index.html?cmd=view&archive=action&msgnum=0005 (first mention).

55. GenderPAC, *50 under 30: Masculinity and the War on America's Youth*, 2006, 2, https://web.archive.org/web/20071007083152/http://www.gpac.org/50under30/50u30.pdf.

56. NCTE, "NCTE in the News," January 16, 2007, https://transequality.org/blog/ncte-in-the-news-transgender-people-face-violence-obstacles.

57. GLAAD, "Transgender Hate Crimes Panel Provides Personal Stories as Well as Advocacy Insight," October 8, 2009, https://web.archive.org/web/20110804054314/http://glaadblog.org/2009/10/08/transgender-hate-crimes-panel-provides-personal-stories-as-well-as-advocacy-insight/.

58. NCAVP, *Hate Violence against the Lesbian, Gay, Bisexual, Transgender and Queer Communities in the United States in 2009*, 2010.

59. NCAVP, *Hate Violence against the Lesbian, Gay, Bisexual, Transgender and Queer Communities in the United States* in 2009, 49.

60. Quoted in HRC, "HRC Decries Two Recent Hate Crimes against GLBT People of Color," May 22, 2003, https://web.archive.org/web/20030804074619 /http://www.hrc.org/newsreleases/2003/030522hatecrimes.asp.

61. Quoted in GenderPAC, "GenderPAC Condemns Murder of African-American NJ Teen," May 11, 2003, https://web.archive.org/web /20030710163937/http://www.gpac.org/archive/news/index.html?cmd=view &archive=news&msgnum=0482.

62. GSA, "Transgender Inclusivity in GSAs," March 1, 2005, https://web .archive.org/web/20050831085248/http://www.gsanetwork.org/resources/pdf /Transgender.pdf.

63. NCAVP, *Hate Violence against the Lesbian, Gay, Bisexual, Transgender and Queer Communities in the United States* in 2009, 32.

64. Alexander John Goodrum, "Gender, Identity Politics & Eating Our Own," *FTMi*, no. 50 (2001): 3.

65. GenderPAC, *50 under 30*, 4.

66. Brown (1995).

67. Nancy Nangeroni, "Trans-Actions," *Transgender Tapestry*, no. 74 (1995): D4 ("a leading activist for our community"); Nancy Nangeroni, "Trans-Actions," *Transgender Tapestry*, no. 78 (1996) (united several trans rights organizations).

68. For example, "In Your Face," *FTMi*, no. 35 (1996); "Interview: Riki Ann Wilchins," *Transgender Tapestry*, no. 81 (1997).

69. "Interview: Riki Ann Wilchins," 8 ("national lobbying arm"); Gender-PAC, "Justice for Christian Paige," May 19, 1996; Nangeroni, "Trans-Actions," *Transgender Tapestry*, no. 78, 11 ("gender, affectional and racial equality").

70. "Interview: Riki Ann Wilchins," 10.

71. Valentine (2007, 213).

72. GenderPAC, "Our Mission and Vision," 2002, https://web.archive.org /web/20020603125232/http://www.gpac.org/gpac/index.html.

73. Pauline Park, "GenderPAC, the Transgender Rights Movement and the Perils of a Post-Identity Politics Paradigm," April 15, 2003, https://paulinepark .com/genderpac-the-transgender-rights-movement-and-the-perils-of-a-post -identity-politics-paradigm/.

74. Valentine (2007); Donna Cartwright, "Whither GPAC? Reflections at My Time of Resignation," *Transgender Tapestry*, no. 93 (2001).

75. Cartwright, "Whither GPAC?"

76. Cartwright, "Whither GPAC?"

77. Riki Wilchins, "Letter to Supporters," May 28, 2009, https://web .archive.org/web/20090707183228/http://www.gpac.org/.

78. "Here's Wilchins' July Letter," *Transgender Tapestry*, no. 89 (2000).

79. For readers who currently exist in activist communities that regularly attend to multiple inequalities, such a conflict may seem baffling. However,

highlighting intersectionality is a relatively new practice in anti-violence activism and, as I detail in chapter 7, is still often done in ways that echo patterns from previous decades. Moreover, as a "transgender organization" GenderPAC focused on gender-based issues faced by those who were not transgender, an approach that is still not accepted within a political field that values identity politics.

80. Goodrum, "Gender, Identity Politics & Eating Our Own," 3.
81. Cartwright, "Whither GPAC?," 57.
82. Cartwright, "Whither GPAC?," 57.
83. Goodrum, "Gender, Identity Politics & Eating Our Own."

CHAPTER 5. VALUABLE AND VULNERABLE

1. Quoted in Gwendolyn Smith, "Day of Remembrance: 14 Cities," *Transgender Tapestry*, no. 93 (2001): 32–33).
2. Smith, "Day of Remembrance: 14 Cities," 33.
3. Smith, "Day of Remembrance: 14 Cities," 34.
4. Polletta and Jasper (2001); Smithey (2009).
5. Hacking (1986, 236); Hunt and Benford (2004).
6. Remembering Our Dead, "About This Site," https://web.archive.org/web/20051124173501/http://www.rememberingourdead.org/about/core.html.
7. NCTE, "It's Official: First Federal Law to Protect Transgender People," 2009, https://web.archive.org/web/20091219004618/http://transequality.org:80/news.html.
8. Kerry Lobel, "Where Have You Been America?," *Transgender Tapestry*, no. 99 (1999, 10).
9. Jasper (1998).
10. Butler (2004, 224).
11. GenderPAC, *50 under 30: Masculinity and the War on America's Youth*, 2006, 9, https://web.archive.org/web/20071007083152/http://www.gpac.org/50under30/50u30.pdf.
12. Butler (1993).
13. Quoted in "Demonstration/Vigil for Christian Paige," in "In Your Face" insert, *FTMi*, no. 35, (1996): 3.
14. Quoted in NTAC, "Transgenders across Country, Globe to Remember Victims of Murder," November 3, 2002, https://web.archive.org/web/20021204224139/http://www.ntac.org:80/pr/release.asp?did=52.
15. Quoted in GenderPAC, "Lambda Legal Defense Fund Will Join Appeal of Meager Award in Brandon Teena Case," February 29, 2000, https://web.archive.org/web/20051111053156/http://www.gpac.org/archive/news/notitle.html?cmd=view&archive=news&msgnum=0215.
16. Quoted in HRC, "HRC Mourns the Murders of Two Transgender Women and Brutal Attack of Another Transgender Woman in Nation's

Capital," August 21, 2003, https://web.archive.org/web/20030903153057 /http://www.hrc.org/newsreleases/2003/030821transgender.asp.

17. GSA, "Transgender Day of Remembrance," June 29, 2007, https://web .archive.org/web/20090219155449/http://www.gsanetwork.org/resources/pdf /DayofRemembrance2.pdf.

18. Quoted in GenderPAC, "Two Murder Convictions in Araujo Case But No Hate Crime," September 13, 2005, https://web.archive.org/web /20071004064923/http://www.gpac.org/archive/news/notitle.html?cmd=view &archive=news&msgnum=0608.

19. Davis and Martinez (1994).

20. GenderPAC, *50 under 30*, 9.

21. Fellows and Razack (1998). For an analysis of how this occurs through the Transgender Day of Remembrance, see Lamble (2008).

22. For a similar argument, see Brown (1995).

23. Allyson Robinson, "Holding My Hand and Watching My Back," HRC, November 2, 2009, https://web.archive.org/web/20091226083450/http://www .hrcbackstory.org/2009/11/allyson-robinson-holding-my-hand-and-watching -my-back/.

24. Mark Potok, "Rage on the Right," *SPLC Intelligence Report* (Winter 2003), https://web.archive.org/web/20040414115327/http://www.splcenter .org/intel/intelreport/article.jsp?aid=141.

25. Bob Moser, "Disposable People," *SPLC Intelligence Report* (Winter 2003), https://web.archive.org/web/20040414161146/http://www.splcenter .org/intel/intelreport/article.jsp?aid=149.

26. Quoted in Tara Culp-Ressler, "Jimmy Carter: Violence against Women Is the Most Pervasive Human Rights Violation in the World." March 24, 2014, https://web.archive.org/web/20140325235903/http://thinkprogress.org /health/2014/03/24/3418277/jimmy-carter-gender-inequality/.

27. *I am a girl*, 2013, https://iamagirl.com.au/the-film.

28. Bureau of Justice Statistics, "Sex," https://www.bjs.gov/index.cfm?ty =tp&tid=923; Federal Bureau of Investigation, "UCR Publications," https:// www.fbi.gov/services/cjis/ucr/publications.

29. Carrie Davis, "Testimony to the New York City Council," *Transgender Tapestry*, no. 99 (2002): 16. Note that the statistic referenced in this quote is false.

30. Beeghley (2003).

31. Wirtz et al. (2018).

32. Factor and Rothblum (2008).

33. Dinno (2017, 1441); cf. Stotzer (2017).

34. GenderPAC, "Trans-Murder in Austin," January 14, 1999, https://web .archive.org/web/20051111050521/http://www.gpac.org/archive/news/notitle .html?cmd=view&archive=news&msgnum=0052.

35. GLAAD, "The Angie Zapata Murder: Violence against Transgender People Resource Kit," 2009, https://web.archive.org/web/20100712224608 /http://www.glaad.org/Page.aspx?pid=571.

36. The original had an orange background, blue writing, and blue tape. I have reproduced it here in black and white without the tape to make it easier to read.

37. Quoted in Smith, "Day of Remembrance: 14 Cities," 34.

38. "FTMI Male Box," *FTMi*, no. 59 (2005): 15.

39. HRC, NGLTF, and NOW, *Examples of Hate Crimes against Transgender Individuals*, March 2002 (document available upon request).

40. Hollander (2001).

41. GSA, "Transgender Inclusivity in GSAs," March 1, 2005, https://web
.archive.org/web/20050831085248/http://www.gsanetwork.org/resources/pdf
/Transgender.pdf.

42. Best (1995).

43. Note that unlike those in the civil rights and lesbian and gay rights movements, those working to reduce violence against women do not tend to center their claims around fatal violence. Instead, they focus on rape, a form of violence seen by many as a fate worse than death (Marcus 1992).

44. Madriz (1997, 354).

45. Britt and Heise (2000) (eliciting fear as a tactic).

46. Ethan St. Pierre, "Remembering Debbie Forte," NTAC, November 28, 2001, https://web.archive.org/web/20020325070932/http://www.ntac.org:80
/newsletter/details.asp?IID=27&AID=149&type=Latest.

47. SPLC, "The Forgotten," *SPLC Intelligence Report* (Spring 2002), https://web.archive.org/web/20040406173020/http://www.splcenter.org/intel
/intelreport/article.jsp?aid=133.

48. HRC, "Hate Violence Continues to Shock the Nation," May 26, 2005, https://web.archive.org/web/20070426052821/http://www.hrc.org/Template
.cfm?Section=Home&Template=/ContentManagement/ContentDisplay.cfm
&ContentID=27103.

49. Riki Wilchins, "Saturday Night Live: Brandon Teena & Friends '. . . Deserve to Die,'" February 28, 1996, http://www.qrd.org/qrd/trans/1996/snl
.slur.response-02.28.96.

50. Quoted in NCTE, "NCTE in the News," January 16, 2007, https://
transequality.org/blog/ncte-in-the-news-transgender-people-face-violence
-obstacles.

51. NCAVP, *Anti-Lesbian, Gay, Bisexual and Transgender Violence in 1997*, 1998, 25.

52. NCAVP, *Hate Violence against the Lesbian, Gay, Bisexual, Transgender and Queer Communities in the United States in 2009*, 2010, 13.

53. Moser, "Disposable People."

54. Wertheimer (2000).

55. Berrill and Herek (1990).

56. Jenness and Broad (1994, 408).

57. Jacobs and Henry (1996).

58. For example, Best (1999, 2004, 2012, 2016).

75. Janet Mock, "Quiet Reflections: Why I Choose Silence on Trans Day of Remembrance," November 22, 2013, https://janetmock.com/2013/11/22/transgender-day-of-remembrance/.

76. GLAAD, "Community Response to Murder of Gwen Araujo," October 22, 2002, https://web.archive.org/web/20060308000056/http://www.glaad.org/publications/resource_doc_detail.php?id=3063&PHPSESSID=0c465e7e78818ca9bd4dac5d9308fd67.

77. Jenness and Broad (1994, 409).

78. www.oneinfourusa.org/ (no longer an active website).

79. Michele Black, Kathleen Basile, Matthew Breiding, Sharon Smith, Mikel Walters, Melissa Merrick, Jieru Chen, and Mark Stevens, *The National Intimate Partner and Sexual Violence Survey: 2010 Summary Report*, National Center for Injury Prevention and Control, 2011, www.niwrc.org/sites/default/files/documents/Resources/Stalking-report2010.pdf.

80. Cermele (2010).

81. NCAVP, *Anti-Lesbian, Gay, Bisexual and Transgender Violence in 1998*, 1999, 6–7.

82. Nancy Nangeroni, "Trans-Actions," *Transgender Tapestry*, no. 79 (1997).

83. See Hale (1998) and Valentine (2007) for analyses of moments in which trans activists label those who do not self-identify as trans as "transgender."

84. For example, Riki Wilchins, "Editorial From GenderPAC's Executive Director," March 1, 1999, https://web.archive.org/web/20051110110938/http://www.gpac.org/archive/news/notitle.html?cmd=view&archive=news&msgnum=0144.

85. GLAAD, "Hate Crimes," October 1, 2003, https://web.archive.org/web/20051119220511/http://www.glaad.org/publications/resource_doc_detail.php?id=3496&PHPSESSID=634260e10ba3d59dd3d319e66a1c8956#patton.

86. Best (1999); Jenness and Grattet (2001).

87. Jenness and Grattet (2001).

88. NCAVP, *Anti-Lesbian, Gay, Bisexual and Transgender Violence in 1998*, 4.

89. Wilchins, "Editorial from GenderPAC's Executive Director" ("meat-grinder"); GenderPAC, "Defense Used Gender to Free Killer of Black Gay Man," March 1, 2000, https://web.archive.org/web/20051111053220/http://www.gpac.org/archive/news/notitle.html?cmd=view&archive=news&msgnum=0216 ("open season").

90. Jacobs and Henry (1996).

91. Jacobs and Henry (1996, 370, 372, 376).

92. NCAVP, *Anti-Lesbian, Gay, Bisexual and Transgender Violence in 2000*, 2001, 8. Note that LGTB was the acronym used by NCAVP that year.

93. Jacobs and Potter (1998).

94. NCAVP, *Anti-Lesbian, Gay, Bisexual and Transgender Violence in 2000*, 8.

95. NCAVP, *Anti-Lesbian, Gay, Bisexual and Transgender Violence in 2004*, 2005, 4–5.

96. NCAVP, *Anti-Lesbian, Gay, Bisexual and Transgender Violence in 2005*, 2006.

97. NCAVP, *Anti-Lesbian, Gay, Bisexual and Transgender Violence in 2005*, 15.

98. NCAVP, *Anti-Lesbian, Gay, Bisexual and Transgender Violence in 2001*, 2002, 10.

99. Wilchins, "Editorial from GenderPAC's Executive Director."

100. Riki Wilchins, "Disposable People," *Transgender Tapestry*, no. 87 (1999); Moser, "Disposable People."

101. Gwendolyn Smith, "Remembering Our Dead: Behind the Website," *Transgender Tapestry*, no. 87 (1999): 35.

102. Monica Helms, ". . . And That's the Way It Is," *Transgender Tapestry*, no. 105 (2004): 14.

103. Remembering Our Dead, "About This Site."

104. GenderPAC, *70 under 30: Masculinity and the War on America's Youth*, 2008, 4.

105. Helms, ". . . And That's the Way It Is," 15.

106. Cooper and Smith (2011).

107. GenderPAC, *50 under 30*, 10.

108. Valentine (2007).

109. Todd Savage, "Requiem for a Teenage Cross-Dresser," *Chicago Reader*, May 19, 1994, www.chicagoreader.com/chicago/requiem-for-a -teenage-cross-dresser/Content?oid=884561; Dian Stojentin, "The True, Fabulous, Radiantly Obnoxious Quona," *Chicago Reader*, June 2, 1994, www .chicagoreader.com/chicago/the-true-fabulous-radiantly-obnoxious-quona /Content?oid=884665.

110. Miqqi Gilbert, "On the Edge of Revolution," *Transgender Tapestry*, no. 87 (1999): 24.

111. Chris Johnson, "HRC Associate Diversity director Allyson Robinson Speaks at National Transgender Day of Remembrance Event in Orlando," HRC, November 20, 2008. https://web.archive.org/web/20081127134149 /http://www.hrcbackstory.org/2008/11/hrc-associate-d.html.

112. Quoted in HRC, "November 20th Is Transgender Day of Remembrance," November 20, 2007, https://web.archive.org/web/20110524152546 /http://www.hrc.org/8318.htm.

113. Abelson (2019, 131).

114. Miles Walser, "Nebraska," 2010, http://thespice-boxofearth.blogspot .com/2012/12/brandon-teena.html.

115. Harwood (2004, 467, 471).

116. Moran et al. (2003, 142).

117. Mehta and Bondi (1999).

118. Hollander (2001).

119. Marcus (1992) (inherently rapable); Helliwell (2000) (baffling in some cultures).

120. Burton (1998).

121. Hill (2002); Perry and Dyck (2014).

122. Hollander (2001); Madriz (1997).

123. Yavorsky and Sayer (2013).

124. Meyer and Grollman (2014).

125. Campbell (2005); Hollander (2001).

126. Madriz (1997, 343).

127. Abelson (2019, 152).

128. Perry and Dyck (2014, 58); see also Yavorsky and Sayer (2013).

129. Grant et al. (2011, 126).

130. Hale (1998, 318–19). In this context, "ftm" refers to "female-to-male" transsexuals or transgender people.

131. Anonymous, "How My Friend John Was Murdered Twice," 1999, https://web.archive.org/web/19991013235855/http://www.gender.org /remember/about/core.html.

132. For example, Geronimus et al. (2006)

133. Campbell (2005); Marcus (1992).

134. Helms, ". . . And That's the Way It Is," 14.

CHAPTER 6. SHAPING SOLUTIONS

1. GLAAD, "The Angie Zapata Murder: Violence against Transgender People Resource Kit," 2009, https://web.archive.org/web/20100712224608/http:// www.glaad.org/Page.aspx?pid=571; GenderPAC, *70 under 30: Masculinity and the War on America's Youth*, 2008, https://www.scribd.com/document /101473531/70-Under-30-Masculinity-and-the-War-on-America-s-Youth.

2. For example, GLAAD, "Transgender Woman Murdered in Colorado," July 23, 2008, https://web.archive.org/web/20081008160602/http://www .glaad.org/publications/archive_detail.php?id=4556; GLAAD, "Spotlight on the Colorado Anti-Violence Program," November 19, 2008, https://web .archive.org/web/20100616115913/http://glaadblog.org/2008/11/19/spotlight -on-the-colorado-anti-violence-program/.

3. Donna Rose, "The Angie Zapata Vigil," The Bilerico Project, August 11, 2008, http://bilerico.lgbtqnation.com/2008/08/the_angie_zapata_vigil.php.

4. GLAAD, "Arrest Made in Murder of Transgender Woman," July 31, 2008, https://web.archive.org/web/20081008161034/http://www.glaad.org /publications/archive_detail.php?id=4584; Chris Johnson, "Update: An Arrest Made in the Murder of Teenage Transgender Woman in Colorado," HRC, July 31, 2008, https://web.archive.org/web/20081127201836/http://www .hrcbackstory.org/2008/07/update-an-arres.html; NCTE, "NCTE Statement on the Greeley Colorado Verdict," April 22, 2009, https://web.archive.org/web /20091219004618/http://transequality.org:80/news.html.

5. Chris Johnson, "Murder of Teenage Transgender Woman in Colorado Raises Flags of Possible Hate Crime," HRC, July 28, 2008, https://web.archive .org/web/20081127180312/http://www.hrcbackstory.org/2008/07/murder-of -teena.html.

6. For example, GLAAD, "Hate Crimes Charge in Murder of Transgender Woman," August 1, 2008, https://web.archive.org/web/20081008155937 /http://www.glaad.org/publications/archive_detail.php?id=4587.

7. GLAAD, "GLAAD Issues Statement on Angie Zapata Murder Verdict," April 22, 2009, https://web.archive.org/web/20100616090608/http://glaadblog .org/2009/04/22/glaad-issues-statement-on-angie-zapata-murder-verdict/.

8. HRC, "Human Rights Campaign Honors Transgender Day of Remembrance," November 19, 2008, https://web.archive.org/web/20081129105503 /http://www.hrc.org/issues/hate_crimes/11574.htm.

9. GLAAD, "GLAAD Issues Statement on Angie Zapata Murder Verdict."

10. NCAVP, *Hate Violence against the Lesbian, Gay, Bisexual, Transgender People in the United States in 2008*, 2009.

11. NCTE, "NCTE Statement on the Greeley Colorado Verdict," April 22, 2009, https://web.archive.org/web/20091219004618/http://transequality.org: 80/news.html

12. Benford and Snow (2000); Berns (2004); Best (1995); Lamble (2008).

13. Gerstenfeld (2004); Jacobs and Potter (1998).

14. Spade (2011).

15. Quoted in GLAAD, "Spotlight on the Colorado Anti-Violence Program."

16. R. Scott Gerdes, "Update: The Brandon Teena Murder," *Transgender Tapestry*, no. 75 (1996): 43.

17. NCTE, "Year in Review," January 2004, https://web.archive.org/web /20040717073838/http://nctequality.org/Jan04Newsletter.pdf ("invisible massacre"); GenderPAC, "HRC Issues Statement on Gender Hate Crimes," May 30, 1999, https://web.archive.org/web/20040701174245if_/http://www.gpac .org/archive/news/notitle.html?cmd=view&archive=news&msgnum=0201 ("silent wave of violence").

18. GenderPAC, "HRC Issues Statement on Gender Hate Crimes" ("time to break the silence"); NTAC, "Day of Remembrance 2001," December 2001, https://web.archive.org/web/20020308064516/http://ntac.org:80/newsletter /details.asp?AID=143&IID=27&type=Latest ("educate the public").

19. NCAVP, *Anti-Lesbian, Gay, Bisexual and Transgender Violence in 1996*, 1997, 1.

20. GLAAD, "Communities Set to Observe National Transgender Day of Remembrance," November 18, 2002, https://web.archive.org/web /20021122132712/https://www.glaad.org/.

21. NTAC, "Day of Remembrance 2001."

22. Quoted in "Second Annual 'Day of Remembrance,'" *FTMi*, no. 48 (2000): 14.

23. GSA, "Transgender Day of Remembrance," 2009, https://web.archive
.org/web/20090211080505/http://gsanetwork.org:80/resources/dayof
remembrance.html.

24. Gwendolyn Smith, "2005 Transgender Day of Remembrance One
Month Away," October 3, 2005, https://web.archive.org/web/20051026184857
/http://www.rememberingourdead.org/day/.

25. Quoted in GenderPAC, "Transgender Violence Study Nearing Launch,"
October 9, 1995, https://web.archive.org/web/20021018101557/http://www
.qrd.org/qrd/trans/1995/violence.study.nears.launch-10.09.95.

26. Nancy Nangeroni, "Trans-Actions," *Transgender Tapestry*, no. 80 (1997).

27. For example, NTAC, "Transgenders, Families Gear Up to Lobby on
Capitol Hill," April 4, 2004, https://web.archive.org/web/20041204120014
/http://www.ntac.org:80/pr/release.asp?did=92.

28. It's Time, Massachusetts!, "If You Thought Your Silence Would Protect You . . . Think Again," in special insert, *Transgender Tapestry*, no. 85
(1998): 1.

29. Campbell (2005, 129); Marcus (1992).

30. Crenshaw (1991); Richie (2000).

31. NCTE, *Responding to Hate Crimes: A Community Resource Manual*,
2006, 15.

32. For example, GenderPAC, "Vigil at Forte Murder Trial, Killer Gets Life,"
September 16, 1996, https://web.archive.org/web/20020629073431/http://
www.qrd.org/qrd/trans/1996/forte.killer.gets.life-09.16.96; GenderPAC, "Vigil
Held for Chanelle Picket," February 27, 1997, https://web.archive.org/web
/20040626204441if_/http://www.gpac.org/archive/news/notitle.html?cmd=
view&archive=news&msgnum=0109; GenderPAC, "Boys Boys Boys," March
16, 2000. https://web.archive.org/web/20040512180130if_/http://www.gpac.org
/archive/news/notitle.html?cmd=view&archive=news&msgnum=0218.

33. Martin Rawlings-Fein, "SF Team: The Driving Force Behind the Trans
March," *FTMi*, no. 56 (2004).

34. NCTE, *Responding to Hate Crimes*, 15.

35. Gould (2009); Harwood (2004).

36. ROD, "Tips for Hosting a Successful Day of Remembrance Event,"
https://web.archive.org/web/20060718133730/http://www.gender.org
/remember/day/files/dor_tips.doc.

37. ROD, "About the Day of Remembrance," 2005, https://web.archive.org
/web/20050204082300/http://www.gender.org/remember/day/what.html.

38. Gwendolyn, Smith, "Day of Remembrance: 14 Cities," *Transgender
Tapestry*, no. 93 (2001).

39. David Steinberg, "Comes Naturally," *Transgender Tapestry*, no. 100
(2002).

40. Garin Wiggins, "Death and Transition," *FTMi*, no. 52 (2002): 12.

41. Monica Taher, "Amazing Grace," GLAAD, October 2002, https://web
.archive.org/web/20081008161201/https://www.glaad.org/publications/op-ed
_archive_year.php?year=2002.

42. HRC, "Transgender Day of Remembrance," 2007, https://web.archive
.org/web/20071225005245/http://www.hrc.org:80/issues/transgender
/transgender_day_of_remembrance.asp.

43. Smith, "2005 Transgender Day of Remembrance One Month Away."

44. Nancy Nangeroni, "Hundreds Turn Out in Boston after Transexual
Murder," GenderPAC, December 22, 1995, https://web.archive.org/web
/20040123162402/http://www.qrd.org/qrd/trans/1995/boston.actions.after
.murders-12.22.95.

45. Gwendolyn Smith, "Remembering Our Dead: Behind the Website,"
Transgender Tapestry, no. 87 (1999): 67.

46. Quoted in GenderPAC, "Vigil at Forte Murder Trial, Killer Gets Life."

47. For example, GLAAD, "Memorial Events for Gwen Araujo," October 22, 2002.

48. ROD, "Day of Remembrance Supply List," August 8, 2002, https://
web.archive.org/web/20060718134229/http://www.gender.org/remember
/day/files/dor_supp.pdf.

49. GLAAD, "An Introduction to the Transgender Day of Remembrance," November 17, 2008, https://web.archive.org/web/20100616115836
/http://glaadblog.org/2008/11/17/an-introduction-to-the-transgender-day-of
-remembrance/.

50. HRC, "Vigil Tomorrow for Transgender Crime Victims in DC,"
August 27, 2009, https://web.archive.org/web/20100203115723/http://www
.hrcbackstory.org/2009/08/vigil-tomorrow-for-transgender-crime-victims
-in-dc/ ("condemn the recent violence"); GLAAD, "UPDATE: Vigil Held to
Mourn Death of Transgender Woman in D.C. Draws Support from Community and National Organizations," August 31, 2009, https://web.archive
.org/web/20110804083134/http://glaadblog.org/2009/08/31/update-vigil
-held-to-mourn-death-of-transgender-woman-in-d-c-draws-support-from
-community-and-national-organizations/ ("denounce the ongoing violence").

51. "Largest Multi-Venue Transgender Event Ever," *Transgender Tapestry*, no. 102 (2003): 57.

52. ROD, "Tips for Hosting a Successful Day of Remembrance Event."

53. The tendency to advocate for after-the-fact solutions is a common
theme in the documents I examined. For example, in 2006 NCTE released with
much fanfare a twenty-eight-page guide for anti-violence activists. Notably,
it was titled *Responding to Hate Crimes: A Community Resource Manual*
(emphasis added) and focused exclusively on what activists should do after a
hate crime had occurred in their community.

54. In 2009, transgender activist Rachel Crandall started the International
Transgender Day of Visibility. This event was created specifically in response
to frustration about Transgender Day of Remembrance being the only national
transgender event.

55. GLAAD, "Hate Crimes," October 1, 2003, https://web.archive.org/web
/20051119220511/http://www.glaad.org/publications/resource_doc_detail.php
?id=3496&PHPSESSID=634260e1oba3d59dd3d319e66a1c8956#patton.

56. Armstrong and Crage (2006).
57. Abelson (2019).
58. Monica Helms, ". . . And That's the Way It Is," *Transgender Tapestry,* no. 105 (2004): 15.
59. Gwendolyn Smith, "Say Their Names," November 30, 2000, https://web.archive.org/web/20010217141018/http://www.gwensmith.com/gender/writings/transmissions3.html.
60. NCTE, *Responding to Hate Crimes,* 7.
61. "S 1105," *Transgender Tapestry,* no. 112 (2007).
62. NCAVP, *Anti-Lesbian, Gay, Bisexual and Transgender Violence in 1997,* 1998, 6 ("comprehensive hate crime legislation"); GenderPAC, "HRC Issues Statement on Gender Hate Crimes" ("some basic protections").
63. For example, Li Anne Taft, "There Is No Safe Way to Be Transgendered," *Transgender Tapestry,* no. 97 (2002).
64. Quoted in HRC, "HRC Expresses Alarm over Recent Spate of Apparent Hate Crimes," March 22, 2005, https://web.archive.org/web/20061205134621/https://www.hrc.org/Template.cfm?Section=Search_the_Database&CONTENTID=26139&TEMPLATE=/ContentManagement/ContentDisplay.cfm.
65. NCTE, "Hate Crimes Bill Becomes a Law Today with President's Signature," October 28, 2009, https://transequality.org/blog/hate-crimes-bill-becomes-a-law-today-with-presidents-signature.
66. Jenness and Grattet (2001).
67. Best (1999); Jacobs and Potter (1998).
68. Best (1999); Jacobs and Potter (1998).
69. Wertheimer (2000).
70. Jenness and Grattet (2001, 26).
71. Jenness and Grattet (2001).
72. Jacobs and Potter (1998); Jenness and Broad (1997).
73. Jenness and Grattet (2001).
74. Jacobs and Henry (1996, 385).
75. For example, Lawrence (1999); Levin and McDevitt (2002); Levin and Rabrenovic (2003); Perry (2001); Streissguth (2009).
76. Gerstenfeld (2004); Jenness and Grattet (2001); Mason (2007).
77. Jenness and Grattet (2001, 3).
78. Jenness and Grattet (2001, 4).
79. Mason (2007, 249).
80. Jacobs and Henry (1996).
81. For a critique of this punishment model, see Spade (2011).
82. Riki Wilchins, Emilia Lombardi, Dana Priesing, and Diana Malouf, *First National Survey of Transgender Violence,* GenderPAC, April 1997, 5.
83. Nancy Nangeroni, "Trans-Actions," *Transgender Tapestry,* no. 76 (1996): 11.

84. GenderPAC, "Transpeople Left Behind on Hate Crimes Again," July 6, 1996, https://web.archive.org/web/20030506171706/http://www.qrd.org/qrd /trans/1996/left.out.again.on.hate.crimes-07.04.96.

85. Quoted in NCTE, "Hate Crimes Bill Becomes a Law Today with President's Signature," October 28, 2009, https://transequality.org/blog/hate -crimes-bill-becomes-a-law-today-with-presidents-signature.

86. NCTE, "Victory: Hate Crimes Bill Passes," October 22, 2009, https:// web.archive.org/web/20091219004618/http://transequality.org:80/news .html.

87. NCTE, "Hate Crimes Bill Passes," April 29, 2009, https://web.archive .org/web/20091219004618/http://transequality.org:80/news.html.

88. NCAVP, "NCAVP Voices Support for Reintroduction of Federal Hate Crime Bill," March 22, 2007, https://web.archive.org/web/20070403035044 /http://www.avp.org:80/.

89. NTAC, "In Memoriam: NTAC Joins Others in Remembering Our Dead," November 17, 2004, https://web.archive.org/web/20041206152613 /http://www.ntac.org:80/pr/release.asp?did=99.

90. Li Anne Taft, "There Is No Safe Way to Be Transgendered," NTAC, June 11, 2001, https://web.archive.org/web/20010724155709/http://www.ntac .org:80/news/01/06/11hi.html.

91. Mara Keisling, "Statement on the Introduction of the Local Law Enforcement Hate Crimes Prevention Act of 2005," NCTE, May 26, 2005, https://web.archive.org/web/20051028082947/http://nctequality.org /hatecrimesintroduction.pdf.

92. GLAAD, "Man Gets Maximum Sentence for the Murder of Transgender Woman," August 18, 2009, https://web.archive.org/web/20100713083751 /http://www.glaad.org/page.aspx?pid=930.; HRC, "Human Rights Campaign Statement on Sentencing in Lateisha Green Murder Trial," August 18, 2009, https://web.archive.org/web/20081127162555/http://www.hrcbackstory.org /2008/08/human-rights--1.html.

93. Wilchins, Lombardi, Priesing, and Malouf, *First National Survey of Transgender Violence*, 5.

94. Quoted in GenderPAC, "Judge Imposes Maximum Sentence for Assault in Chanelle Pickett Murder," May 16, 1997, https://web.archive.org /web/20051110105542/http://www.gpac.org/archive/news/notitle.html?cmd= view&archive=news&msgnum=0086.

95. NCAVP, *Anti-Lesbian, Gay, Bisexual and Transgender Violence in 1998*, 1999, 3.

96. NTAC, "NTAC Urges Passage of Hate Crimes Proposal after Colorado Attack," March 30, 2002, https://web.archive.org/web/20021224071311 /http://www.ntac.org:80/pr/020330denver.html.

97. GenderPAC, *50 under 30: Masculinity and the War on America's Youth*, 2006, https://web.archive.org/web/20071007083152/http://www.gpac .org/50under30/50u30.pdf.

98. NCAVP, *Anti-Lesbian, Gay, Bisexual and Transgender Violence in 2003, 2004*, 9.

99. HRC, "Human Rights Campaign Responds to Murder of Syracuse Man," November 17, 2008, https://web.archive.org/web/20081129105448 /http://www.hrc.org/issues/hate_crimes/11550.htm.

100. Kleiman (2009).

101. Valentine (2007).

102. Westbrook (2008).

103. Starr (1992).

104. Westbrook (2008).

105. For example, Denise Leclair, "The Back of the Bus," *Transgender Tapestry*, no. 113 (2007).

106. GLAAD, "Man Sentenced to 25 Years for the Killing of Lateisha Green," August 18, 2009, https://web.archive.org/web/20110804083128 /http://glaadblog.org/2009/08/18/man-sentenced-to-25-years-for-the-killing -of-lateisha-green/.

107. Beeghley (2003); Franklin (2002); Spade (2011); Strout (2012). Cf. Levy and Levy (2017).

108. Spade (2011).

109. Gerstenfeld (2004); Jacobs and Potter (1998).

110. NCTE, "It's Official: First Federal Law to Protect Transgender People," 2009, https://web.archive.org/web/20091219004618/http://transequality.org: 80/news.html.

111. NCTE, "Testimony Regarding Senate Bill 698," March 17, 2004, https://web.archive.org/web/20050528231425/http://www.nctequality.org /MDHateTestimony.pdf.

112. Allyson Robinson, "Holding My Hand and Watching My Back," HRC, November 2, 2009, https://web.archive.org/web/20091226083450/http://www .hrcbackstory.org/2009/11/allyson-robinson-holding-my-hand-and-watching -my-back/.

113. There are exceptions made for state-sanctioned violence, such as the death penalty, wars, and certain violent actions by police officers.

114. Gerstenfeld (2004).

115. Ashley (2018).

116. Quoted in NCTE, "Verdict in Lateisha Green Court Trial," July 17, 2009, https://transequality.org/blog/verdict-in-lateisha-green-court-trial.

117. Vipond (2015b).

118. Franklin (2002).

119. The murders of Angie Zapata and Lateisha Green in 2008 resulted in hate crime convictions in 2009 under Colorado and New York state law, respectively. However, the verdict in the case of Lateisha Green was overturned on appeal in 2013, and the accused perpetrator was found not guilty in a retrial in 2016.

120. Quoted in Chris Johnson, "A Tragedy in California," HRC, February 15, 2008, https://web.archive.org/web/20080216053544/http://www.hrc backstory.org:80/2008/02/a-tragedy-in--1.html.

121. NCTE, "The Power of Language," June 5, 2009, https://transequality .org/blog/the-power-of-language.

122. Robinson, "Holding My Hand and Watching My Back."

123. Franklin (2002); Jacobs and Potter (1998).

124. Franklin (2002).

125. Jacobs and Henry (1996, 391).

126. NCAVP, *Hate Violence against the Lesbian, Gay, Bisexual, Transgender and Queer Communities in the United States in 2009*, 2010, 14.

127. NCAVP, *Hate Violence against the Lesbian, Gay, Bisexual, Transgender and Queer Communities in the United States in 2009*, 15 and 49.

128. In its 2006 and 2008 reports, GenderPAC, a previous advocate for enhanced penalties, took a neutral stance, stating: "There is ongoing concern that laws which allow for enhanced penalties may be disproportionately invoked against defendants who are of color, and are thus controversial; this report does not endorse them and takes no position on them." GenderPAC, *50 under 30*, 7.

129. Ashley (2018); Franklin (2002); Kohn (2001); Lamble (2013); Meyer (2014); Moran and Sharpe (2002); Spade (2011); Spade and Willse (1999); Vipond (2015b). See Richie (2000) and Creek and Dunn (2011) for similar arguments about criminalization of violence against women.

130. Jenness and Grattet (2001).

131. Jenness and Grattet (2001).

132. Jenness and Broad (1994, 414).

133. Burton (1998, 195); see also Marcus (1992).

134. This book focuses on social movement organizations working to reduce violence. It should be noted, however, that there are also less-organized responses to violence experienced by an identity group that are also forms of "fighting back." In the 1960s there were a number of riots by people who were gay, queer, and/or gender nonnormative in response to police brutality and harassment. The best known of these are the Compton's Cafeteria Riot of 1966 in San Francisco (Stryker 2017) and the Stonewall Rebellion of 1969 in New York (Armstrong and Crage 2006). Other identity groups have also rioted in response to violence by the police, such as in 1992 in Los Angeles after the acquittal of the officers who beat Rodney King (Gooding-Williams 1993) and the protests sparked by the murder of George Floyd by a police officer in 2020.

135. Austin (2008).

136. Hanhardt (2013).

137. Hanhardt (2013, 117).

138. Jenness and Broad (1994).

139. Marcus (1992, 387).

CHAPTER 7. FACILITATING LIVABLE LIVES

1. Although 2019 would mark a full ten years since 2009, I collected and analyzed materials from 2018 because I was writing this chapter in early 2019.

By 2018, *FTMi*, GEA, GenderPAC, NTAC, the ROD website, and *Transgender Tapestry* were no longer operating.

2. The only mentions of nonfatal violence were cases of sexual assault and relationship violence. See, for example, Jay Wu, "Fighting for Survivors of Sexual Assault," NCTE, September 25, 2018, https://web.archive.org/web/20190301202408/https://www.hrc.org/resources/a-national-epidemic-fatal-anti-transgender-violence-in-america-in-2018.

3. HRC, *A National Epidemic: Fatal Anti-Transgender Violence in America in 2018*, 2018, https://web.archive.org/web/20190301202408/https://www.hrc.org/resources/a-national-epidemic-fatal-anti-transgender-violence-in-america-in-2018.

4. NCAVP, *A Crisis of Hate: A Report on Lesbian, Gay, Bisexual, Transgender and Queer Hate Violence Homicides in 2017*, 2018, https://avp.org/2017-hv-ipv-report/.

5. For example, GLAAD, "GLAAD Calls for Increased and Accurate Media Coverage of Transgender Murders," October 20, 2018, https://www.glaad.org/blog/glaad-calls-increased-and-accurate-media-coverage-transgender-murders-0.

6. Rokia Hassanein, "HRC Mourns Keanna Mattel," December 10, 2018, www.hrc.org/blog/hrc-mourns-keanna-mattel-transgender-woman-killed-in-detroit.

7. NCAVP, *Lesbian, Gay, Bisexual, Transgender, Queer and HIV-Affected Hate and Intimate Partner Violence in 2017*, 2018, 6.

8. Meredith Talusan, "What the Media Gets Wrong about Trans Murders," March 28, 2018, www.them.us/story/what-the-media-gets-wrong-about-trans-murders.

9. NCAVP, *A Crisis of Hate*, 13.

10. HRC "Transgender Day of Remembrance," 2018, www.hrc.org/campaigns/transgender-day-remembrance.

11. For example, GLAAD, "GLAAD Calls for Increased and Accurate Media Coverage."

12. Crenshaw (1991).

13. HRC, *A National Epidemic*. Counter to this trend, NCAVP consistently marked white victims as such. For example, NCAVP, *Lesbian, Gay, Bisexual, Transgender, Queer and HIV-Affected Hate and Intimate Partner Violence in 2017*.

14. NCTE, "NCTE Statement on the 20th Transgender Day of Remembrance," November 20, 2018, https://transequality.org/press/releases/ncte-statement-on-the-20th-transgender-day-of-remembrance.

15. Hassanein, "HRC Mourns Keanna Mattel" ("particularly transgender women of color"); HRC, "Violence against the Transgender Community in 2018," 2018, www.hrc.org/resources/violence-against-the-transgender-community-in-2018 ("disproportionately affects transgender women of color").

16. NCTE, "NCTE Statement on the 20th Transgender Day of Remembrance."

17. To achieve the goal of improving the livability of all transgender lives, such activism from points of privilege would have to be coupled with efforts to ensure that activists did not reproduce the forms of inequality that provide them with relative safety.

18. Vidal-Ortiz (2009, 101). See also Snorton and Harritaworn (2013).

19. Orion Ibert, "Embroidered on Our Hearts: Creating the Trans Wings Quilt Project," GLAAD, November 20, 2018, www.glaad.org/amp/embroidered -hearts-creating-trans-quilt-project.

20. Sawyer Stephenson, "The Importance of Trans Day of Remembrance," GLAAD, November 20, 2018, www.glaad.org/amp/importance-trans-day -remembrance.

21. Hough and McCorkle (2016) (since the early 1990s); Rosenfeld (2016) (increased slightly in 2015).

22. Lauritsen and Heimer (2008) (both cisgender men and women); Barker (2010, 496–97) ("across all . . .").

23. Flores et al. (2016); Stotzer (2017).

24. See appendix B for details.

25. For example, Bernstein (1997); Crenshaw (1991).

26. Butler (2004).

27. Cermele (2010). See also Hollander (2005).

28. Marcus (1992).

29. Ullman (2007). Notably, women who resist "fare better, both physically and psychologically," than victims of completed rape" (Cermele 2010, 1166). See also Brecklin and Ullman (2005).

30. Hollander and Rodgers (2014, 358).

31. Goodmark (2008).

32. Goodmark (2008).

33. Buist and Stone (2014).

34. Sunnivie Brydum and Mitch Kellaway, "This Black Trans Man Is in Prison for Killing His Rapist," *Advocate*, April 8, 2015, www.advocate.com /politics/transgender/2015/04/08/black-trans-man-prison-killing-his-rapist.

35. Jenness and Fenstermaker (2014).

36. *Nation*, June 23–30, 2014, www.thenation.com/issue/june-23-30 -2014/.

37. Of all of the anti-violence organizations studied for this book, NCAVP is the only one that regularly called for research into patterns of violence experienced by transgender people as a vital tool for reducing that violence. See, for example, NCAVP, *Anti-Lesbian, Gay, Bisexual and Transgender Violence in 2006*, 2007.

38. Crenshaw (1989).

39. Beeghley (2003); Pridemore (2008).

40. Bettcher (2007, 52) ("whores"); Lyons et al. (2015) (shame about their own desires); Bettcher (2007); Schilt and Westbrook (2009) (deserve to be punished).

41. Hough and McCorkle (2016).

42. Serano (2007).

43. Massey (1995).

44. Blau and Blau (1982, 123).

45. Anderson (1999).

46. James et al. (2016).

47. James et al. (2016).

48. James et al. (2016).

49. Grant et al. (2011); James et al. (2016); Koken, Bimbi, and Parsons (2009); Meyer (2015); Saffin (2011).

50. For example, Hallinan (2001).

51. Ferguson (2001).

52. Chapman et al. (2011) (higher dropout rates); Wald and Losen (2003) ("school-to-prison pipeline").

53. Graham (2014); James et al. (2016); Wyss (2004).

54. James et al. (2016).

55. Bertrand and Mullainathan (2004); Pager, Bonikowski, and Western (2009) (race-based); James et al. (2016) (against transgender people).

56. Spade (2006).

57. For example, Xavier et al. (2005).

58. James et al. (2016).

59. James et al. (2016).

60. Grant et al. (2011); Schilt (2011); Xavier et al. (2005).

61. Schilt and Wiswall (2008).

62. James et al. (2016); Saffin (2011); Spade (2006).

63. Meyer (2015); Saffin (2011); Xavier et al. (2005).

64. James et al. (2016).

65. Grant et al. (2011); Hwahng and Nuttbrock (2014); James et al. (2016); Kattari and Begun (2017); Saffin (2011); Sausa, Keatley, and Operario (2007).

66. Graham (2014); Grant et al. (2011); James et al. (2016).

67. Hwahng and Nuttbrock (2014); Sausa, Keatley, and Operario (2007). Due to employment discrimination, among other factors, body modification is not equally distributed across racial groups. White trans women are much more likely to have genital surgery than trans women of color (Xavier et al. 2005), as well as other forms of permanent body modification (Meier and Labuski 2013). To the extent that body modifications may reduce risk of experiencing violence, this increases the racial inequality in homicides.

68. Cohan et al. (2006); Weitzer (2009).

69. Grant et al. (2011); James et al. (2016).

70. Beeghley (2003); Rogers and Pridemore (2013).

71. Brents and Hausbeck (2005); Weitzer (2009).

72. HRC, *A National Epidemic*, 57.

73. Grant et al. (2011); HRC (2015); Lombardi et al. (2001); Stotzer (2008); Waters, Jindasurat, and Wolfe (2016); Xavier et al. (2005).

74. Acemoglu and Angrist (2001); DeLeire (2000); Lahey (2008). On June 15, 2020, the US Supreme Court ruled that the 1964 Civil Rights Act protects

gay, lesbian, and transgender employees from discrimination based on sex, a decision that was widely celebrated. Due to the potential pitfalls of antidiscrimination legislation, future research should examine whether and how this decision affects transgender employment.

75. Kalev, Dobbin, and Kelly (2006); Lindsey et al. (2013).

76. GenderPAC (2007); Graham (2014); Grant et al. (2011); Griffin (2016); HRC (2015).

77. Flores (2015); Flores et al. (2018); Tadlock et al. (2017) and Walch et al. (2012) (interpersonal contact); Broockman and Kalla (2016) and Tompkins et al. (2015) (short activities); Case and Stewart (2013) and Mizock et al. (2017) (educational programs).

78. Butler (2004).

79. Burton (1998); Campbell (2005); Marcus (1992).

80. Janet Mock, "Quiet Reflections: Why I Chose Silence on Trans Day of Remembrance," November 22, 2013, https://janetmock.com/2013/11/22 /transgender-day-of-remembrance/.

81. Kai Cheng Thom, "Someone Tell Me That I'll Live: On Murder, Media, and Being a Trans Woman in 2015," https://web.archive.org/web /20150302221659/https://www.xojane.com/issues/someone-tell-me-that-ill -live-murdered-trans-women-2015.

82. "3 Transgendered Persons Murdered in Atlanta," *Transgender Tapestry*, no. 61 (1991): 74.

83. HRC, *A National Epidemic*, 10, 12, 17, 18, 20, 21, and 26.

84. NCAVP, *A Crisis of Hate*, 19.

85. Harwood (2004, 471). See also Sedgwick (1993).

86. Tey Meadow, "Queer Children Are Dying . . . But Many More Are Living," *HuffPost*, January 20, 2012, www.huffingtonpost.com/tey-meadow -jd-phd/gay-suicide_b_1218124.html.

87. Tey Meadow, "Gay Is Great (Not Just Tolerable)," Social (In)Queery, January 31, 2012, https://socialinqueery.com/2012/01/31/gay-is-great-not -just-tolerable/.

88. Nico Lang, "Interview with Jen Richards, Creator of We Happy Trans," *HuffPost*, November 12, 2013, www.huffpost.com/entry/we-happy-trans_b _2101627.

89. https://twitter.com/WeHappyTrans and https://www.facebook.com /WeHappyTrans/.

90. Dani Heffernan, "GLAAD Sponsors Trans 100 Launch, Produced by We Happy Trans and This Is HOW," GLAAD, March 29, 2013, https://www .glaad.org/blog/glaad-sponsors-trans-100-launch-produced-we-happy-trans -and-how.

91. Vance (1984).

92. Hollander (2004).

93. "Interview: Riki Anne Wilchins," *Transgender Tapestry*, no. 81 (1997): 11.

94. Forward Together, "About Trans Day of Resilience," https://web .archive.org/web/20190219192508/https://www.tdor.co/about.

95. Forward Together, "About Trans Day of Resilience."

96. Bettcher (2007); Schilt and Westbrook (2009).

97. Bob Moser, "Disposable People," *SPLC Intelligence Report* (Winter 2003) ("bogus"); NCTE, "NCTE Statement on the Greeley Colorado Verdict," April 22, 2009 ("absurd"); GLAAD, "Hate-Crimes against Transgender People Grow but Community Response Deepens," October 11, 2008 ("defamatory").

98. HRC, "HRC Strongly Disappointed and Saddened at Araujo Mistrial," June 22, 2004, https://web.archive.org/web/20040625123509/https://www.hrc.org/Template.cfm?Section=Press_Room&CONTENTID=20241&TEMPLATE=/ContentManagement/ContentDisplay.cfm.

99. GenderPAC, "ABC News 20/20 on Brandon Teena: Good Reporting But Still No Respect" February 11, 2000, https://web.archive.org/web/20010118003400/http://www.gpac.org/archive/action/index.html?cmd=view&archive=action&msgnum=0001.

100. Note that although doctors and cisgender people may refer to those body parts in that way, those are not necessarily the terms used by individual transgender people.

101. Britt and Heise (2000).

102. Gwendolyn Smith, "Where's the Pride in Being Transgendered?," June 14, 2001, https://web.archive.org/web/20020426071736/http://www.gwensmith.com:80/gender/writings/transmissions17.html.

103. Monica Roberts, "Address to the New England Transgender Pride March and Rally," *Transgender Tapestry*, no. 115 (2009): 13.

104. Roberts, "Address to the New England Transgender Pride March and Rally," 13.

105. Britt and Heise (2000).

106. Britt and Heise (2000).

107. Gould (2009).

108. A notable exception is the outpouring of anger toward police violence witnessed in 2020. By focusing on police brutality, Black Lives Matter activists provided a target for anger that facilitated mass protests and encouraged a nationwide narrative of black pride. Included in these protests were Black Trans Lives Matter rallies and the replacement of the usual LGBT Pride parades with Black Lives Matter marches. Future research should examine whether (and how) this identity-based anti-violence movement fostered long-term changes in policies and cultural beliefs.

109. Spade (2011).

110. Remembering Our Dead, "About This Site," https://web.archive.org/web/20051124173501/http://www.rememberingourdead.org/about/core.html.

111. Snorton and Haritaworn (2013) ("trans necropolitics"). Notably, rage was a key element of early transgender narratives (e.g., Stryker 1994), but it is not a central emotion in current mainstream trans activism.

112. Many people whom we would now call "transgender" were involved in the Stonewall riots. However, the riots are rarely used as an origin story for the modern transgender rights movement. By the "modern" movement,

I mean activism that started in the 1990s after what historian Susan Stryker (2017) has called "The Difficult Decades" of the 1970s and 1980s, in which little progress was made with regard to trans rights.

113. "Transgender Shabbat," *FTMi*, no. 63 (2007): 5.

114. Quoted in Jessica Carreras, "Transgender Day of Visibility Plans Erupt Locally, Nationwide," Between the Lines, March 26, 2009, www.pridesource .com/article.html?article=34351.

115. Carreras, "Transgender Day of Visibility Plans Erupt Locally, Nationwide."

116. Trans Women of Color Collective (TWOCC), 2019, www.twocc.us/.

117. Lombardi et al. (2001, 98).

118. GLAAD, "Victim's Mother to Speak at San Francisco Vigil in Memory of Fred C. Martinez, Jr.," August 22, 2001, https://web.archive.org/web /20060514122910/http://www.glaad.org:80/publications/archive_year.php ?year=2001&PHPSESSID=ca96685ba5eb2330c1fb3b94e17f026d.

119. SPLC, "The Forgotten," *SPLC Intelligence Report* (Spring 2002), https://web.archive.org/web/20040406173020/http://www.splcenter.org/intel /intelreport/article.jsp?aid=133.

120. Being out may, however, increase the risk for street harassment, job discrimination, and romantic rejection. Future research should examine whether being out as transgender increases the risk for nonfatal violence.

121. This pride month does include bisexuals and transgender people, at least in name (i.e., LGBT Pride Month). However, such inclusion is often in name only.

122. Westbrook (2014).

123. Jeff Taylor, "Don't Miss These Transgender Pride Events," June 13, 2018, www.newnownext.com/dont-miss-these-transgender-pride-events/06/2018/.

124. For example, NCAVP, *Hate Violence against the Lesbian, Gay, Bisexual, Transgender and Queer Communities in the United States in 2009*, 2010.

125. Capuzza and Spencer (2017).

126. GLAAD, "Victims or Villains: Examining Ten Years of Transgender Images on Television," November 2012, www.glaad.org/publications /victims-or-villains-examining-ten-years-transgender-images-television. See also Sam Feder and Amy Scholder, dirs., *Disclosure* (Netflix, 2020), www .disclosurethemovie.com/.

127. GLAAD, "Two Transgender Women Stabbed in Broad Daylight, One Dead," August 28, 2009, https://web.archive.org/web/20110804083137 /http://glaadblog.org/2009/08/28/two-transgender-women-stabbed-in-broad -daylight-one-dead/.

128. For example, GLAAD, "Hate-Crimes against Transgender People Grow but Community Response Deepens," October 11, 2008.

129. GLAAD Transgender Media Program, www.glaad.org/transgender.

130. Heather Dockray, "Vice's Broadly Creates a Free, Gender-Inclusive Stock Photo Library," March 26, 2019, https://mashable.com/article/vice -broadly-stock-photo-library/.

131. Flores et al. (2018); Gillig et al. (2018).

132. Vipond (2015a).

133. Ray Filar, "Trans™: How the Trans Movement Got Sold Out," 2015, www.opendemocracy.net/en/transformation/how-trans-movement-sold-out/.

134. Akwaeke Emezi, *Pet* (New York: Make Me a World, 2019).

135. Concepción de León, "'This Is a Possibility': Akwaeke Emezi Writes a Trans Story Where Nobody Gets Hurt," *New York Times*, September 9, 2019.

136. Tai Gooden. "Why Angel & Papi's Romance on 'Pose' Isn't Just Adorable—It's Revolutionary," June 26, 2019, www.bustle.com/p/angel-papis-relationship-on-pose-is-both-sweet-revolutionary-18143064. Note that, due to the time period the show is set in, the characters would not likely have identified as "trans" and definitely would not have identified as "cis," but that is how they are interpreted now.

137. Butler (1993; 2004); Spade and Willse (1999).

138. Butler (2004, 231 and 8).

139. Brown (1995, 55).

140. Brown (1995, 51).

141. Fabj and Sobnosky (2014).

142. Crenshaw (1989; 1991).

143. Campbell (2005).

144. For example, Patrick Coleman, "How to Teach Young Kids about Consent," July 9, 2019, www.fatherly.com/parenting/teach-young-kids-consent-respect-sex/.

145. Jenness and Broad (1994).

146. Hollander (2004).

147. Spade (2011).

148. NCAVP, *Hate Violence against the Lesbian, Gay, Bisexual, Transgender and Queer Communities in the United States in 2009.*

149. Rosenbaum et al. (2005).

150. For some exceptions, see https://stoppolicebrutalitynow.org/ and www.joincampaignzero.org/.

151. For an excellent examination of these factors, see Beeghley (2003).

152. Best (2016); Goss (2006).

153. Taylor, Haider-Markel, and Lewis (2018).

APPENDIX A

1. Bob Moser, "Disposable People," *SPLC Intelligence Report* (Winter 2003), https://web.archive.org/web/20040414161146/http://www.splcenter.org/intel/intelreport/article.jsp?aid=149 ("the most powerful hatred on the planet"); and Mark Potok, "Rage on the Right," *SPLC Intelligence Report* (Winter 2003), https://web.archive.org/web/20040414115327/http://www.splcenter.org/intel/intelreport/article.jsp?aid=141 ("most despised people in America").

2. International Foundation for Gender Education, *Transgender Tapestry*, www.ifge.org/tgmag/tgmagtop.htm.
3. Dallas Denny, "Deceit and Betrayal at IFGE," September 19, 2011, http://dallasdenny.com/Chrysalis/2011/09/19/deceit-and-betrayal-at-ifge/.
4. GLAAD, "Our History," 2005, www.glaad.org.
5. "Welcome to Our First Issue!," *FTMi*, no. 13 (1990): 1; and *FTMi*, no. 59 (2005): 1.
6. https://web.archive.org/web/20050204044035/http://www.gender.org/.
7. GenderPAC, "Who We Are," https://web.archive.org/web/19971021171100/http://www.gpac.org/.
8. GenderPAC, home page, https://web.archive.org/web/20000511053412/http://www.gpac.org/.
9. Remembering Our Dead, "About This Site," https://web.archive.org/web/20051124173501/http://www.rememberingourdead.org/about/core.html.
10. Remembering Our Dead, "About the Day of Remembrance," https://web.archive.org/web/20050215183548/http://www.rememberingourdead.org/day/what.html.
11. Gary Barlow, "Some Transgender Advocates Angered by National Group," NTAC, January 18, 2001, https://web.archive.org/web/20010221045948/http://www.ntac.org:80/news/010118dallas.html.
12. NTAC, "About NTAC," https://web.archive.org/web/20020201205833/http://ntac.org/index.html.
13. National Center for Transgender Equality, "Mission," https://web.archive.org/web/20050205015717/http://nctequality.org/about.asp.
14. National Center for Transgender Equality, "About Us," www.transequality.org/About/about.html.

APPENDIX B

1. Federal Bureau of Investigation, *Uniform Crime Report Hate Crime Statistics, 2013* (Washington, DC: US Department of Justice, 2014).
2. The phrases in italics are direct quotes from news articles collected in this study.
3. For example, Robert Eads, a trans man who died in 1999 after being denied treatment for ovarian cancer.
4. In six cases, police ruled the death an accident, but activists argued that the evidence pointed to murder. Those deaths are Jill Seidel (February 3, 2000, Honolulu, HI), Alicia Sandoval (March 27, 2005, Lodi, CA), Vanessa Facen (November 17, 2005, San Diego, CA), Erika Keels (March 21, 2007, Philadelphia, PA), Ruby Molina (September 21, 2008, Sacramento, CA), and Kayla Moore (February 12, 2013, Berkeley, CA). Police reported that Seidel died of a drug overdose, Sandoval died in a drunk driving accident, Facen was killed by sheriff's deputies while in jail, Keels was struck and killed by a car, Molina

drowned in the Sacramento River, and Moore died while being forcefully restrained by police officers who were responding to a disturbance call at her home. Activists, pointing to suspicious circumstances, argued that all six deaths were homicides rather than accidents.

In four cases, police ruled the death a suicide, but activists argued that the victim was not suicidal and highlighted evidence indicating that the death was actually homicide. Those deaths are Marsha P. Johnson (July 6, 1992, New York, NY); Mara Duvouw (1995, New York, NY); Aimee Wilcoxson (October 31, 2008, Aurora, CO); and Selma Dias (May 16, 2010, Chicago, IL).

5. Mya Hall accidentally crashed an SUV into a security checkpoint at the National Security Agency in Fort Mead, Maryland, on March 30, 2015, and was shot and killed by guards who thought she was a terrorist.

6. Stotzer (2017).

7. Parkin and Gruenewald (2017) (replicate official homicide data); Lowman (2000) (prostitutes); Gruenewald (2012) (LGBT people); Malphurs and Cohen (2002) (homicide-suicide cases).

8. Roshco (1979).

9. Cain (1982); Chermak (1995); Meyers (1996).

10. Paulsen (2003).

11. See Gruenewald, Chermak, and Pizarro (2013) for a review.

12. Paulsen (2003).

13. It should be noted that many of the ways homicide is studied rely on datasets that are neither censuses nor random samples. For example, studies using arrest data to explore patterns of perpetration rely on datasets that are systematically biased, as not all homicides result in arrests, and arrests are unlikely to be randomly distributed across the population of perpetrators.

14. Parkin and Gruenewald (2017).

15. In order to raise awareness of violence against transgender people and to demonstrate to policy makers the scope of the problem, anti-violence activists have compiled extensive lists of transgender murder victims.

16. Note that not all of these organizations were active during the whole period studied. This list differs slightly from the list of organizations analyzed for the main part of this book because some of the organizations listed here were not engaged in transgender anti-violence activism from 1990 to 2009 but did such work after 2009. Most of these organizations are described in detail in appendix A.

17. To compile these sources for the entire period studied, I accessed them via the internet when they were available online and via physical archives when they were not. The physical archives I searched included those at the Bancroft Library at the University of California, Berkeley; the Gay, Lesbian, Bisexual, Transgender Historical Society in San Francisco; and the San Francisco Public Library.

18. Although LexisNexis is more commonly used by scholars, Access World News is particularly appropriate for this study because it includes numerous

local papers, which are more likely to cover local homicides than are national publications (Chermak 1995).

19. GenderPAC (2007); MacKenzie and Marcel (2009).

20. Meyers (1996). Sometimes printed copies of newspapers include a photo of the victim and/or perpetrator from which race could be inferred, but searchable databases of news stories such as LexisNexis and Access World News do not include photos, and inferring race from photographs is likely to be inaccurate.

21. Some police departments destroy reports after ten years, even if the case is unsolved.

22. Each source of information has its own biases, but the activist accounts, mainstream news stories, and government documents rarely contradicted each other. When they did, the most common variations were slight differences in the date of the murder and the age of the victim. Discrepancies were handled on a case-by-case basis, treating the source that seemed to know the most about the murder as the most "true."

23. HRC, *Addressing Anti-Transgender Violence: Exploring Realities, Challenges and Solutions for Policymakers and Community Advocates*, 2015; NCAVP, *Lesbian, Gay, Bisexual, Transgender, Queer, and HIV-Affected Hate Violence in 2015*, 2016.

24. Prunas et al. (2015).

25. Prunas et al. (2015) did not explain how they determined that a victim was transgender.

26. West and Zimmerman (1987) ("doing gender"); Connell (2010) ("doing transgender").

27. The "Asian/Pacific Islander" category includes people whose families originated from South Asia, including India, Afghanistan, and Pakistan. For research showing that these five categories are the best for measuring inequality, see Howell and Emerson (2017).

28. Patricia Murphy (January 8, 2008, Albuquerque, NM) was described as "half Acoma American Indian and half black" (Shepard 2008); Latisha King (February 12, 2008, Oxnard, CA) was described as "half African-American" (Setoodeh 2008); and Kyra Cordova Kruz (September 3, 2012, Philadelphia, PA), whose mother is white and father is black, was described as "biracial" (Williams 2012). I recoded each as black, based on physical appearance in photos and descriptions by friends and family.

29. Many cisgender people, including journalists and police officers, often assume that transgender women are sex workers (Nadal, Skolnik, and Wong 2012). Homicides were only coded as sex work related when it was confirmed, not just hypothesized, that the victim was charging the perpetrator money for sexual services. Thus, if anything, my dataset underestimates the number of sex-work-related deaths. In addition, although the code was intended to comprise all forms of sex work, including exotic dancing and pornography, all the victims who were killed while engaging in sex work were working as prostitutes.

References

Abelson, Miriam. 2019. *Men in Place: Trans Masculinity, Race, and Sexuality in America*. Minneapolis: University of Minnesota Press.

Acemoglu, Daron, and Joshua Angrist. 2001. "Consequences of Employment Protection? The Case of the Americans with Disabilities Act." *Journal of Political Economy* 109 (5): 915–57.

Anderson, Elijah. 1999. *Code of the Street: Decency, Violence, and the Moral Life of the Inner City*. New York: W. W. Norton.

Anderson, Kristin, and Debra Umberson. 2001. "Gendering Violence: Masculinity and Power in Men's Accounts of Domestic Violence." *Gender & Society* 15 (3): 358–80.

Andersson, Kjerstin. 2008. "Constructing Young Masculinity: A Case Study of Heroic Discourse on Violence." *Discourse & Society* 19 (2): 139–61.

Armstrong, Elizabeth, and Suzanna Crage. 2006. "Movements and Memory: The Making of the Stonewall Myth." *American Sociological Review* 71 (5): 724–51.

Ashley, Florence. 2018. "Don't Be So Hateful: The Insufficiency of Anti-Discrimination and Hate Crime Laws in Improving Trans Well-Being." *University of Toronto Law Journal* 68 (1): 1–36.

Austin, Curtis. 2008. *Up Against the Wall*. Fayetteville: University of Arkansas Press.

Banerjee, Sukanya, Angana Chatterji, Lubna Nazir Chaudhry, Manali Desai, Saadia Toor, and Kamala Visweswaran. 2004. "Engendering Violence." *Cultural Dynamics* 16 (2–3): 125–39.

Barker, Vanessa. 2010. "Explaining the Great American Crime Decline: A Review of Blumstein and Wallman, Goldberger and Rosenfeld, and Zimring." *Law & Social Inquiry* 35 (2): 489–516.

Beauchamp, Toby. 2007. "The Limits of Virtual Memory: Nationalisms, State Violence, and the Transgender Day of Remembrance." *InterAlia: Pismo Poświęcone Studiom Queer*, no. 2: 1–16.

Beeghley, Leonard. 2003. *Homicide: A Sociological Explanation*. Lanham, MD: Rowman & Littlefield.

Benford, Robert, and David Snow. 2000. "Framing Processes and Social Movements: An Overview and Assessment." *Annual Review of Sociology* 26:611–39.

Berns, Nancy. 2001. "Degendering the Problem and Gendering the Blame: Political Discourse on Women and Violence." *Gender & Society* 15 (2): 262–81.

Berrill, Kevin, and Gregory M. Herek. 1990. "Primary and Secondary Victimization in Anti-Gay Hate Crimes Official Response and Public Policy." *Journal of Interpersonal Violence* 5 (3): 401–13.

Bertrand, Marianne, and Sendhil Mullainathan. 2004. "Are Emily and Greg More Employable Than Lakisha and Jamal? A Field Experiment on Labor Market Discrimination." *American Economic Review* 94 (4): 991–1013.

Best, Joel, ed. 1995. *Images of Issues: Typifying Contemporary Social Problems*. 2nd ed. New York: Aldine Transaction.

———. 1999. *Random Violence: How We Talk about New Crimes and New Victims*. Berkeley: University of California Press.

———. 2004. *More Damned Lies and Statistics: How Numbers Confuse Public Issues*. New ed. Berkeley: University of California Press.

———. 2012. *Damned Lies and Statistics: Untangling Numbers from the Media, Politicians, and Activists*. Updated ed. Berkeley: University of California Press.

———. 2016. *Social Problems*. 3rd ed. New York: W. W. Norton.

Best, Joel, and Gerald T. Horiuchi. 1985. "The Razor Blade in the Apple: The Social Construction of Urban Legends." *Social Problems* 32 (5): 488–99.

Bettcher, Talia Mae. 2007. "Evil Deceivers and Make-Believers: On Transphobic Violence and the Politics of Illusion." *Hypatia* 22 (3): 43–65.

Blau, Judith, and Peter Blau. 1982. "The Cost of Inequality: Metropolitan Structure and Violent Crime." *American Sociological Review* 47 (1): 114–29.

Blee, Kathleen. 2005. "Racial Violence in the United States." *Ethnic and Racial Studies* 28 (4): 599–619.

Boonzaier, Floretta. 2008. "'If the Man Says You Must Sit, Then You Must Sit': The Relational Construction of Woman Abuse: Gender, Subjectivity and Violence." *Feminism & Psychology* 18 (2): 183–206.

Bourdieu, Pierre. 1991. "On Symbolic Power." In *Language and Symbolic Power*, edited by J. B. Thompson, 163–70. Cambridge, MA: Harvard University Press.

———. 1998. *On Television*. New York: New Press.

Brecklin, Leanne R., and Sarah E. Ullman. 2005. "Self-Defense or Assertiveness Training and Women's Responses to Sexual Attacks." *Journal of Interpersonal Violence* 20 (6): 738–62.

Brents, Barbara, and Kathryn Hausbeck. 2005. "Violence and Legalized Brothel Prostitution in Nevada: Examining Safety, Risk, and Prostitution Policy." *Journal of Interpersonal Violence* 20 (3): 270–95.

Britt, Lory, and David Heise. 2000. "From Shame to Pride in Identity Politics." In *Self, Identity, and Social Movements*, edited by S. Stryker, T. Owens, and R. White, 252–67. Minneapolis: University of Minnesota Press.

Broad, Kendal. 2002. "GLB + T? Gender/Sexuality Movements and Transgender Collective Identity (De)Constructions." *International Journal of Sexuality and Gender Studies* 7 (4): 241–64.

Brody, Jennifer Devere. 2002. "Boyz Do Cry: Screening History's White Lies." *Screen* 43 (1): 91–96.

Broockman, David, and Joshua Kalla. 2016. "Durably Reducing Transphobia: A Field Experiment on Door-to-Door Canvassing." *Science* 352 (6282): 220–24.

Brown, Wendy. 1995. *States of Injury.* Princeton, NJ: Princeton University Press.

———. 2001. *Politics Out of History.* Princeton, NJ: Princeton University Press.

Buist, Carrie, and Codie Stone. 2014. "Transgender Victims and Offenders: Failures of the United States Criminal Justice System and the Necessity of Queer Criminology." *Critical Criminology* 22 (1): 35–47.

Burton, Nadya. 1998. "Resistance to Prevention: Reconsidering Feminist Antiviolence Rhetoric." In *Violence against Women: Philosophical Perspectives*, edited by S. G. French, L. M. Purdy, and W. Teays, 182–200. Ithaca, NY: Cornell University Press.

Butler, Judith. 1993. *Bodies That Matter: On the Discursive Limits of "Sex."* New York: Routledge.

———. 2004. *Undoing Gender.* New York: Routledge.

Cain, Stephen. 1982. "Murder and the Media." In *The Human Side of Homicide, Foundation of Thanatology Series*, edited by B. Danto, J. Bruhns, and A. Kutscher, 73–84. New York: Columbia University Press.

Campbell, Alex. 2005. "Keeping the 'Lady' Safe: The Regulation of Femininity through Crime Prevention Literature." *Critical Criminology* 13 (2): 119–40.

Capuzza, Jamie C., and Leland G. Spencer. 2017. "Regressing, Progressing, or Transgressing on the Small Screen? Transgender Characters on U.S. Scripted Television Series." *Communication Quarterly* 65 (2): 214–30.

Carrabine, Eamonn, Pamela Cox, Nigel South, Maggy Lee, Jackie Turton, and Ken Plummer. 2009. *Criminology: A Sociological Introduction.* 2nd ed. London: Routledge.

Case, Kim, and Briana Stewart. 2013. "Intervention Effectiveness in Reducing Prejudice Against Transsexuals." *Journal of LGBT Youth* 10 (1–2): 140–58.

Cermele, Jill. 2010. "Telling Our Stories: The Importance of Women's Narratives of Resistance." *Violence Against Women* 16 (10): 1162–72.

Cerulo, Karen. 2002. "Deciphering Violence: The Cognitive Structure of Right and Wrong." In *Cultural Sociology*, edited by L. Spillman, 257–71. Malden, MA: Wiley-Blackwell.

Chancer, Lynn S. 2005. *High-Profile Crimes: When Legal Cases Become Social Causes.* Chicago: University of Chicago Press.

Chapman, Chris, Jennifer Laird, Nicole Ifill, and Angelina KewalRamani. 2011. *Trends in High School Dropout and Completion Rates in the United States: 1972–2009*. Washington, DC: National Center for Education Statistics.

Chermak, Steven. 1995. *Victims in the News: Crime and the American News Media*. Boulder, CO: Westview Press.

Christie, Nils. 1986. "The Ideal Victim." In *From Crime Policy to Victim Policy*, 17–30. Basingstoke, UK: Macmillan.

Cohan, D., A. Lutnick, P. Davidson, C. Cloniger, A. Herlyn, J. Breyer, C. Cobaugh, D. Wilson, and J. Klausner. 2006. "Sex Worker Health: San Francisco Style." *Sexually Transmitted Infections* 82 (5): 418–22.

Collins, Patricia Hill. 1998. "The Tie That Binds: Race, Gender and US Violence." *Ethnic and Racial Studies* 21 (5): 917–38.

Connell, Catherine. 2010. "Doing, Undoing, or Redoing Gender? Learning from the Workplace Experiences of Transpeople." *Gender & Society* 24 (1): 31–55.

Cooper, Alexia, and Erica Smith. 2011. *Homicide Trends in the United States, 1980–2008*. Washington, DC: Bureau of Justice Statistics.

Correia, David. 2008. "'Rousers of the Rabble' in the New Mexico Land Grant War: La Alianza Federal De Mercedes and the Violence of the State." *Antipode* 40 (4): 561–83.

Creek, S. J., and Jennifer L. Dunn. 2011. "Rethinking Gender and Violence: Agency, Heterogeneity, and Intersectionality." *Sociology Compass* 5 (5): 311–22.

Crenshaw, Kimberlé. 1989. "Demarginalizing the Intersection of Race and Sex: A Black Feminist Critique of Antidiscrimination Doctrine, Feminist Theory and Antiracist Politics." *University of Chicago Legal Forum* 1989: 139.

———. 1991. "Mapping the Margins: Intersectionality, Identity Politics, and Violence against Women of Color." *Stanford Law Review* 43 (6): 1241–99.

Davis, Angela, and Elizabeth Martinez. 1994. "Coalition Building among People of Color." *Inscriptions* 7: 42–53.

Day, Kristen. 1999. "Strangers in the Night: Women's Fear of Sexual Assault on Urban College Campuses." *Journal of Architectural and Planning Research* 16 (4): 289–312.

D'Cruze, Shani, and Anupama Rao. 2004. "Violence and the Vulnerabilities of Gender." *Gender & History* 16 (3): 495–512.

DeLeire, Thomas. 2000. "The Wage and Employment Effects of the Americans with Disabilities Act." *Journal of Human Resources* 35 (4): 693–715.

Denny, Dallas. 2006. "Transgender Communities of the United States in the Late Twentieth Century." In *Transgender Rights*, edited by P. Currah, R. Juang, and S. Minter, 171–91. Minneapolis: University of Minnesota Press.

Dinno, Alexis. 2017. "Homicide Rates of Transgender Individuals in the United States: 2010–2014." *American Journal of Public Health* 107 (9): 1441–47.

Dixon, Travis L., and Keith B. Maddox. 2005. "Skin Tone, Crime News, and Social Reality Judgments: Priming the Stereotype of the Dark and

Dangerous Black Criminal." *Journal of Applied Social Psychology* 35 (8): 1555–70.

Eileraas, Karina. 2002. "The Brandon Teena Story: Rethinking the Body, Gender Identity and Violence Against Women." *Michigan Feminist Studies* 16: 85–116.

Fabj, Valeria, and Matthew Sobnosky. 2014. "Responses from the Street: ACT UP and Community Organizing Against AIDS." In *Aids: Effective Health Communication for the 90s*, edited by S. C. Ratzan, 91–108. New York: Routledge.

Factor, Rhonda, and Esther Rothblum. 2008. "A Study of Transgender Adults and Their Non-Transgender Siblings on Demographic Characteristics, Social Support, and Experiences of Violence." *Journal of LGBT Health Research* 3 (3): 11–30.

Fanon, Frantz. 1963. *The Wretched of the Earth*. New York: Grove Press.

Fellows, Mary Louise, and Sherene Razack. 1998. "The Race to Innocence: Confronting Hierarchical Relations among Women." *Journal of Gender, Race and Justice* 1: 335.

Ferguson, Ann. 2001. *Bad Boys: Public Schools in the Making of Black Masculinity*. Ann Arbor: University of Michigan Press.

Ferree, Myra Marx, William Anthony Gamson, Jürgen Gerhards, and Dieter Rucht. 2002. *Shaping Abortion Discourse: Democracy and the Public Sphere in Germany and the United States*. New York: Cambridge University Press.

Flores, Andrew. 2015. "Attitudes toward Transgender Rights: Perceived Knowledge and Secondary Interpersonal Contact." *Politics, Groups, and Identities* 3 (3): 398–416.

Flores, Andrew R., Donald P. Haider-Markel, Daniel C. Lewis, Patrick R. Miller, Barry L. Tadlock, and Jami K. Taylor. 2018. "Challenged Expectations: Mere Exposure Effects on Attitudes About Transgender People and Rights." *Political Psychology* 39 (1): 197–216.

Flores, Andrew, Jody Herman, Gary Gates, and Taylor Brown. 2016. *How Many Adults Identify as Transgender in the United States?* Los Angeles: The Williams Institute.

Foucault, Michel. 1977a. *Discipline and Punish: The Birth of the Prison*. New York: Vintage Books.

———. 1977b. "Nietzsche, Genealogy, History." In *Language, Counter-Memory, Practice: Selected Essays and Interviews*, edited by D. Bouchard, 139–64. Ithaca, NY: Cornell University Press.

———. 1982a. *The Archaeology of Knowledge; and the Discourse on Language*. New York: Pantheon Books.

———. 1982b. "The Subject and Power." *Critical Inquiry* 8 (4): 777–95.

———. 1990. *The History of Sexuality: An Introduction*. New York: Vintage Books.

Franklin, Karen. 2002. "Good Intentions: The Enforcement of Hate Crime Penalty-Enhancement Statutes." *American Behavioral Scientist* 46 (1): 154–72.

Franzosi, Roberto. 1998. "Narrative Analysis—or Why (and How) Sociologists Should Be Interested in Narrative." *Annual Review of Sociology* 24:517–54.

Garrison, Spencer. 2018. "On the Limits of 'Trans Enough': Authenticating Trans Identity Narratives." *Gender & Society* 32 (5): 613–37.

GenderPAC. 2007. *70 under 30: Masculinity and the War on America's Youth, A Human Rights Report.* www.scribd.com/document/101473531/70-Under -30-Masculinity-and-the-War-on-America-s-Youth.

Geronimus, Arline T., Margaret Hicken, Danya Keene, and John Bound. 2006. "'Weathering' and Age Patterns of Allostatic Load Scores Among Blacks and Whites in the United States." *American Journal of Public Health* 96 (5): 826–33.

Gerstenfeld, Phyllis B. 2004. *Hate Crimes: Causes, Controls, and Controversies.* Thousand Oaks, CA: Sage.

Gilchrist, Kristen. 2010. "'Newsworthy' Victims?" *Feminist Media Studies* 10 (4): 373–90.

Gillig, Traci K., Erica L. Rosenthal, Sheila T. Murphy, and Kate Langrall Folb. 2018. "More Than a Media Moment: The Influence of Televised Storylines on Viewers' Attitudes toward Transgender People and Policies." *Sex Roles* 78 (7): 515–27.

Goffman, Erving. 1986. *Frame Analysis: An Essay on the Organization of Experience.* Boston: Northeastern University Press.

Gooding-Williams, Robert. 1993. *Reading Rodney King/Reading Urban Uprising.* New York: Routledge.

Goodmark, Leigh. 2008. "When Is a Battered Woman Not a Battered Woman? When She Fights Back." *Yale Journal of Law and Feminism* 20: 75–129.

Goss, Kristin A. 2006. *Disarmed: The Missing Movement for Gun Control in America.* Princeton, NJ: Princeton University Press.

Gould, Deborah B. 2009. *Moving Politics: Emotion and ACT UP's Fight against AIDS.* Chicago: University of Chicago Press.

Graham, Louis. 2014. "Navigating Community Institutions: Black Transgender Women's Experiences in Schools, the Criminal Justice System, and Churches." *Sexuality Research and Social Policy* 11 (4): 274–87.

Grant, Jaime, Lisa Mottet, Justin Tanis, Jack Harrison, Jody Herman, and Mara Keisling. 2011. *Injustice at Every Turn: A Report of the National Transgender Discrimination Survey.* Washington, DC: National Center for Transgender Equality.

Greenwald, Anthony G., Mark A. Oakes, and Hunter G. Hoffman. 2003. "Targets of Discrimination: Effects of Race on Responses to Weapons Holders." *Journal of Experimental Social Psychology* 39 (4): 399–405.

Griffin, Michael. 2016. "Intersecting Intersectionalities and the Failure of the Law to Protect Transgender Women of Color in the United States." *Tulane Journal of Law and Sexuality* 25:123.

Gruenewald, Jeff. 2012. "Are Anti-LGBT Homicides in the United States Unique?" *Journal of Interpersonal Violence* 27 (18): 3601–23.

Gruenewald, Jeff, Steven Chermak, and Jesenia Pizarro. 2013. "Covering Victims in the News: What Makes Minority Homicides Newsworthy?" *Justice Quarterly* 30 (5): 755–83.

Hacking, Ian. 1986. "Making Up People." In *Reconstructing Individualism*, edited by T. Heller, M. Sosna, and D. Wellbery, 222–36. Stanford, CA: Stanford University Press.

Halberstam, Jack. 2005. *In a Queer Time and Place: Transgender Bodies, Subcultural Lives*. New York: New York University Press.

Hale, C. Jacob. 1998. "Consuming the Living, Dis(Re)Membering the Dead in the Butch/FTM Borderlands." *GLQ: A Journal of Lesbian and Gay Studies* 4 (2): 311–48.

Hallinan, Maureen. 2001. "Sociological Perspectives on Black-White Inequalities in American Schooling." *Sociology of Education* 74: 50–70.

Hamermesh, Daniel S. 2013. *Beauty Pays: Why Attractive People Are More Successful*. Princeton, NJ: Princeton University Press.

Hanhardt, Christina B. 2013. *Safe Space: Gay Neighborhood History and the Politics of Violence*. Durham, NC: Duke University Press.

Harris, Angela P. 2000. "Gender, Violence, Race, and Criminal Justice." *Stanford Law Review* 52 (4): 777–807.

Hartman, Saidiya V. 1997. *Scenes of Subjection: Terror, Slavery, and Self-Making in Nineteenth-Century America*. New York: Oxford University Press.

Harwood, Valerie. 2004. "Telling Truths: Wounded Truths and the Activity of Truth Telling." *Discourse: Studies in the Cultural Politics of Education* 25 (4): 467.

Helliwell, Christine. 2000. "'It's Only a Penis': Rape, Feminism, and Difference." *Signs* 25 (3): 789–816.

Herek, Gregory M. 1990. "The Context of Anti-Gay Violence: Notes on Cultural and Psychological Heterosexism." *Journal of Interpersonal Violence* 5 (3): 316–33.

Herman, Dianne. 1989. "The Rape Culture." In *Women: A Feminist Perspective*, edited by J. Freeman, 45–53. Mountain View, CA: Mayfield.

Hill, Darryl B. 2002. "Genderism, Transphobia, and Gender Bashing: A Framework for Interpreting Anti-Transgender Violence." In *Understanding and Dealing with Violence: A Multicultural Approach*, edited by B. C. Wallace and R. T. Carter, 113–36. Thousand Oaks, CA: Sage.

Hollander, Jocelyn A. 2001. "Vulnerability and Dangerousness: The Construction of Gender through Conversation about Violence." *Gender & Society* 15 (1): 83–109.

———. 2004. "'I Can Take Care of Myself': The Impact of Self-Defense Training on Women's Lives." *Violence Against Women* 10 (3): 205–35.

———. 2005. "Challenging Despair: Teaching about Women's Resistance to Violence." *Violence Against Women* 11 (6): 776–91.

Hollander, Jocelyn A., and Katie Rodgers. 2014. "Constructing Victims: The Erasure of Women's Resistance to Sexual Assault." *Sociological Forum* 29 (2): 342–64.

Hough, Richard, and Kimberly McCorkle. 2016. *American Homicide*. Los Angeles: Sage.

Howell, Junia, and Michael O. Emerson. 2017. "So What 'Should' We Use? Evaluating the Impact of Five Racial Measures on Markers of Social Inequality." *Sociology of Race and Ethnicity* 3 (1): 14–30.

HRC. 2015. *Addressing Anti-Transgender Violence: Exploring Realities, Challenges and Solutions for Policymakers and Community Advocates.* www.hrc.org/resources/addressing-anti-transgender-violence-exploring-realities-challenges-and-sol.

Hunt, Scott, and Robert Benford. 2004. "Collective Identity, Solidarity, and Commitment." In *The Blackwell Companion to Social Movements*, edited by D. Snow, S. Soule, and H. Kriesi, 433–57. Malden, MA: Blackwell Publishing.

Hwahng, Sel, and Larry Nuttbrock. 2014. "Adolescent Gender-Related Abuse, Androphilia, and HIV Risk Among Transfeminine People of Color in New York City." *Journal of Homosexuality* 61 (5): 691–713.

Jacobs, James, and Jessica Henry. 1996. "The Social Construction of a Hate Crime Epidemic." *Journal of Criminal Law and Criminology* 86 (2): 366–91.

Jacobs, James, and Kimberly Potter. 1998. *Hate Crimes: Criminal Law & Identity Politics*. New York: Oxford University Press.

Jacobs, Ronald N. 1996. "Civil Society and Crisis: Culture, Discourse, and the Rodney King Beating." *American Journal of Sociology* 101 (5): 1238–72.

James, Sandy, Jody Herman, Susan Rankin, Mara Keisling, Lisa Mottet, and Anafi Ma'ayan. 2016. *The Report of the 2015 U.S. Transgender Survey*. Washington, DC: National Center for Transgender Equality.

Jasper, James M. 1998. *The Art of Moral Protest: Culture, Biography, and Creativity in Social Movements*. Chicago: University of Chicago Press.

Jenkins, Philip. 1994. *Using Murder: The Social Construction of Serial Homicide*. New York: A. de Gruyter.

Jenness, Valerie, and Kendal Broad. 1994. "Antiviolence Activism and the (In) Visibility of Gender in the Gay/Lesbian and Women's Movements." *Gender & Society* 8 (3): 402–23.

———. 1997. *Hate Crimes: New Social Movements and the Politics of Violence*. New York: Aldine de Gruyter.

Jenness, Valerie, and Sarah Fenstermaker. 2014. "Agnes Goes to Prison: Gender Authenticity, Transgender Inmates in Prisons for Men, and Pursuit of 'The Real Deal.'" *Gender & Society* 28 (1): 5–31.

Jenness, Valerie, and Ryken Grattet. 2001. *Making Hate a Crime: From Social Movement to Law Enforcement*. New York: Russell Sage Foundation.

Juang, Richard. 2006. "Transgendering the Politics of Recognition." In *The Transgender Studies Reader*, edited by S. Stryker and S. Whittle, 706–20. New York: Routledge.

Kalev, Alexandra, Frank Dobbin, and Erin Kelly. 2006. "Best Practices or Best Guesses? Assessing the Efficacy of Corporate Affirmative Action and Diversity Policies." *American Sociological Review* 71 (4): 589–617.

Kattari, Shanna, and Stephanie Begun. 2017. "On the Margins of Marginalized: Transgender Homelessness and Survival Sex." *Affilia* 32 (1): 92–103.

Kindt, Tom, and Hans-Harald Müller. 2003. *What Is Narratology? Questions and Answers Regarding the Status of a Theory.* New York: Walter de Gruyter.

Kleiman, Mark A. R. 2009. *When Brute Force Fails: How to Have Less Crime and Less Punishment.* Princeton, NJ: Princeton University Press.

Kohn, Sally. 2001. "Greasing the Wheel: How the Criminal Justice System Hurts Gay, Lesbian, Bisexual and Transgendered People and Why Hate Crime Laws Won't Save Them." *New York University Review of Law & Social Change* 27 (2–3): 257–80.

Koken, Juline, David Bimbi, and Jeffrey Parsons. 2009. "Experiences of Familial Acceptance–Rejection among Transwomen of Color." *Journal of Family Psychology* 23 (6): 853–60.

Lahey, Joanna. 2008. "State Age Protection Laws and the Age Discrimination in Employment Act." *Journal of Law and Economics* 51 (3): 433–60.

Lamble, Sarah. 2008. "Retelling Racialized Violence, Remaking White Innocence: The Politics of Interlocking Oppressions in Transgender Day of Remembrance." *Sexuality Research and Social Policy* 5 (1): 24–42.

———. 2013. "Queer Necropolitics and the Expanding Carceral State: Interrogating Sexual Investments in Punishment." *Law and Critique* 24 (3): 229–53.

Lauritsen, Janet, and Karen Heimer. 2008. "The Gender Gap in Violent Victimization, 1973–2004." *Journal of Quantitative Criminology* 24 (2): 125–47.

Lawrence, Frederick M. 1999. *Punishing Hate: Bias Crimes under American Law.* Cambridge, MA: Harvard University Press.

Levin, Jack, and Jack McDevitt. 2002. *Hate Crimes Revisited: America's War on Those Who Are Different.* Boulder, CO: Basic Books.

Levin, Jack, and Gordana Rabrenovic. 2003. *Why We Hate.* Amherst, NY: Prometheus Books.

Levy, Brian, and Denise Levy. 2017. "When Love Meets Hate: The Relationship between State Policies on Gay and Lesbian Rights and Hate Crime Incidence." *Social Science Research* 61:142–59.

Lindsey, Alex, Eden King, Tracy McCausland, Kristen Jones, and Eric Dunleavy. 2013. "What We Know and Don't: Eradicating Employment Discrimination 50 Years after the Civil Rights Act." *Industrial and Organizational Psychology* 6 (4): 391–413.

Lombardi, Emilia, Riki Wilchins, Dana Priesing, and Diana Malouf. 2001. "Gender Violence." *Journal of Homosexuality* 42 (1): 89–101.

Lowman, John. 2000. "Violence and the Outlaw Status of (Street) Prostitution in Canada." *Violence Against Women* 6 (9): 987–1011.

Lyons, Christopher. 2008. "Individual Perceptions and the Social Construction of Hate Crimes: A Factorial Survey." *Social Science Journal* 45 (1): 107–31.

Lyons, Tara, Andrea Krüsi, Leslie Pierre, Thomas Kerr, Will Small, and Kate Shannon. 2015. "Negotiating Violence in the Context of Transphobia and

Criminalization: The Experiences of Trans Sex Workers in Vancouver, Canada." *Qualitative Health Research* 27 (2): 182–90.

MacKenzie, Gordene, and Mary Marcel. 2009. "Media Coverage of the Murder of U.S. Transwomen of Color." In *Local Violence, Global Media: Feminist Analyses of Gendered Representations*, edited by L. Cuklanz and S. Moorti, 79–108. New York: Peter Lang.

Madriz, Esther I. 1997. "Images of Criminals and Victims: A Study on Women's Fear and Social Control." *Gender & Society* 11 (3): 342–56.

Malphurs, Julie E., and Donna Cohen. 2002. "A Newspaper Surveillance Study of Homicide-Suicide in the United States." *Journal of Forensic Medicine* 23 (2): 142–48.

Maratea, R. J. 2013. *The Politics of the Internet: Political Claims-Making in Cyberspace and Its Effect on Modern Political Activism*. Lanham, MD: Lexington Books.

Marcus, Sharon. 1992. "Fighting Bodies, Fighting Words: A Theory and Politics of Rape Prevention." In *Feminists Theorize the Political*, edited by J. Butler and J. W. Scott, 385–403. New York: Routledge.

Mason, Gail. 2002. *The Spectacle of Violence: Homophobia, Gender, and Knowledge*. London: Routledge.

———. 2007. "Hate Crime as a Moral Category: Lessons from the Snowtown Case." *Australian & New Zealand Journal of Criminology* 40 (3): 249–71.

———. 2014. "The Symbolic Purpose of Hate Crime Law: Ideal Victims and Emotion." *Theoretical Criminology* 18 (1): 75–92.

Massey, Douglas. 1995. "Getting Away with Murder: Segregation and Violent Crime in Urban America." *University of Pennsylvania Law Review* 143 (5): 1203–32.

Mehta, Anna, and Liz Bondi. 1999. "Embodied Discourse: On Gender and Fear of Violence." *Gender, Place and Culture* 6 (1): 67–84.

Meier, Stacey, and Christine Labuski. 2013. "The Demographics of the Transgender Population." In *International Handbook on the Demography of Sexuality*, edited by A. Baumle, 289–327. Dordrecht, Netherlands: Springer.

Meyer, Doug. 2014. "Resisting Hate Crime Discourse: Queer and Intersectional Challenges to Neoliberal Hate Crime Laws." *Critical Criminology* 22 (1): 113–25.

———. 2015. *Violence against Queer People: Race, Class, Gender, and the Persistence of Anti-LGBT Discrimination*. Princeton, NJ: Rutgers University Press.

Meyer, Doug, and Eric Anthony Grollman. 2014. "Sexual Orientation and Fear at Night: Gender Differences among Sexual Minorities and Heterosexuals." *Journal of Homosexuality* 61 (4): 453–70.

Meyerowitz, Joanne. 2002. *How Sex Changed: A History of Transsexuality in the United States*. Cambridge, MA: Harvard University Press.

Meyers, Marian. 1996. *News Coverage of Violence against Women: Engendering Blame*. Thousand Oaks, CA: Sage.

Mills, Sara. 1997. *Discourse*. London: Routledge.

Mizock, Lauren, Ruben Hopwood, Heather Casey, Ellen Duhamel, Alyssa Herrick, Geraldine Puerto, and Jessica Stelmach. 2017. "The Transgender Awareness Webinar: Reducing Transphobia Among Undergraduates and Mental Health Providers." *Journal of Gay & Lesbian Mental Health* 21 (4): 292–315.

Moran, Leslie J., and Andrew N. Sharpe. 2002. "Policing the Transgender/ Violence Relation." *Current Issues in Criminal Justice* 13 (3): 269–85.

———. 2004. "Violence, Identity and Policing: The Case of Violence against Transgender People." *Criminal Justice* 4 (4): 395–417.

Moran, Leslie J., Beverley Skeggs, Paul Tyrer, and Karen Corteen. 2003. "The Formation of Fear in Gay Space: The 'Straights' Story." *Capital & Class* 27 (2): 173–98.

Morash, Merry. 2006. *Understanding Gender, Crime, and Justice*. Thousand Oaks, CA: Sage.

Nadal, Kevin, Avy Skolnik, and Yinglee Wong. 2012. "Interpersonal and Systemic Microaggressions Toward Transgender People: Implications for Counseling." *Journal of LGBT Issues in Counseling* 6 (1): 55–82.

Nagel, Joane. 2003. *Race, Ethnicity, and Sexuality: Intimate Intersections, Forbidden Frontiers*. New York: Oxford University Press.

Namaste, Viviane. 2000. *Invisible Lives: The Erasure of Transsexual and Transgendered People*. Chicago: University of Chicago Press.

Nichols, Lawrence T. 1997. "Social Problems as Landmark Narratives: Bank of Boston, Mass Media and Money Laundering." *Social Problems* 44 (3): 324–41.

Nixon, Jennifer, and Cathy Humphreys. 2010. "Marshalling the Evidence: Using Intersectionality in the Domestic Violence Frame." *Social Politics: International Studies in Gender, State & Society* 17 (2): 137–58.

Pager, Devah, Bart Bonikowski, and Bruce Western. 2009. "Discrimination in a Low-Wage Labor Market: A Field Experiment." *American Sociological Review* 74 (5): 777–99.

Parkin, William, and Jeff Gruenewald. 2017. "Open-Source Data and the Study of Homicide." *Journal of Interpersonal Violence* 32 (18): 2693–2723.

Paulsen, Derek. 2003. "Murder in Black and White: The Newspaper Coverage of Homicide in Houston." *Homicide Studies* 7 (3): 289–317.

Perry, Barbara. 2001. *In the Name of Hate: Understanding Hate Crimes*. New York: Routledge.

Perry, Barbara, and D. Ryan Dyck. 2014. "'I Don't Know Where It Is Safe': Trans Women's Experiences of Violence." *Critical Criminology* 22 (1): 49–63.

Peterson, Elicka S. L. 2010. "Vicarious Victimization." In *Encyclopedia of Victimology and Crime Prevention*, edited by B. Fischer and S. Lab, 963–64. Thousand Oaks, CA: Sage.

Polletta, Francesca. 2006. *It Was like a Fever: Storytelling in Protest and Politics*. Chicago: University of Chicago Press.

Polletta, Francesca, and James M. Jasper. 2001. "Collective Identity and Social Movements." *Annual Review of Sociology* 27 (1): 283–305.

Pridemore, William. 2008. "A Methodological Addition to the Cross-National Empirical Literature on Social Structure and Homicide: A First Test of the Poverty-Homicide Thesis." *Criminology* 46 (1): 133–54.

Prunas, Antonio, Carlo Alfredo Clerici, Guendalina Gentile, Enrico Muccino, Laura Veneroni, and Riccardo Zoja. 2015. "Transphobic Murders in Italy: An Overview of Homicides in Milan in the Past Two Decades." *Journal of Interpersonal Violence* 30 (16): 2872–85.

Rader, Nicole, and Stacy Haynes. 2011. "Gendered Fear of Crime Socialization: An Extension of Akers's Social Learning Theory." *Feminist Criminology* 6 (4): 291–307.

Ray, Raka. 1999. *Fields of Protest: Women's Movement in India*. Minneapolis: University Of Minnesota Press.

Rich, Adrienne. 1993. "Compulsory Heterosexuality and Lesbian Existence." In *The Lesbian and Gay Studies Reader*, edited by H. Abelove, M. A. Barale, and D. M. Halperin, 227–54. New York: Routledge.

Richie, Beth E. 2000. "A Black Feminist Reflection on the Antiviolence Movement." *Signs* 25 (4): 1133–37.

Rickford, Russell. 2016. "Black Lives Matter: Toward a Modern Practice of Mass Struggle." *New Labor Forum* 25 (1): 34–42.

Rogers, Meghan, and William Pridemore. 2013. "The Effect of Poverty and Social Protection on National Homicide Rates: Direct and Moderating Effects." *Social Science Research* 42 (3): 584–95.

Rosenbaum, Dennis P., Amie M. Schuck, Sandra K. Costello, Darnell F. Hawkins, and Marianne K. Ring. 2005. "Attitudes Toward the Police: The Effects of Direct and Vicarious Experience." *Police Quarterly* 8 (3): 343–65.

Rosenfeld, Richard. 2016. *Documenting and Explaining the 2015 Homicide Rise: Research Directions*. Washington, DC: National Institute of Justice.

Roshco, Bernard. 1979. *Newsmaking*. Chicago: University of Chicago Press.

Saffin, Lori. 2011. "Identities Under Siege: Violence against Transpersons of Color." In *Captive Genders: Trans Embodiment and the Prison Industrial Complex*, edited by E. A. Stanley and N. Smith, 141–62. Oakland, CA: AK Press.

Sausa, Lydia, JoAnne Keatley, and Don Operario. 2007. "Perceived Risks and Benefits of Sex Work among Transgender Women of Color in San Francisco." *Archives of Sexual Behavior* 36 (6): 768–77.

Schilt, Kristen. 2011. *Just One of the Guys? Transgender Men and the Persistence of Gender Inequality*. Chicago: University of Chicago Press.

Schilt, Kristen, and Laurel Westbrook. 2009. "Doing Gender, Doing Heteronormativity: 'Gender Normals,' Transgender People, and the Social Maintenance of Heterosexuality." *Gender & Society* 23 (4): 440–64.

Schilt, Kristen, and Matthew Wiswall. 2008. "Before and After: Gender Transitions, Human Capital, and Workplace Experiences." *B.E. Journal of Economic Analysis & Policy* 8 (1): 1–26.

Scott, Ellen K. 2000. "Everyone against Racism: Agency and the Production of Meaning in the Anti-Racism Practices of Two Feminist Organizations." *Theory and Society* 29 (6): 785–818.

Sedgwick, Eve Kosofsky. 1993. "How to Bring Your Kids Up Gay." In *Fear of a Queer Planet: Queer Politics and Social Theory*, edited by M. Warner, 69–81. Minneapolis: University of Minnesota Press.

Serano, Julia. 2007. *Whipping Girl: A Transsexual Woman on Sexism and the Scapegoating of Femininity*. Emeryville, CA: Seal Press.

Setoodeh, Ramin. 2008. "Young, Gay and Murdered in Junior High." *Newsweek*, July 18.

Shapiro, Eve. 2004. "'Trans' Cending Barriers." *Journal of Gay & Lesbian Social Services* 16 (3–4): 165–79.

Shepard, Maggie. 2008. "Shooting Victim Was Local Drag Icon." *Albuquerque Tribune*, January 12.

Shepherd, Laura J. 2007. "'Victims, Perpetrators and Actors' Revisited: Exploring the Potential for a Feminist Reconceptualisation of (International) Security and (Gender) Violence." *British Journal of Politics and International Relations* 9 (2): 239–56.

Smithey, Lee A. 2009. "Social Movement Strategy, Tactics, and Collective Identity." *Sociology Compass* 3 (4): 658–71.

Snorton, C. Riley. 2017. *Black on Both Sides: A Racial History of Trans Identity*. Minneapolis: University of Minnesota Press.

Snorton, C. Riley, and Jin Haritaworn. 2013. "Trans Necropolitics: A Transnational Reflection on Violence, Death, and the Trans of Color Afterlife." In *The Transgender Studies Reader 2*, edited by S. Stryker and A. Aizura, 66–76. New York: Routledge.

Spade, Dean. 2006. "Compliance Is Gendered: Struggling for Gender Self-Determination in a Hostile Economy." In *Transgender Rights*, edited by P. Currah, R. Juang, and S. Minter, 217–41. Minneapolis: University of Minnesota Press.

——. 2011. *Normal Life: Administrative Violence, Critical Trans Politics, and the Limits of the Law*. Brooklyn, NY: South End Press.

Spade, Dean, and Paisley Currah. 2008. "The State We're In: Locations of Coercion and Resistance in Trans Policy, Part 2." *Sexuality Research and Social Policy: Journal of NSRC* 5 (1): 1–4.

Spade, Dean, and Craig Willse. 1999. "Confronting the Limits of Gay Hate Crimes Activism: A Radical Critique." *Chicano-Latino Law Review* 21: 38–52.

Stanko, Elizabeth. 2003. Introduction to *The Meanings of Violence*, edited by E. A. Stanko, 1–11. New York: Routledge.

Stanko, Elizabeth A., and Paul Curry. 1997. "Homophobic Violence and the Self 'At Risk': Interrogating the Boundaries." *Social & Legal Studies* 6 (4): 513–32.

Starr, Paul. 1992. "Social Categories and Claims in the Liberal State." *Social Research* 59 (2): 263–95.

Stone, Amy L. 2019. "Frame Variation in Child Protectionist Claims: Constructions of Gay Men and Transgender Women as Strangers." *Social Forces* 97 (3): 1155–76.

Stotzer, Rebecca. 2008. "Gender Identity and Hate Crimes: Violence against Transgender People in Los Angeles County." *Sexuality Research and Social Policy* 5 (1): 43–52.

———. 2017. "Data Sources Hinder Our Understanding of Transgender Murders." *American Journal of Public Health* 107 (9): 1362–63.

Strauss, Anselm, and Juliet M. Corbin. 1990. *Basics of Qualitative Research: Grounded Theory Procedures and Techniques.* Thousand Oaks, CA: Sage.

Streissguth, Tom. 2009. *Hate Crimes.* New York: Facts on File.

Strout, Jean. 2012. "The Massachusetts Transgender Equal Rights Bill: Formal Legal Equality in a Transphobic System." *Harvard Journal of Law & Gender* 35: 515–21.

Stryker, Susan. 1994. "My Words to Victor Frankenstein above the Village of Chamounix: Performing Transgender Rage." *GLQ: A Journal of Lesbian and Gay Studies* 1 (3): 237–54.

———. 2017. *Transgender History, Second Edition: The Roots of Today's Revolution.* Berkeley, CA: Seal Press.

Tadlock, Barry L., Andrew R. Flores, Donald P. Haider-Markel, Daniel C. Lewis, Patrick R. Miller, and Jami K. Taylor. 2017. "Testing Contact Theory and Attitudes on Transgender Rights." *Public Opinion Quarterly* 81 (4): 956–72.

Taylor, Jami Kathleen, Donald P. Haider-Markel, and Daniel Clay Lewis. 2018. *The Remarkable Rise of Transgender Rights.* Ann Arbor: University of Michigan Press.

Taylor, Verta, and Nella Van Dyke. 2007. "'Get Up, Stand Up': Tactical Repertoires of Social Movements." In *The Blackwell Companion to Social Movements*, edited by D. A. Snow, S. A. Soule, and H. Kriesi, 262–93. Malden, MA: Wiley-Blackwell.

Tompkins, Tanya, Chloe Shields, Kimberly Hillman, and Kadi White. 2015. "Reducing Stigma toward the Transgender Community: An Evaluation of a Humanizing and Perspective-Taking Intervention." *Psychology of Sexual Orientation and Gender Diversity* 2 (1): 34–42.

Travers, Ann. 2018. *The Trans Generation: How Trans Kids (and Their Parents) Are Creating a Gender Revolution.* New York: New York University Press.

Ullman, Sarah E. 2007. "A 10-Year Update of 'Review and Critique of Empirical Studies of Rape Avoidance.'" *Criminal Justice and Behavior* 34 (3): 411–29.

Valenti, Jessica. 2007. *Full Frontal Feminism: A Young Woman's Guide to Why Feminism Matters.* Emeryville, CA: Seal Press.

Valentine, David. 2007. *Imagining Transgender: An Ethnography of a Category.* Durham, NC: Duke University Press Books.

Valentine, Gill. 1989. "The Geography of Women's Fear." *Area* 21 (4): 385–90.

———. 1992. "Images of Danger: Women's Source of Information about the Spatial Distribution of Male Violence." *Area* 24 (1): 22–29.

Valier, Claire. 2004. *Crime and Punishment in Contemporary Culture.* New York: Routledge.

Vance, Carol S., ed. 1984. *Pleasure and Danger: Exploring Female Sexuality.* Boston: Routledge and Kegan Paul.

Varshney, Ashutosh. 2008. *Ethnic Conflict and Civic Life: Hindus and Muslims in India.* New Haven, CT: Yale University Press.

Vidal-Ortiz, Salvador. 2009. "The Figure of the Transwoman of Color through the Lens of 'Doing Gender.'" *Gender and Society* 23 (1): 99–103.

Vipond, Evan. 2015a. "Resisting Transnormativity: Challenging the Medicalization and Regulation of Trans Bodies." *Theory in Action* 8 (2): 21–44.

Vipond, Evan. 2015b. "Trans Rights Will Not Protect Us: The Limits of Equal Rights Discourse, Antidiscrimination Laws, and Hate Crime Legislation." *Western Journal of Legal Studies* 6 (1): 1–20.

Walch, Susan, Kimberly Sinkkanen, Elisabeth Swain, Jacquelyn Francisco, Cassi Breaux, and Marie Sjoberg. 2012. "Using Intergroup Contact Theory to Reduce Stigma against Transgender Individuals: Impact of a Transgender Speaker Panel Presentation." *Journal of Applied Social Psychology* 42 (10): 2583–2605.

Wald, Johanna, and Daniel Losen. 2003. "Defining and Redirecting a School-to-Prison Pipeline." *New Directions for Youth Development* 2003 (99): 9–15.

Waters, Emily, Chai Jindasurat, and Cecilia Wolfe. 2016. *Lesbian, Gay, Bisexual, Transgender, Queer, and HIV-Affected Hate Violence in 2015.* New York: National Coalition of Anti-Violence Programs.

Weitzer, Ronald. 2009. "Sociology of Sex Work." *Annual Review of Sociology* 35 (1): 213–34.

Welch, Kelly. 2007. "Black Criminal Stereotypes and Racial Profiling." *Journal of Contemporary Criminal Justice* 23 (3): 276–88.

Weldon, S. Laurel. 2006. "Women's Movements, Identity Politics, and Policy Impacts: A Study of Policies on Violence against Women in the 50 United States." *Political Research Quarterly* 59 (1): 111–22.

Wertheimer, David. 2000. "The Emergence of a Gay and Lesbian Antiviolence Movement." In *Creating Change: Sexuality, Public Policy, and Civil Rights,* edited by J. D'Emilio, W. B. Turner, and U. Vaid, 261–78. New York: St. Martin's Press.

West, Candace, and Don Zimmerman. 1987. "Doing Gender." *Gender & Society* 1 (2): 125–51.

Westbrook, Laurel. 2008. "Vulnerable Subjecthood: The Risks and Benefits of the Struggle for Hate Crime Legislation." *Berkeley Journal of Sociology* 52: 3–23.

———. 2010. "Becoming Knowably Gendered: The Production of Transgender Possibilities in the Mass and Alternative Press." In *Transgender Identities:*

Towards a Social Analysis of Gender Diversity, edited by S. Hines and T. Sanger, 43–63. London: Routledge.

———. 2014. "What Kind of Work Does Women's History Month Value?" Sociological Images, March 19. https://thesocietypages.org/socimages/2014/03/19/whats-wrong-with-womens-history-month/.

Whittle, Stephen. 1998. "The Trans-Cyberian Mail Way." *Social & Legal Studies* 7 (3): 389–408.

Wilcox, Lauren. 2015. *Bodies of Violence: Theorizing Embodied Subjects in International Relations*. Oxford: Oxford University Press.

Williams, Rick. 2012. "Who Killed Kyra Cordova?" *6ABC News*, December 1.

Wirtz, Andrea L., Tonia C. Poteat, Mannat Malik, and Nancy Glass. 2018. "Gender-Based Violence against Transgender People in the United States: A Call for Research and Programming." *Trauma, Violence, & Abuse.* 21 (2): 227–41.

Witten, Tarynn M., and A. Evan Eyler. 1999. "Conflicting Identities and TransGender Violence." *Peace Review* 11 (3): 461–68.

Wyss, Shannon. 2004. "'This Was My Hell': The Violence Experienced by Gender Non-Conforming Youth in US High Schools." *International Journal of Qualitative Studies in Education* 17 (5): 709–30.

Xavier, Jessica, Marilyn Bobbin, Ben Singer, and Earline Budd. 2005. "A Needs Assessment of Transgendered People of Color Living in Washington, DC." *International Journal of Transgenderism* 8 (2–3): 31–47.

Yavorsky, Jill E., and Liana Sayer. 2013. "'Doing Fear': The Influence of Hetero-Femininity on (Trans)Women's Fears of Victimization." *Sociological Quarterly* 54 (4): 511–33.

Zangrando, Robert L. 1980. *The NAACP Crusade against Lynching, 1909–1950*. Philadelphia: Temple University Press.

Index

Abelson, Miriam, 119, 135
abject, 89
accentuating the negative, 113–15
activist networks: importance of established, 45–47
ACT UP (the AIDS Coalition to Unleash Power), 180, 187
Age Discrimination in Employment Act, 171
age of victims, 41–42, 71–72
"always already" victims, 26, 32, 136. *See also* vulnerable subjecthood
Americans with Disabilities Act, 142, 171
Anderson, Elijah, 168
Anderson, Jacqueline Julita, 109
Anderson, Kristin, 28
Andrade, Allen, 124–25
anger: pride facilitated by, 180–81
anomie, 168
anti-violence activism, alternative approaches to: address the deception narrative, 177–78; alter academia, 185–86; attend to patterns of violence, 166–72; boycott the oppression Olympics, 165–66; construct a multifaceted subjecthood, 172–73; highlight successful resistance, 162–65; highlight transgender joy and celebrate the living, 173–77; improve media narratives, 183–85; make all victims matter, 165; pride,

178–83; separate from identity politics, 186–91. *See also* identity-based anti-violence activism
Araujo, Gwen: activism mentioning, 71, 90, 108, 128, 132–33, 177, 179, 195; different from the average victim, 41–42; famousness of, 14, 36–37; "ideal" victim, 42–45, 48–49; influence on anti-violence strategies, 57–59; influence on beliefs about transgender lives, 53–56; influence on scholarship, 56–57; life and death of, 39; media coverage of, 50–52; similarity to other victims, 40–41
arena, 12–13
Armstrong, Elizabeth, 45, 135

backstage, 12
Barragan, Alina Marie, 43, 51, 95
Best, Joel, 5, 26, 98, 103, 106
Bettcher, Talia Mae, 216n27
Biden, Joe, 1
Birch, Elizabeth, 73, 90
bisexuals: ignored within LGBT activism, 209n4, 241n121
Black Lives Matter, 7, 150, 240n108
Black Panther Party, 151
Blair, Timothy, Jr., 95, 199
Blau, Judith, 168
Blau, Peter, 168
Blee, Kathleen, 9, 29
Bodfish, Emmon, 67, 71

Hall, Mya, 244n5
Harwood, Valerie, 6, 120
hate crime legislation: anti-violence
strategy of, 137; convictions, 125,
147, 234n119; counting victims
through, 140–41; crime deterrent,
seen as, 143–44; enhanced penalties,
140, 143–44, 147, 149, 235n128;
factors encouraging, 144–45; history of, 9, 137–39; ineffectiveness
of, 126, 146–48, 160–61; process of
getting enacted, 1–2, 26; valuable
subjecthood and, 139–44, 145–46;
violence caused by, 148–50
Hate Crimes Statistics Act, 138–41
hatred: seen as motivating violence, 2,
9, 24, 31, 34–35, 62–63, 65–66, 69,
76, 144, 158
Haynes, Stacy, 30
Heise, David, 30, 180
Helms, Monica, 45, 76, 87, 115, 123,
126, 136
Henderson, Tyra, 86, 95
Henry, Jessica, 113
hero, 19, 32
Hester, Rita, 73, 179
heterogeneous subjecthood, 83
hierarchy of victimization, 37
Hollander, Jocelyn, 26, 28, 163
homicide. *See* murder
homogeneous subjecthood, 15, 63, 65,
70–75, 118
honor contests, 167
Hughes, Joy Vannelia, 43, 51
Human Rights Campaign (HRC),
10, 55, 69, 79, 84, 90–91, 96, 100,
124, 133–34, 137, 143–44, 146, 148,
157–58, 171, 174, 177, 194–95, 199,
204–5
Hunter, Tyra, 95, 118, 179

"ideal" perpetrator, 37, 40
"ideal" victims, 14, 37, 43; age of, 44;
attractiveness, 45; bias motivation
and, 49; focus on, 47; gender conformity and, 48; identity and, 48,
53; race of, 43–44; sex and gender
of, 44–45

identify with the dead, 16, 32, 102,
118–19, 121–22
identify with the victim, 29–30, 32
identity: focus on, in anti-violence
activism, 63–64; frame of, 24; seen
as a motivation for violence, 64–66
identity-based anti-violence activism:
definition of, 2, 4–5
identity politics: academic debates
about, 5–6; activist debates about,
81–84; combined with anti-violence
activism (*see* identity-based anti-
violence activism)
International Foundation for Gender
Education (IFGE), 194
intersectionality, 4, 6, 12, 16, 27, 62,
77–78, 80–82, 144, 158; attention to,
77–81, 158–59, 166–72; failure to
attend to, 6, 67–72, 221, 222n79
irony of social movement success, 113

Jacobs, James, 76, 113
Jacques, Cheryl, 177
Jasper, James, 89
Jenner, Caitlyn, 48
Jenness, Valerie, 26, 103, 139, 150
Jimenez, Stephen, 25
Johnson, Duanna, 94
Johnson, Marsha P., 67, 110, 244n4
Johnson, Nireah, 44, 95
joy, transgender, 27, 173–77, 183–86

Keels, Erika, 243n4
Keisling, Mara, 65, 101, 142, 146
Kilbourn, Seth, 79
King, Latisha, 71, 94, 147–48, 194,
245n28
King, Martin Luther, Jr., 163
King, Rodney, 235n134
Kruz, Kyra Cordova, 245n28

Laing, Alison, 143
Lambert, Lisa, 38
Lamble, Sarah, 70
landmark narratives, 14, 37–38, 43, 47,
55–56, 59. *See also* famous victims
Lavender Panthers, 151
Leno, Mark, 86

people, 15, 39–40, 92–93, 160–61; produces gender, race, and sexuality, 27–29; produces resistance, 33; productive power and, 18–23, 27–29; 31–32; repressive power and, 21–22; sexual interactions and, 41, 73–74; structural causes of, 190; symbolic, 11; "us versus them" mentality increasing, 77
Violence Against Women Act, 1, 138, 150
violence reduction strategies, 9, 151–53. *See also* celebrate transgender people; education about levels of violence; hate crime legislation; joy; remembering the dead
vulnerability: highlighted by activists, 3, 117–23; perceptions of transgender people and, 29, 117–23; perceptions of women and, 28–30, 120–22
vulnerability rituals, 135
vulnerable subjecthood, 15–16, 30, 34, 54, 88, 117–23, 145–46

Walser, Miles, 119
war, metaphor of, 75–77, 84, 89, 135

Warren, J.R., 79
Washington, Kareem, 95–96
We Happy Trans, 175
Whitaker, Ebony, 94
Wilchins, Riki, 44, 79, 81–83, 93, 101, 104, 111, 115, 128, 133, 175, 194–95, 197
Wilcoxons, Aimee, 110, 244n4
Williams, Christian, 94
Williams, Nakhia, 94
Williams, Simmie, 71, 94
Williams, Vianna Faye, 73, 93
Women's History Month, 152, 182
women's rights movement, 1–2, 6–7, 26–30, 59, 62, 74–76, 91–92, 98–99, 106, 108–9, 112–13, 120–23, 129, 130, 138, 150–53, 163–64, 166, 182, 188, 209n3, 224n43
wounded truths, 6, 120, 132, 174

X, Malcolm, 163
Xavier, Jessica, 74–75, 91

Yavorsky, Jill, 121

Zapata, Angie, 93, 124–25, 148, 153, 234n119

Founded in 1893,
UNIVERSITY OF CALIFORNIA PRESS
publishes bold, progressive books and journals
on topics in the arts, humanities, social sciences,
and natural sciences—with a focus on social
justice issues—that inspire thought and action
among readers worldwide.

The UC PRESS FOUNDATION
raises funds to uphold the press's vital role
as an independent, nonprofit publisher, and
receives philanthropic support from a wide
range of individuals and institutions—and from
committed readers like you. To learn more, visit
ucpress.edu/supportus.

Made in the USA
Las Vegas, NV
05 February 2024

85358545R00173